PRAISE FOR UP!

It only takes just a little bit of light, or truth, or good wisdom to get my day going in the right direction. I find it in the Word. And I also find it in devotionals like "Up!" Matthew's daily flashes of hope and inspiration open my eyes a bit more to the most important things, and help set my heart on True North. I'm thankful for his calling, and the impact it has on me and countless others.

— BRETT BEAVERS, HIT SONGWRITER AND
GRAMMY-NOMINATED RECORD PRODUCER
(DIERKS BENTLEY, DUSTIN LYNCH)

Matthew's voice is one of the bright and encouraging ones in the Canadian church today. I'm one of the many who are grateful for him. I think you'll find him as encouraging as I do.

— CAREY NIEUWHOF, AUTHOR AND FOUNDING
PASTOR, CONNEXUS CHURCH, BARRIE, ONTARIO

"Espresso for the soul." That how I think of "Up" Devos. Matthew Ruttan packs a lot of spiritual wisdom into a few words. Always biblical, thoughtful, understandable, and on point.

— JOHN A. VISSERS, PRINCIPAL AND PROFESSOR
OF HISTORICAL THEOLOGY, KNOX COLLEGE,
TORONTO SCHOOL OF THEOLOGY, UNIVERSITY
OF TORONTO

I've really been enjoying starting my morning off with a coffee and The "Up!" Devotional to help set my heart and mind right for the day ahead. The Up Devo is spiritual nourishment, grounded in Bible-based truth and encouragement. Highly recommend.

— JASON BLAINE, CANADIAN COUNTY SINGER
AND SONGWRITER

Up! is a spark of scripture, applied to life, to launch you into your day. It takes and applies God's word to encourage, challenge, and inspire.

— BRIAN IRWIN, ASSOCIATE PROFESSOR OF OLD
TESTAMENT/HEBREW SCRIPTURES, KNOX
COLLEGE, TORONTO SCHOOL OF THEOLOGY,
UNIVERSITY OF TORONTO

In a world where days can become so easily lost in hustle and hype, The Up Devotional is the perfect bite-sized Faith reality to kick start my mind and day in the right direction.

— RUSTY GASTON, MUSIC INDUSTRY EXECUTIVE

UP!

Thicket Books, PO Box 46052 Westdale PO, Winnipeg, MB R3R 3S3

www.thicketbooks.com

Photo of M. Ruttan by Charlene Hammond

CONNECT

The "Up!" daily devotional is published five days a week.

Sign up at www.MatthewRuttan.com/Up or www.TheUpDevo.com.

YOU CAN ALSO FOLLOW ON SOCIAL MEDIA:

facebook.com/MatthewRuttanUp

twitter.com/theupdevo

instagram.com/theupdevo

PROFITS

100% of the profits from this book will be given to Fight4Freedom, an organization "dedicated to battling human trafficking in the sex trade, seeing victims set free, and giving beauty from ashes."

Learn more at www.fight4freedom.ca and become a modern abolitionist.

UP! – 313 DEVOTIONALS TO HELP YOU START YOUR DAY IN A BIBLICAL, RELEVANT WAY

MATTHEW RUTTAN

Thicket Books

I dedicate this book to my wife Laura,

whose light beats back the darkness of the world,

and whose faithfulness is evidence of the faithfulness of God.

FOREWORD

Maybe it's weird for a person to have a motto, but I do. And I'm okay with that. Here it is: "A pulse doesn't mean you're alive." I just don't think that having a heartbeat is enough. Life on this side of the soil is a short game—and all of us have one chance to do it well.

One of my favourite movies is *The Shawshank Redemption*. There's a scene where Andy Dufresne, played by Tim Robbins, says "Get busy living or get busy dying." He's fed up with his situation and, as the viewers soon find out, has taken steps to break open his life to a whole new level. In other words, get on with what's important or else you're wasting what precious little time you have on earth.

In one of my first years as a pastor I went to the hospital to visit a man who was dying. I gathered around his bed with the family. We made a circle, held hands, and prayed together. The cardiac monitor—or whatever it's called—was beeping away in the background. As we prayed, its beep-beep-beeping started to slow like a wind-up music box coming to the end of its tune. And then he took his final breath.

Only an hour later, in the very same hospital, I walked over to the maternity ward to welcome a new baby into the fold. The new parents cried tears of joy, took frantic pictures, and entered a new version of their own lives that they could never have anticipated or planned for. One person had taken their final breath and another gasped their first. That day reminded me that heartbeats come and heartbeats go—quickly. The events surrounding the start of life and the end of life are powerful moments you never forget. But my question for all of us is this: *Are the moments in between just as powerful?*

Enter Jesus.

Ever since high school I've been captivated by Jesus. I had grown up in the church—although I must admit that it didn't always beat out hockey or girls in the competition for my time, attention and loyalty. But it wasn't really until my time in Bracebridge and Muskoka Lakes Secondary School that I started to examine him more closely.

Jesus was bold and fierce and loving and against-the-grain. The reason I eventually made him my number one priority was because his words and actions gave me the most hope for my life and for the wider world. In John 10:10 (ESV) he says, "I came that they may have life and have it abundantly." In other words, a pulse by itself doesn't mean you're truly alive.

As I started to read the Bible during lunch hours and between hockey practices, and as I started writing spacey spiritual songs on my guitar with my friend Jeff,[1] I became increasingly captivated by this God-Man Jesus. The great literary critic and author C.S. Lewis once said that in Christianity you're not faced "with an argument which demands your assent, but with a Person who demands your confidence."[2] And I totally got that. I felt that Jesus, standing tall and radiating integrity, was a power unto himself of incomparable magnetism. It wasn't about a religious system or a specific tradition or a set of well-oiled arguments—it was about him, someone who demanded my confidence, and someone who earned it.

But as the years grew—and as I went through the usual distractions, embarrassments and semi-successes of a young person discovering his way in the world—I kept coming back to the same spiritual frustration: *Why did my day-to-day life sometimes seem so disconnected from this almighty and awesome God?* If my faith was going to be meaningful, and if my journey with God was going to be meaningful, it needed to be tangible, immediate, and down-to-earth—something that would make a relevant difference in my daily life and in the lives of the people around me.

In 1930 King George was supposed to give a radio address to the London Arms Conference. Apparently, a few minutes before he was to begin, an important wire was broken in the CBS control room. But the chief control operator, Harold Vidian, grabbed the two wires and held them together to restore the circuit. As a result, the world heard the King's speech. All the while, two hundred and fifty volts of electricity coursed through Vidian's body![3] I wanted a faith with that kind of connection and power—but without the physical pain!

A faith that is powerful, practical and relevant to daily life. That's what motivates me. And now that I'm a pastor, that's what I try to do. I try to help people live out a powerful and relevant faith in practical ways today. Yes, Christians believe in life *after* death—but we also believe in life *before* life after death.[4] It's not just about waiting on earth for heaven—it's working for heaven on earth. After all, our time in this world is a short game—and all of us have one chance to do it well. Get busy living or get busy dying.

One of the ways we can do that is to intentionally seek God. And when you intentionally seek God, you see God. Or, put another way, the more you actively seek God in your daily thoughts, the more you see God active in your daily life. And that's where a daily devotional can help.

THE UP! DEVOTIONAL

Over the years I've subscribed to a few different devotionals. Some of them were great. But the thing that didn't sit well with me was that many of them were too theoretical and abstract—and too long. I was often left wondering, 'So how does that apply to my daily life?'

So as I went about my days as a pastor, husband and father, I started to write my own daily devotionals in my head. I didn't realize I was doing it, but that's what was happening. And then one day the idea became a little more concrete. I prayed about it and felt God giving me a nudge. So I cobbled together a crude logo and asked my wife, Laura, what she thought of the name "Up!" "I like it," she said. "Kind of like, 'Get up, look up and be up!'" As you can tell, she has a way with words. (Thanks honey!)

So in April 2015 I started sending out devotionals through an email subscription list. Over the past three years, the list has grown every month and now has multiple platforms. (See the "Connect" page.) It comes out five mornings a week and the goal is simple. I want it to be something you can read, generally in a minute or less, that will help you start in each day in a biblical, relevant way.

THE BOOK

In 2015 people started asking if the devotionals would ever be published as a book. I hadn't really thought about it until recently. But since I've always wanted to write a book, and since three years of writing were already in the bag, it made sense. Even though I do a lot of stuff online, I still like to hold a book in my hands, mark it up, and put it on a shelf. A hard-copy book of devotionals could be another means to accomplish the same end.

Through leadership in the church I got to know Matt Brough, a creative pastor in Manitoba, Canada, who hosts the *Spirituality for Ordinary People* podcast,[5] writes theological books as well as the *Del Ryder* fantasy adventure series, and who owns Thicket Books along with his wife Cheryl. At first I had some conversations with Matt simply to find out more about publishing. But then I started to wonder if he could coordinate the project himself. After all, we already knew each other, he had the know-how, and Matt was a subscriber to the devotional. He agreed.

313?

The subtitle of this book is, "313 Devotionals To Help You Start Your Day in a Biblical, Relevant Way." So what's the deal with 313, you might ask? It's one devotional for every day of the year minus Sundays. 365 - 52 = 313. It's my way of encouraging us to worship and rest one day a week.

STYLE

The style of the devotionals is conversational. I break some grammatical rules (sorry Mom), because I want you to read what I'm writing as if you're hearing me say it. I just think that a conversational style makes something more 'real,' down-to-earth and personal. I also don't use conventional paragraphs. Since "Up!" began and continues as a web-based devotional, it's roughly organized on a line-per-thought basis instead of a paragraph-per-thought basis like you might find in a novel. I think that the internet is changing how we read. We tend to 'scroll.' So that's how the text appears in the book too. I wanted to preserve that same experience.

USE OF SCRIPTURE

Every daily devotional includes at least one quote from the Bible. I think that's important because the Bible is the primary place where we learn about God's will. But a devotional is different from a sermon. A sermon includes sustained study of a biblical passage to uncover some meaning and includes an application to daily life in a specific context. But each devotional isn't the result of that kind of sustained study. Some of them are; but the majority are inspired by, or related to, a biblical passage or theme. In either case, I've done my best to be faithful to the spirit of a passage and never misrepresent it. Throughout this book I usually use the New International Version of the Bible, quite simply because it's the version most English readers have. When I quote another version I make a note of it in brackets.

A BROAD AUDIENCE

Generally speaking, when I write the devotionals I have a broad, mostly middle-class, Western audience in mind. These are people—probably like you and me—trying to navigate modern life in a changing time. Some readers are in their teens, some are seniors, some are in-between. Some are mature Christians, some are new Christians, and some are just curious. Most are in North America, some are in Europe, and some are from who-knows-where. In light of that diversity, I try to get as specific as I can on certain topics, but not so specific that what I say wouldn't apply in a variety of situations. I also tend to include a fair amount of conditional language (i.e. "such-and-such *might* mean that..."). I do this because each reader is unique and may be in very different circumstances than the next person. Just as I have all this in mind as a writer, I think you should have it in mind as a reader too. So if you are navigating a specific and difficult situation or question, I suggest you do some sustained biblical study, pray, reach out to some wise friends, and speak to your pastor for more guidance.

THE BASICS

In these devotionals I tend to stick to the basics. Much more could be said about all of these topics, but here I keep it fairly simple. You won't find me getting into the specifics of the lesser-known spiritual disciplines, the nuances of building relational trust with those who live on the street, or the five points of Calvinism. My personal passion is to help people live out their faith in a practical way today. So in these devotionals I tend to focus on short bursts of the basics which can be clearly applied to daily life.

THANK YOU!

If you don't personally know me, this is the point in the Forward when you usually tune out. Why? Because you probably don't know the people I'm about to name. And I admit it. Up until now I've been a book-Forward-thank-you-skipper too. But don't do it! These people are awesome.

Thankful people thank people. And I am very thankful to the many people who have supported me and this project since it began in April 2015.

I thank my wife, Laura, because she has always and whole-heartedly supported this devotional and what it's about. Her faith in me never fails; and more importantly, neither does her faith in God. She is the heart of our home, and her generous attitude and honest feedback help cultivate a climate of creativity without which nothing I do would be possible.

I thank my children, Sarah, Ben and Anna, because they have given me new eyes to see the world. And that kind of gift is beyond value for someone who likes to create. I love to watch who they are becoming as our Creator God crafts them and calls them forward in life.

I thank my mom, Donna, who always encouraged me to do my best and whose unwavering support is the stuff of legends. And I thank my dad, Eric, for his unconditional encouragement, and who taught me to treat each day like a new life, and to live it like it is.

I thank my brothers, Deric and Jason, who I've always looked up to, and who are consistent pillars in my life. It's rare to have loyal friends as brothers, but I do.

I thank my feedback writers who I ask to give me occasional feedback about whether or not my writing is clear and makes sense. Sean O'Toole was my high school English Teacher at Bracebridge and Muskoka Lakes Secondary School. Andrew Faiz was the Senior Editor of the Presbyterian

Record magazine. Brian Irwin is the Associate Professor of Old Testament/Hebrew Scriptures at Knox College, at the University of Toronto. And Jeff Loach is the pastor at St. Paul's Presbyterian Church in Nobleton, Ontario, and is a spiritual director who formerly served as Central Ontario District Director for the Canadian Bible Society. I consider all of them friends and value the helpful wisdom they've given over the past three years.

I thank my friend Jeff Einboden, Professor of 19th-century American Literature and Comparative Literature at Northern Illinois University. His friendship and meaningful encouragement have buoyed me along the way. Plus, he's way smarter than me—and it's always good to have someone like that around to both keep you humble and at your best!

I thank Lauren Walsh and Caitlin Cone, members of the congregation at Westminster Presbyterian Church, who have kept records of the themes, Bible verses and quotes from each daily devotional over the past three years. This has been very helpful as I've tried to find past content, stay organized, and assemble this book.

I thank the elders and congregation at Westminster Church in Barrie, Ontario where I've served as the pastor since 2008. Their support and enthusiasm for the "Up!" devotional has been steadfast—and I continue to learn so much from them. Plus, their prayers have surrounded me every single day.

I thank Jeff Walther, also a member at Westminster Presbyterian Church, whose love for "Up!" has brought it to many more thousands of listeners through the Life Radio Network in Central Ontario. I love his outward-focussed mind.

I thank Matt Brough, the co-owner of Thicket Books, for his enthusiasm about this project, for his intelligence and sense of humour, and for how his eyes light up when he gets a creative idea for connecting more people with God.

I thank you, the readers, not only for your confidence, but for your commitment to the kingdom come, and to God's will being done on earth as it is in heaven.

And I thank Jesus. He is everything.

Enjoy, be lifted Up, and remember: *A pulse doesn't mean you're alive.*

UP!

MONDAY - THE MEANS TO LIVE (BUT NO MEANING TO LIVE FOR)

Holocaust survivor, neurologist and psychiatrist Victor Frankl said that, "Ever more people today have the means to live, but no meaning to live for."[6]

He was referring to what I call the *crisis of purpose*. I think it's a huge part of the general malaise and apathy which can seep into so many people's minds these days.

One straightforward way to fight against this cultural landslide is to go out of your way to serve and help other people.

Recently I sent out an email and asked subscribers to the 'Up!' daily devotional to reply to this question: "How has serving or helping others given you a stronger sense of purpose?"

Here are a few of the responses:

"When I serve or help others I realize that I am alive for a reason..."

"The ways I help and pitch in are often things other people don't want to do. But that's what makes it important. It's behind-the-scenes. But it builds up the hospital and my church for God's glory."

1

"I try to make the day better for complete strangers. I go out of my way to offer help, buy them food, or just listen to someone who doesn't have anyone to talk to."

"I advocate for people who have been abused. They are God's children too, but often fly under the radar because they don't want to draw attention to their situation."

"I coach sports for the kids. Winning is nice, but it's really about building our young people into men and women of character, who will make our world a better place down the line."

Wow!

The bottom line is this: *Service gives purpose*. Since God hasn't given up on the world, neither should we. So when you go out of your way to serve and help others on a daily basis, it breathes greater purpose into your life.

Colossians 2:9 says that "For in [Jesus] all the fullness of Deity dwells in bodily form." God became flesh in Jesus, which is an incredible confirmation not only that God loves his world, but that it has value and is worth redeeming and fighting for.

"Ever more people today have the means to live, but no meaning to live for." But that's not you. Do you want your days to escape the general malaise and apathy of our time?

Service gives purpose.

TUESDAY - CONTINUOUS PARTIAL ATTENTION

We live in the information age. And there are some positive things about that.

But there are some negative things too.

Linda Stone, a former senior executive with Apple and Microsoft, coined the phrase "continuous partial attention." She writes that we're "much more motivated by not wanting to miss anything... we want to be part of this broader set of connections that are out there. And the unfortunate cost of that... is when you're on top of everything, it's hard to get to the bottom of anything."[7]

So when we try to stay plugged in to everything that's going on we end up with a lack of sustained connection. And that can undermine the depth of our attention spans and even the depth of our relationships.

It matters because getting to know and love people matters. A life spent loving God is a life spent loving the people God loves. And that's very hard to do when we're spinning around in a whirlpool of data and distraction. If we want to really connect and care for others, we need to take the time to listen to them, get to know them, and be a godly presence in their lives.

In Luke 6:31 (NLT) Jesus says, "Do to others as you would like them to do to you." If you want others to get to know you and take your life seriously, don't you think others want the same?

In the information age, "continuous partial attention" threatens this possibility. It can undermine the depth of our attention spans and even the depth of our relationships. Let's not let that happen.

A life spent loving God is a life spent loving the people God loves.

WEDNESDAY - HELP FOR THE RELAXATION IMPAIRED

I have a confession to make. I'm not very good at relaxing.

What I mean is that it takes some work to calm my mind. When I'm supposed to be mellow in a semi-trance of blissfulness with my uber-cool sunglasses, my brain easily wanders back to my gargantuan to-do list. Can you relate?

If not, consider yourself blessed. But if so, maybe what I'm about to say will help.

Since I've been impaired in the relaxation department for about twenty years, I've learned a few tricks. One of them is this: Get your mind on the *right* things to get your mind off the *wrong* things.

Let me explain:

The human mind is proficient. If you're used to operating at a certain speed, your mind will continue to operate at a certain speed—even if you're trying to relax. If you sit there just trying to think of nothingness you'll probably fail because your brain will simply stuff a lot of other information into the void—information which includes annoying things to worry about or a growing to-do list.

So when my mind gets overactive in all the wrong ways, I direct my thoughts to biblical truth that preaches the peace of God into my soul.

One of my favourites is repeating the twenty-third psalm to myself. "The Lord is my shepherd, I lack nothing. He makes me lie down in green pastures…" Another is Psalm 131: "My heart is not proud, Lord, my eyes are not haughty; I do not concern myself with great matters or things too wonderful for me…"

If you're relaxation impaired, direct your thoughts to biblical truth that preaches the peace of God into your soul.

Get your mind on the right things to get your mind off the wrong things.

THURSDAY - ORDER OF OPERATIONS

I forget which grade I was in but it was definitely high school. And it was the day of the big math test.

I remember that the problems were complicated. You had to follow all the mathematical rules, what the teacher called the "order of operations." If you didn't, your entire answer would get messed up.

But guess what? I totally blanked and forgot everything I had learned! And since I didn't get the first part of the equation right, the rest of the equation was wrong.

That's like life. If you don't get the first and most important part of the equation right, everything else gets messed up too. And to be clear, the first and most important part of the equation is your relationship with God. It makes all the difference.

When you give God first place other things fall into place.

That doesn't mean your life will always be easy; it means it will be more godly.

If you seek God's will in your decisions, they will be wiser. If you seek God's will with your health, you will be stronger. If you seek God's will in your relationships, they will be godlier. If you seek God's will in your nine-to-five, they will have more integrity.

But if you don't give God first place, the various compartments of your life will bear the consequence and stench of confused priorities.

"Order of operations" matter—in mathematics, and in life.

Today, with whatever you're facing, remember Proverbs 3:6 (NRSV): "In all your ways acknowledge him, and he will make straight your paths."

When you give God first place other things fall into place.

FRIDAY - UFFGEVVA

Lately I've been thinking a lot about how individualistic our society has become. Basically, "individualism" is a way of thinking. It's living like your own immediate needs and wants are more important than the needs of the wider community.

It's a Me-Myself-and-I way of life.

I'm not saying your own needs aren't important. But they're not *more* important than the needs of the wider community.

Consider a contrast. The Amish call it *uffgevva*. Loosely translated it means that you are less important than others. In a book about Amish parenting, an Amish tour guide describes how this concept is passed on to new generations:

"Amish children are taught from an early age, by example as well as words, that their needs and wants are important, but not *more* important than those of the family, the church, and the community. It is the exact opposite of individualism... It involves a surrendering of the will rather than emphasizing the importance of the person over the group. Ultimately, it makes a major difference in the way children behave."[8]

If you think that sounds harsh maybe that's because you've been thoroughly soaked and saturated with the prevailing illness of our society known as Individualism.

But what the Amish teach their children shouldn't alarm us. Here's what Paul says to the Philippians in chapter 2, verse 3: "Do nothing out of selfish ambition or vain conceit, but in humility consider others better than yourselves."

Today, as you make decisions and set priorities, and as you go about your school, work and conversations, remember that your needs are important —but they're not *more* important than the needs of the wider community.

Let's call it *uffgevva*.

"Do nothing out of selfish ambition or vain conceit, but in humility consider others better than yourselves."

SATURDAY - BOTH EXTREMES ARE HYPOCRITICAL

"You're a hypocrite." Has anyone ever said that to you? It's a nasty and unpleasant thing!

A hypocrite is a pretender—someone who says they believe certain ideals but doesn't actually live them out in their own life. Hypocrites were the people Jesus often railed against.

But guess what? Regardless of your theological leanings, it's easy to become one!

So how do you guard against it? How do you become more like Jesus and less like the hypocrites he warned us against?

John 1:14 says that Jesus came into the world "full of grace and truth." Not grace and no truth, and not truth and no grace. But both grace *and* truth.

I think some people focus on just half of the equation. They mentally agree with the right doctrines but don't live in a loving, gracious way. Or they focus on loving (in a vague sense) while disregarding God's truth and right and wrong.

Both extremes are hypocritical.

Truth without love isn't really truth; and love without truth isn't really love.

So where are you on the spectrum? Come on, be honest: Do you need to be more loving toward the people around you, or do you need to take God's truth more seriously?

Jesus was full of both grace *and* truth. When we humbly make a serious effort to grow both of those things within ourselves, we're making a move to be more like Jesus and less like the hypocrites he warned us against.

The more truth, the more love; the more love, the more truth.

SUNDAY...

MONDAY - NEVER TRUST YOUR SELF-DEFEATING THOUGHTS

I think there can be a darkness within each one of us that loves to reach up, take hold of our confidence, and pull it down into an abyss of self-pity.

You know the days. The bad thoughts or feelings start to steamroll. It's the opposite of positive momentum. You feel deflated. Then you catch an unflattering glimpse in the mirror... Then a friend says something spiteful...

Next thing you know you start to believe the darkness. And instead of it coming from an outside source, it comes from within. You start to pick on yourself, beat yourself up, and un-believe who you are and what you can do.

Today I'm here to tell you this: Never trust your self-defeating thoughts on the days you feel most defeated.

None of us are immune to bad days. They happen. That's life. But those are definitely not the days when we're thinking most clearly.

So what you need to do is (a) acknowledge that your day is junky and that your thoughts are going south, and (b) take Paul's advice for peace in Philippians 4:8 (ESV): "whatever is true... think about these things."

And what is true? That you are a child of God. That you are valuable. That your life has purpose. That in Christ you are a new creation—forgiven, saved, made holy, and a living, breathing ambassador of God's love.

Darkness loves to suck at your soul. As the saying goes, misery loves company. But don't be hospitable to untruth. It needs a firm deportation notice to the other side of the galaxy. To do that, acknowledge what's going on, and take Paul's advice for peace: "whatever is true... think about these things."

Never trust your self-defeating thoughts on the days you feel most defeated.

TUESDAY - IF YOU'RE NOT DEAD

A lot of people make "New Year's Resolutions." When the year behind gives way to the year-to-come, they "resolve" to do something differently.

Some people love to make these kinds of resolutions. Some don't.

Either way, many of us make personal goals. And a new year is a time to look forward to the next 365 days and wonder what we can do differently —and better.

As you think about your goals—formally or informally—I want to encourage you to make them consistent with who God wants you to be. Think about it. If you're going to shoot for something, don't make it lame or irrelevant.

Aim high. Don't waste your mental time and energy on the kind of change that doesn't really matter or make a difference.

Writing to the Philippians, Paul said, "I am sure of this, that he who began a good work in you will bring it to completion at the day of Jesus Christ" (Philippians 1:6, ESV).

God has begun a good work in you...

He wants you to become more like Jesus. He wants you to not only be a disciple but to make disciples. He wants you to love him with all you've got, and to love your neighbour big. He wants you to be a person of prayer and integrity. He wants you to bring him glory and help bring heaven to earth.

So whether you make a New Year's Resolution or not, as you think about your goal, remember that God has begun a good work in you. Resolve to help the Master Craftsman with what he wants to do.

God finishes what he starts. He keeps his promises. He is faithful to the end. Carry that kind of confidence into your next 365 days.

As pastor Craig Goeschel puts it, "If you're not dead, you're not done."[9]

WEDNESDAY - THINGS THAT RENEW YOU (NOT DRAIN YOU)

Learning how to rest.

In the church I pastor, that's something I've been teaching and talking about lately. Why? Because of what it says in Exodus 20:8: "Remember the Sabbath day by keeping it holy."

But this can be hard. Many of us know rest is important, but we don't do it as much as we should. Life gets busy, and the faster you go on the hamster wheel of modern life the harder it is to get off.

After talking about this on a Sunday, a few different people approached me for some advice about *how* to rest. What kinds of things *should* we do, and what kinds of things should we *avoid* doing if we're to truly cease and desist from the rat race pace?

Although there are several important nuances to Sabbath rest, here's a good guideline when planning some of your activities: *Do things that renew you not drain you*.

You probably already know what they are. If something takes mountains of planning or leaves you utterly exhausted, I can virtually guarantee it's not restful. But if something helps you connect with God, lifts your spirit, or bonds you to the important people around you, it may very well be a great and godly use of your time.

God doesn't command rest because he wants to make life *harder* for you; he does it because he wants to make life *better* for you. God is a loving Parent who wants his children to experience purpose, joy, peace... and to be at their best.

To do that he knows we need rest.

So what is your next day of rest? Seriously, picture your schedule. Identify the day. When you have it in mind, and as you consider the kinds of things you may or may not do...

Do things that renew you not drain you.

THURSDAY - TIRRITATED

Every once in a while people feel compelled to invent a new word.

One of them is "Hangry." Have you heard of it? It's a combination of "hungry" and "angry." As you may very well know from personal experience, when you're hungry you're not at your best—and sometimes angry. Hence, hangry! Lol

So recently I decided to make up a word of my own. When you put together "tired" plus "irritated" you get "tirritated"!

Let's face it. When we're tired we get easily irritated. And it's not usually because what we're dealing with is overly unsolvable. It's often because we're tired and don't have the mental capacity to think clearly. Fatigue runs sour buttermilk through the engine of your brain.

That's why rest is so important. In fact, it's so important that God commands it. He doesn't do it to make life harder, but better!

But first you need to acknowledge the problem: That you're neglecting godly rest.

"But Matthew," I can hear some of you saying, "if you only knew how busy my life was you'd know that I just can't slow down!"

I think God anticipated that line of thinking. That's why Exodus 20:11 says, "in six days the LORD made the heavens and the earth... but he rested on the seventh day." Even *God himself* rested. So here's the thing. The moment you become busier than God you have the right to say you're too busy to slow down.

(Crickets.)

So, do you get tired or irritated? It can happen to any of us. That's why it's important to acknowledge the problem and trust the Bible when it says it's best to rest.

Join with me in the fight against tirritation.

FRIDAY - WHY DOING NOTHING IS DOING SOMETHING

Rest.

It's something many of us think is a good thing... but don't do as much as we should.

Even though it's a command. Yup, God commands rest.

In Exodus 20: 8-10 God says, "Remember the Sabbath day by keeping it holy. Six days you shall labor and do all your work, but the seventh day is a sabbath to the LORD your God. On it you shall not do any work..."

When God gave the commandments, he began by reminding his people that he had brought them "out of the land of slavery." In contrast, this new way of life was to be one of faithfulness... and *freedom*.

So a part of the meaning of Sabbath rest is to remind us that we're *not* slaves anymore.

However, when we never rest that's exactly how we're acting—like we're still slaves. Maybe not to the Egyptian Pharaoh, but certainly to busyness and complication!

But when we make an effort to rest we renew ourselves in God, think more clearly, enjoy life more fully, and find more peace.

Friends, doing nothing is doing something.

So "Remember the Sabbath day by keeping it holy." If this isn't a part of your routine, it might take some re-organizing of your life to make it happen—but it's worth it. Renew yourself in God. Think more clearly. Enjoy life more fully. And find more peace. In our modern rush-around world, who can argue with that?

Doing nothing is doing something.

SATURDAY - SMASHED TROPHIES

I once heard a story about a college student who *really* wanted to be the school tennis champion. It was all he wanted. He focused exclusively on that goal to the detriment of his relationships, grades and everything else.

And he did it. He won the championship! And the trophy was prominently displayed in the school's trophy cabinet.

After several years he got a package in the mail. It was the trophy he had won—but smashed and dirty! It seems they remodeled the school and threw it out. Someone recognized the name that was engraved on the bottom and sent it to the former champ.

As he held it in his hands, here is what he said: "Given enough time, all your trophies will be trashed by someone else!"

I like that story because it's a reminder about what does (and doesn't) matter most. I think of 1 Corinthians 9:25 (NLT) where Paul writes, "All athletes are disciplined in their training. They do it to win a prize that will fade away, but we do it for an eternal prize."

So many things in life will not last. But the genius of wise and faithful living is to continually ask yourself this question: Am I spending my life contributing to something that matters?

I'm not suggesting you'll never have to do hum-drum tasks. But what I'm suggesting is that our faith in God continually draws our time, attention and energy back to the things that matter most.

(And if you don't feel good about your current trajectory, don't worry, it's never too late to start.)

Today, ask yourself this: Am I spending my life contributing to something that matters?

SUNDAY...

MONDAY - BEING A CHRISTIAN WOULD BE EASY IF IT WEREN'T FOR THIS

I remember having a conversation with someone who said, "Being a Christian would be easy if you didn't have to deal with actual people."

He was being funny, of course. But what he meant was that following Jesus and God's commands are easy... until you have to put them into practice with actual flesh and blood people—flawed people who sometimes rub you the wrong way or disagree with you.

But we live in a world with... people. We are called to live out our values amidst other... people. We worship with other... people. We work and go to school alongside other... people. We live in families with other... people.

With that in mind, Scripture comes along to help re-frame our thinking. In Romans 15:7 (NRSV) Paul gave this advice to the Roman Christians about receiving people into the church they disagreed with: "Welcome one another, therefore, just as Christ has welcomed you, for the glory of God."

The reason I think that's helpful is because it reminds us that our attitude toward others should be based on Jesus' attitude toward us. In other words, deal with people based on what Jesus has done for you, not on what people have done to you or for you.

Someone will bother, upset or frustrate you. And you'll probably bother, upset or frustrate someone else! But Paul teaches that we should re-think how we form our attitudes toward others in our faith communities. After all, if Jesus had treated all of us like we deserved to be treated, none of us would have a hope!

So be gracious.

Deal with people based on what Jesus has done for you, not on what people have done to you or for you.

TUESDAY - WHEN YOU THINK EVERYTHING IS IMPORTANT

When you think everything is important you live like nothing is important.

If that sounds confusing, here's what I mean.

If you think that everything in your life is a priority, you're not actually making anything a true priority. Imagine your time and energy divided up into a pie chart. If you say your relationship with God is important, but so is your family, your career or grades, your friendship circle, your reputation, your soccer skills, your travel schedule, your looks, your bank account, and your hobbies... you've just divided yourself equally in ten different ways!

But the very word "priority" suggests that some things need to occupy a larger percentage of the pie.

Unfortunately, many of us struggle with lives that are too busy or complicated. And that complication is often a result of not knowing what our true priorities. As a result, we let other things bully their way into our brains and schedules.

Proverbs 4:25 says, "Let your eyes look straight ahead; fix your gaze directly before you." It's a warning against the distraction of lesser pursuits.

That's why I think you should pray about and write down your priorities.

I talk to a lot of people, and I've never heard a single one say that priorities aren't important. But the people who actually have a wise, godly focus in their weekly routine, are the ones who have taken the time to identify what's truly key and re-organize their lives as a result of what they've learned.

Friends, when you think everything is important you live like nothing is important.

So prayerfully think about your priorities, write them down, and start to live differently as a result.

WEDNESDAY - PRIORITIES: WHERE THE RUBBER MEETS THE ROAD

Yesterday I talked about setting priorities. Hopefully you were able to think it through and name some of your non-negotiables.

But let's take the next step: *Start to adjust your weekly routine to better reflect those priorities.*

Friends, this is where the rubber meets the road. Why? Because it involves change.

Maybe a priority for you is getting out of your comfort zone and serving God more boldly. If so, what in your weekly routine are you going to *change* to make that happen?

Maybe a priority is a career path (or friends) who better reflect your values. If so, what in your weekly routine are you going to *change* to make that happen?

Maybe a priority is to not spend money you don't already have. If so, what in your weekly routine are you going to *change* to make that happen?

A part of the reason this can be difficult is because saying Yes to important things means saying No to less important things. Author and speaker Lysa TerKeurst says it like this: "The best Yes is sometimes No."[10]

In other words, you need to say no to certain demands on your time and energy if you're truly going to be available for what matters most. If you don't, your commitment is a watered-down shrug of limited value.

Proverbs 4:26 says, "Give careful thought to the paths for your feet and be steadfast in all your ways." Notice how it says to give "careful" thought to the paths for your feet, not "careless" thought.

I realize this is hard, and that it may take time. But set the wheels in motion. *Start to adjust your weekly routine to better reflect your priorities.* And remember, in a world of demands and distractions, the best Yes is sometimes No.

THURSDAY - THE PRIVATIZATION OF FREE TIME

Harvard professor Robert Putnam has researched how communities are changing. One of the significant shifts is something he refers to as the privatization of free time.[11]

In previous decades, people would generally come home from work or school and spend their free time with other people as a part of their wider community.

For example, they'd gather at baseball parks or arenas *together*, or participate in community organizations or events *together*.

But something happened. With the advent of television, more and more people started coming home from work or school, going inside, closing the doors, and watching TV.

Alone.

I'm not saying all TV is bad. Although I don't watch a tonne of it, I generally enjoy it when I do. What concerns me is how exclusive devotion to screens can, if we're not careful, undermine community and our capacity to connect and show compassion to those around us.

In 1 Corinthians 10:24 (ESV) Paul wrote, "Let no one seek his own good, but the good of his neighbour." And that's very hard to do if we never interact with people or know what challenges they may be facing in life.

So when an opportunity arises take some time to get to know those around you.

The privatization of free time may be a powerful force in modern life, but so is the power of community in the heart of Christ's people who have been transformed by his outgoing love.

"Let no one seek his own good, but the good of his neighbour."

FRIDAY - WHEN YOU DON'T FEEL GOD'S PRESENCE

There's a compelling passage in 2 Chronicles 32:31 (NLT) about a king named Hezekiah. It says that "God withdrew from Hezekiah in order to test him and to see what was really in his heart."

Many things happened when Hezekiah was king. But in this verse we're told that God "withdrew" from him. It was a test. It was to "see what was really in his heart."

A season came into Hezekiah's life where he didn't *feel* God's nearness. That doesn't mean God abandoned him. It means God sent a test to see how Hezekiah would act even if he didn't feel God's presence.

Can you relate to that feeling? I can. There are times when God simply feels close—when you can powerfully sense his nearness. But there are other times when he seems distant. When it seems like he has withdrawn from us.

I'm not saying God is testing you every time you feel like God is far away. I don't know enough about your personal situation. But one of the things I take from this verse about Hezekiah is that not sensing God's presence is not evidence of his absence.

It's kind of like any other relationship. Are you loyal to a friend, partner or spouse only when you're with them? Or are you loyal even when you're not? Do you do the right thing only when everyone is looking, or even when you're behind closed doors?

No matter what you *feel*, continue to pray, serve, study the Bible, love, worship, and give.

Not sensing God's presence is not evidence of his absence.

SATURDAY - CONNECT IN CONVERSATION

"I want to grow in my faith."

I hear some variation of that statement almost every week. And I think it's awesome. It's a desire to learn more about God, about how to live in a way that honours him, or about spiritual progress and following Jesus more closely.

Each person is a bit different of course. But one of the biggest ways for you to grow spiritually is to connect in conversation. That means seeking out opportunities to connect with other people and consciously talk about God and faith.

It could be in a formal setting like in a prayer group, Bible study, mission group, or small group. But it could also be in an informal setting, like getting together with some other people who share your faith and asking questions like, 'How can we pray for each other?' or 'What do you think God is doing in your life lately?'

Proverbs 27:17 (NLT) is one of my favourites: "As iron sharpens iron, so a friend sharpens a friend." In other words, trusted spiritual friends make you stronger, wiser and sharper—not more dull!

Consider it a challenge: Connect in conversation.

"As iron sharpens iron, so a friend sharpens a friend."

SUNDAY...

MONDAY - HOW PERFECT OR SPIRITUALLY MATURE EVERYONE IS

A lot of people think the church is based on how perfect or spiritually mature everyone is.

If you think that way, you're always going to be disappointed in God's church. Why? Because people continually fall short of what you think the appropriate moral standard is.

Should we have standards? Of course! But keep this in mind...

In Romans 15:1-2 Paul writes, "We who are strong ought to bear with the failings of the weak and not to please ourselves. Each of us should please our neighbors for their good, to build them up."

When he says "strong" he doesn't mean physical strength; he means *spiritual maturity*. Although he was writing about a specific situation that concerned the church in Rome, one of the things it underscores is that the church includes people who are at various points along the path of discipleship.

So where do we go from here?

First, our common bond as Christians and churches is the risen Jesus. That's beyond dispute.

Second, if you're new to the faith, the church community is a place where you should be able to find wise mentors who can help and guide you.

Third, if you're one of the spiritually mature ones, the church community is a place where you can guide newer Christians as they try to identify and follow the footsteps of Jesus.

The church isn't based on how perfect or spiritually mature everyone is. If it was, none of us would make the grade. It's based on the risen Jesus. He's the only one who gets an A+ on his report card under "Always Does God's Will."

But as for the rest of us, our congregations are profoundly enriched when we see each other as fellow-travelers, reach out when we need counsel, give counsel when it's needed...

And compassionately pray for each other in the process.

TUESDAY - THE IDOLATRY OF OUR FEELINGS

In Jonah 1:1-2 we read, "The word of the LORD came to Jonah... 'Go to the great city of Ninevah and preach against it, because its wickedness has come up before me.'"

Jonah didn't want to do it, so he fled on a ship in the exact opposite direction. He was thrown overboard and swallowed by a huge fish. After three days it spat him out, and Jonah did an about face, went to Ninevah, and proclaimed to everyone that the city would be overthrown if they didn't repent.

And it worked!

But a detail people often miss is what happens next. Instead of being happy, Jonah was angry. It seemed wrong that God was so compassionate that he saved everyone. Even though an amazing thing happened, it didn't make him feel good. In fact, it made him feel *bad*.

It's easy to succumb to the idolatry of our feelings. I realize we can learn a lot from our feelings, but whenever we say or believe things like, 'God just wants you to be happy,' we're not honouring God with our feelings—we're making our feelings into gods, as if they're the only source of truth.

There are times when being courageous, obedient and even loving will not make you *feel* good. After all, doing the godly thing sometimes brings you into conflict with others, and might even go against what your own sinful nature wants.

That's why it's important to remember that *how faithful you are is more important than what your feelings are*. Yes, you can learn from your feelings, but they're not your Commander.

WEDNESDAY - "JUDGY"

Has anyone ever called you "judgy"? It's short for "being judgmental."

Whenever I write about being judgmental, I'm obviously not in favour of it. As Jesus says in Luke 6:37 (NLT), "Do not judge others, and you will not be judged." Sounds like good policy!

But today I'd like to focus on another angle.

Sometimes people call you "judgy" or think you're being "judgy"...

When you're *not*.

Here's the thing. You're allowed to think differently than other people. You're allowed to express an opinion that goes against the majority.

That doesn't make you "judgy." That makes you a thoughtful human being.

Granted, you should never come across as superior. If the love you exude can barely fit into a thimble, and if your words make Carla from the T.V. show *Cheers* look like Mother Teresa, you may need an attitude adjustment. So yes, you need to speak humbly with respect and love.

But if you do, it's okay to have a different perspective.

Quite often, thinking and acting in a way that is consistent with your beliefs—and not what everyone else thinks is popular or trendy—is the faithful and right thing to do. If you talk and act in a gracious way, and people still say you're being "judgy," it may be a case of someone trying to silence you because they simply don't like what you're saying.

Just because someone says you're "judgy" doesn't necessarily mean you are.

Be humble, speak respectfully, and act lovingly.

Don't be intimidated.

You're not defined by how liked you are by others, but by how loved you are by God.

THURSDAY - ASK NOT WHAT YOUR FELLOWSHIP CAN DO FOR YOU...

One of the most famous speeches in American history was by John F Kennedy in 1961. He said, "Ask not what your country can do for you—ask what you can do for your country."

It was a call to community, to think about something more than just your own individual needs.

Thinking about faith, I'd like to substitute the word "fellowship" for "country." *Ask not what your fellowship can do for you—ask what you can do for your fellowship.*

In the New Testament, the word "fellowship" has a few different implications: (a) getting together with other believers, (b) coming together because of a common bond (the resurrected Jesus), and (c) contributing to the well-being of the group.

So the reason I play on JFK's dictum is because the community of faith is something you need to *contribute* to—not just receive from.

Should you be fed? Yes. But you also need to *feed*. Should you be blessed? Yes. But you also need to *bless*.

Since we live in a consumeristic society it's easy to treat the church like any other product which exists to serve us and make us happy. As a result, the church (God's fellowship) can seem optional. But can you imagine what Jesus or the apostle Paul would have said about that?

I'm reminded of Hebrews 10:25 (NLT): "And let us not neglect our meeting together, as some people do, but encourage one another..."

I simply invite you to ponder this statement seriously, and to prayerfully think through how you might respond as a part of Christ's body here on earth:

Ask not what your fellowship can do for you—ask what you can do for your fellowship.

FRIDAY - YOU'RE NOT STARTING AT GROUND ZERO

In North America depression is on the rise. But why?

It's a complicated topic, but psychologist Martin Seligman suggests we have replaced church, faith, and community with something smaller that simply cannot do the job—and that something is "the self."[12]

What I think he means is that when people used to try to figure out who they were and what their purpose in life was, they were quicker to lean on and benefit from the wisdom of their wider community and faith tradition.

But today, since many people devalue those things, they try to make it all up on their own from scratch. And since they can't handle the weight of this task by themselves it often crushes and depresses them!

We need to take into account the deep, biblical wisdom that God has generously given to his people throughout all generations. And here's a taste:

You are his. Your value is uncontested. Because of your faith in Christ, your eternity is secure. And in this life you're enlisted in his incredible, renovating cause to make our society and relationships reflect something more of heaven on earth.

Sound meaningful? Absolutely!

So as you try to figure out who you are and what your purpose is, remember that you're not starting at ground zero. You are starting at the empty tomb; and you are standing on the shoulders of a faithful risen Saviour who is unrelentingly committed to spreading hope throughout the world.

When you feel overwhelmed by life remember the overwhelming love of God. You are his. Your value is uncontested. And your purpose is wonderfully tied to the God who is making all things new.

And know this. As you walk the path, you are not alone. As Jesus says in Matthew 28:20 (NKJ): "I am with you always, even to the end of the age."

SATURDAY - AREN'T THEY ALL OUR CHILDREN?

Several years ago a reporter was covering the conflict in Sarajevo when he saw a young girl get shot.

He rushed over to help. By the time he got there another man also wanted to assist. They lifted her into the reporter's car and set off to the hospital. The reporter drove, and the other man stayed in the back holding the wounded girl.

As they drove the man in the back called out, "Hurry, my friend. My child is still alive." A few minutes later, "Hurry, my friend, my child is still warm." A little later, "Hurry... my child is getting cold."

By the time they got to the hospital she had died.

Later, as the two men were washing the blood off of their hands, the man who had been in the back of the car said he wasn't looking forward to telling the girl's father that his daughter was dead.

The reporter was surprised. Since the other man kept referring to the girl as his "child" he assumed *he* was the father.

"No," the man replied, "but aren't they all our children?"[13]

What I find so moving about this story is that it speaks to the profound truth that we are all connected on a level beyond biology. And not only that, but that we should have a Christ-centred concern for each other's well-being—even when we don't know each other.

Writing in Philippians 2:4 (ESV) Paul says, "Let each of you look not only to his own interests, but also to the interests of others."

Today, as you interact with people who are as broken and as precious as you, know the profound truth that we are all connected on a level beyond biology—and that we should have a Christ-centred concern for each other's well-being.

The result is a world which is a little less impersonal, and a lot more compassionate.

SUNDAY...

MONDAY - AGAINST THE NOISE

I once went on a monastic-style retreat. There was a lot of silence. I mean, a lot.

Other people seemed to instantly enter into a state of relaxation and calm. But for me it didn't come so easy.

When I tried to calm my mind and enter a time of Christian meditation or prayer, things kept jumping into my head. The harder I tried to enter into silence, the louder my thoughts became! I couldn't help think of needing to call so-and-so, or planning the next series of sermons, or needing more laundry detergent, or how interest rates might impact my mortgage...

So to centre myself I kept repeating a powerful scripture verse: "Come, Lord Jesus." Over and over. It's from the second last verse in the Bible, Revelation 22:20.

So that's what I think you should do too.

Find three minutes. For the first minute, simply breathe deeply with your eyes closed. For the following two minutes, slowly repeat this powerful prayer from the early church: "Come, Lord Jesus."

You're not only praying for Jesus to return and make everything right again; you're inviting him to come powerfully into your soul—right now.

The point of silence isn't silence. The point of silence is to bring you back to un-bustled stillness at the foot of God's awesome and awe-inspiring throne.

Won't you pray it with me? Come, Lord Jesus...

TUESDAY - SHOCKED AND SADDENED, BUT NOT AFRAID

A friend posted this on Twitter: "When will all this crazy stuff stop?"

He was referring to the ten deaths and sixteen injuries that resulted when a man drove over pedestrians in Toronto, Ontario, on April 23, 2018. But the backdrop included the Humboldt Broncos tragedy on April 6 and the shooting in Nashville on April 22.

In the midst of this, I think there are big reasons for hope in our world— like how communities can band together; like how women are treated more equally than they used to be; like how medicine reaches places it didn't before.

But even still, it seems easy to find reasons for despair. The original version of this devotional included a list of examples ranging from misguided government policies to the rise of human trafficking. But I had to take it out because I exceeded my word limit!

So, back to my friend's question: When will all this crazy stuff stop?

The short answer is *when Jesus returns*.

But until then, I believe it's important to use our voices and actions to advocate for a better, more hopeful world.

Everything in our society is not hunky-dory. And I refuse to pretend it is. Sin continues to run rampant, and it is even sometimes re-dressed by communication pundits as something admirable.

2000 years ago, referring to his own victory over Satan and evil on the cross, Jesus said: "Now is the time for judgment on this world; now the prince of this world will be driven out" (John 12:31).

To me, it's a reminder that God's undying truth, inseparably partnered with unrelenting and self-sacrificial love, is already victorious and continues to be on the move.

In response to the Toronto deaths, I remember a commentator on *Hockey Night in Canada* reflecting on all of the tragedy and saying something like this: 'We are shocked and we are saddened, but we are not afraid.'

Hope is never fully eclipsed. And you are one of its light-wielding warriors.

WEDNESDAY - THE ESAU COMPLEX

In Genesis 25 we read about the ever-clever Jacob who was cooking some stew. His brother Esau came in from the fields famished and desperately wanted to have some.

Seeing an opportunity, Jacob said, "First sell me your birthright." In exchange for some stew, Jacob wanted Esau to give him his rank and rights as the firstborn son.

What a ridiculous proposal. It'd be like paying a million dollars for a hamburger at McDonald's!

But Esau actually agreed! Instead of acting with wise self-control, he acted with impulse—and it cost him dearly.

How many of us can do the same thing and fall victim to impulse?

In Galatians 5:23 "self-control" is listed as a quality that God grows in Christians. But what is it? Let me put it this way. Someone who has self-control is someone who doesn't let urgency body check their larger priorities.

Self-control means keeping your eye on the goal. It means not getting pushed around by temporary distractions. It means doing the right thing instead of the easy thing.

The Esau complex runs rampant.

So in a society of distraction, know what's important, know what's not, keep your eye on Jesus, and your head in the game.

Someone who has self-control is someone who doesn't let urgency body check their larger priorities.

THURSDAY - CONSISTENCY IN THE STORM

In 1911 two explorers and their teams set out on a 1400 mile journey to be the first in modern times to reach the South Pole.

Roald Amundsen led one team. And Robert Falcon Scott led the other. They were pretty much equally matched. But they had different strategies.

Scott traveled based on the weather conditions. If it was sunny they went further—sometimes up to 50 miles in a day! But if it was stormy, they kept travelling to a minimum.

But Amundsen had a different approach. He and his team would travel fifteen to twenty miles a day no matter what. Rain or shine, fifteen to twenty miles. Sometimes his team would complain by saying things like,

'The weather is good, let's take advantage and keep going!' But he refused. They needed to remain consistent.

So do you want to know who got there first?

Amundsen's team. They beat Scott's team by *thirty four* days. Not only that, but on the return trip, every one of the members of Scott's team died!

To me, one of the lessons from this tragic story is that *consistency is king*.

Regular spiritual habits set you up for victory in life. Prayer, Bible reading, worship, rest, giving, serving others. When you do that, no matter what the external conditions are in your life, you've established a consistent pattern that reminds you to be faithful, and which reminds you about God's continuing faithfulness.

In Psalm 57:7 David said, "My heart is steadfast..." There's the word: *Steadfast*. Would you like to be steadfast? You can be.

Regular spiritual habits set you up for victory in life. Consistency is king.

FRIDAY - HUMAN PRICE TAGS

I like to shop at thrift stores.

At this one place, whichever clerk is working that day chooses the price for items based on what they think they're worth. As a result, prices vary depending on the clerk.

Last year I found a fifty dollar shirt for just five dollars!

We put price tags on humans too. In Matthew 9:11 (NRSV), some Pharisees asked Jesus' disciples, "Why does your teacher eat with tax collectors and sinners?"

Those are price tags—"tax collector," "sinner." They may not have a dollar amount, but they are definitely about value. Bottom of the barrel. Scum.

Do you have invisible tags you put on others? Back-stabber? Bum? Liar? Lunatic? Home-wrecker? Have-not? Drunk? Disaster? Suck up? Sloth?

And yet each is cherished by the same God who made you. Jesus died for them all.

Today, why not take a few moments with someone who has an invisible price tag, and speak to them as a sibling.

I think it would be world-changing if we were to see like Jesus sees—every man, woman and child as God's bundle of joy.

He rips off price tags. So should we.

SATURDAY - SOMEONE WHO NEEDS TO KNOW THEY MATTER

When most people hear the word "hospitality" they think of the "hospitality industry" where guests of some sort are treated well.

But hospitality comes up in the Bible too. Romans 12:13 (NLT) says, "When God's people are in need, be ready to help them. Always be eager to practice hospitality."

But it doesn't mean being Martha Stewart all the time, or having a perfect house, or the conversational nuance of a Victorian-era socialite.

In the Bible, "hospitality" means being welcoming, with special attention not only to other Christians, but to people who aren't in your immediate family or friendship circle.

And practicing hospitality isn't as intimidating as you might think. It involves inviting a new person into a conversation you're having with some friends; asking questions about someone's life because you actually care who they are or what they do; not jumping to judgments about what may have happened in someone's past; taking the time to respond to someone's needs—maybe a ride, or maybe just someone to talk to.

The world is a lonely place to more people than you think. The world is a scary place to more people than you think. The world is a grey place to more people than you think. The world is an anxious place to more people than you think.

So practice hospitality.

Your hospitality can feel like the friendship of God to someone who needs to know they matter.

SUNDAY...

MONDAY - DOING SOMETHING "BENEATH" YOU

There are two kinds of pride.

The first is simply being proud of your country or a child. I get that. It's pretty innocent.

But the second kind of pride is problematic and has to do with ego. It's an over-inflated sense of self. It's having a puffed-up attitude, never admitting you're wrong, and thinking you're superior.

Granted, none of us would admit that we're proud—at least not in that negative kind of way. But when we pretend to have all the answers, always put ourselves first instead of God, and never value the contributions of others... that's pride.

In Galatians 6:3 Paul writes: "If anyone thinks he is something, when he is nothing, he deceives himself." In other words, if you go around thinking and acting superior you're simply not being honest with yourself, with others, or with God. In the schema of life, God is at the top, and the rest of us stand shoulder-to-shoulder. Do we have different roles and responsibilities? Absolutely. But we all have the same value in the eyes of our Creator.

So to guard against pride, make a habit of doing things you think are "beneath" you.

Do a common task or chore that you think isn't worth your time or energy. Do a favour for someone who has done nothing to deserve it...

Pride is like an infection that, if left alone, will spread and contaminate your soul. So guard against it.

Make a habit of doing things you think are "beneath" you.

TUESDAY - THOUGHT-LIFE SPRINGBOARD

In Matthew 5:8 Jesus says, "Blessed are the pure in heart, for they will see God."

This line has always captured me. I sometimes say it to myself quietly as I go about my day, usually when I feel like I'm mentally wandering or unsure.

Not only is it a goal to achieve (purity of heart), but it's a promise to look forward to (seeing God, which is way of saying you'll understand God and his ways more clearly in your daily life).

But the heart needs to be *pure* for that to happen. In other words, it needs to be uncluttered with thoughts and priorities that aren't from God.

So what in your thought-life dishonours God? Be honest. Develop a zero tolerance policy for ungodly squatters in your brain. Once they get comfortable they have a habit of morphing into words and actions that you know are beneath you.

Next, develop a pure heart. Think godly thoughts. Pursue them. As you go about your day pray, "Lord, what do you want me to say and do in this situation?"

Jesus says, "Blessed are the pure in heart, for they will see God." So make the godliness of your thoughts a priority.

What you'll find is this: The more you actively seek God in your daily thoughts, the more you'll see God active in your daily life.

WEDNESDAY - ON THE WALL OF A SLAVE'S CELL

If you go out of your way to worship God, and if someone asked you *why* you did that, what would you say?

That it spiritually feeds you? That you like the music? That it helps you pray? That the sense of community is meaningful? That it's a sense of duty? That God deserves it?

Let me share another reason that might be new to you.

A young woman from Southeast Asia named Elisabeth was 16 when she was kidnapped and sold into sexual slavery. She was forced to work as a prostitute against her will. I could never imagine the horror of that kind of experience.

Fortunately, International Justice Ministries learned about Elisabeth's plight and was able to secure her freedom. The workers came in and helped Elisabeth get her belongings from her tiny, wretched cell. That's when they noticed something she had written on one of the walls in her native language:

> *The LORD is my light and my salvation;*
> *whom shall I fear?*
> *The LORD is the stronghold of my life;*
> *of whom shall I be afraid?*

It was verse 1 from Psalm 27 (ESV). Despite having no music, no sermon, no cushy seat, no fancy bulletin or visuals, and no other people around her, Elisabeth worshiped God faithfully. In so doing, she rooted herself in a strength, hope and wisdom bigger than herself.[14]

Do you worship God? If so, *why* do you worship God? There are many good reasons. But consider this.

Worshiping God roots you in a strength, hope and wisdom bigger than yourself.

It was true for Elisabeth. And it's true for you too.

THURSDAY - WHEN THE FEELING OF LOVE IS LACKING

I think I'm a pretty loving person. Usually. As long as I'm well-rested, un-rushed, and not feeling overwhelmed by my life!

But as soon as I'm tired, rushed, and overwhelmed, I'm a lot less loving!

But even in those moments we are called to be the hands and feet of Christ to one another. Even when we're not at our best. And even when we don't *feel* like it.

Psychiatrist M Scott Peck says that "real love often occurs in a context in which the feeling of love is lacking..."[15] That's helpful. It's easy to honour and serve others when you *feel* like it. It's discipleship to honour and serve others when you don't.

1 John 4:11 (ESV) says, "Beloved, if God so loved us, we also ought to love one another." In other words, the love we have for one another isn't based on our fluctuating impulses. It's based on the fact that our good and stead-fast Lord loved us first.

We love because we're loved.

Today, an opportunity will probably present itself to honour and serve someone. You may not feel like it. You can let it pass. But I think you should seize it. Those opportunities might just be the bread crumbs God leaves for you on the abundant path of Jesus to draw you forward.

So seize the opportunity. Be the hands and feet of Christ. Not because you always feel like it, but because you've been loved first.

FRIDAY - THE RIGHT THINGS OR THE WRONG THINGS

We all want things. But what kinds of things do you spend your time and energy wanting?

Exodus 20:17 says, "You shall not covet..." It's a command against obsessing about things you don't have. After all, if you keep mentally drooling after other people's things, it undermines your belief that God can and will provide for you.

Dietrich Bonhoeffer was a theologian who was murdered by the Nazis in the closing days of World War Two. In his inspiring book, *The Cost of Discipleship*, he wrote: "The covetous man seeks dominion and power, but only to become a slave to the world on which he has set his heart."[16]

So if you spend your time coveting what other people have, you end up forfeiting some of your freedom and become a slave to your desires.

And do you know what? I think we all have wants. But the richness of life is found in wanting the *right* things—not the *wrong* ones.

Many people in our world were shocked after the tragic bus accident on April 6, 2018 in Saskatchewan, Canada that killed sixteen people from the Humboldt Broncos hockey organization. Do you want to know what that news makes me want more of? Meaningful friends and community.

So what do you spend your time and energy wanting?

Fancy clothes, popularity, the latest device... Or lasting friendships, meaningful opportunities to volunteer and serve others, personal integrity, a closer walk with Jesus?

We all want things. But what kinds of things do you spend your time and

31

energy wanting? The richness of life is found in wanting the *right* things—not the *wrong* ones.

SATURDAY - YOU DON'T DIE FOR A LIE

The famous mathematician and physicist Blaise Pascal said: "I [believe] those witnesses that get their throats cut."

He meant that people who are willing to die for their beliefs are more likely to be telling the truth. In other words, people don't tend to die for a lie.

People will, however, give their lives for something they hold incredibly dear—like a loved one, or a God-given truth.

That's why the words and example of the disciples were so important after they saw the resurrected Jesus. Virtually all of them were martyred for their faith. They would rather be executed than renounce the good news of the resurrected Jesus.

Consider the Christians living in Rome when the brutal Nero was Emperor. They were arrested and burned publicly with tar. They could have recanted—but didn't.

Or think of Pliny the Younger who governed Bythynia in the early second century. He led trials of Christians and had them put to death if they didn't renounce Christ. Many didn't. And he even gave each of them three chances to renounce or face death! All of those early witnesses are gone.

But you aren't.

You are today's witnesses for the resurrected Jesus. 2 Timothy 3:12 (ESV) says that "all who desire to live a godly life in Christ Jesus will be persecuted." So it's not always going to be easy. But the benefits are immeasurable.

You are the ones to carry the news of his victory over death into this dark world. *You* are the ones to speak his hope into the caverns of despair. *You* are the ones to live his love in the morbid playgrounds of anger and hate.

You may not die for your faith. But you can stand out, and risk something great for the resurrected Jesus and his message of victory, truth and love.

People don't die for a life. They do, however, give their lives for something they hold incredibly dear—like a loved one, or a God-given truth.

That's exactly what we have in Jesus.

SUNDAY...

MONDAY - REASONS FOR THE RESURRECTION

The resurrection of Jesus is central to the Christian faith. It's not in the outfield somewhere picking at ant hills. It's home plate.

So whether or not you take it seriously is *very* important. In fact, in 1 Corinthians 15:17 Paul said that "if Christ has not been raised, your faith is futile..."

Futile.

So you need to plant your feet firmly on the empty tomb.

But to be honest, a lot of us have been told things that undermine our belief. There are tonnes of conspiracy theories out there designed to shake our faith in the risen Jesus.

So today I'm here to tell you that if a doubt has crept into your mind, and if you leave it alone and don't explore it further, it's like discovering a growing tumor in your body and deciding not to do anything about it. It can prove disastrous.

The good news is that every major conspiracy theory about the resurrection has a sound and reasonable rebuttal. In fact, what a lot of people think are stumbling blocks to belief turn out to be evidences *for* belief.

To that end, I've produced a blog that responds to the four major conspiracy theories about the resurrection. I've also presented several others arguments which bolster your faith in the resurrected Jesus. You can read it at MatthewRuttan.com.[17]

I just really believe that how you use your brain is a part of your devotion to God. Reason to your faith is like walls to your house—it gives it strength, structure, and guards against collapse.

So use your brain and let God build you up on the firm foundation of the resurrected Jesus.

TUESDAY - NEVER TOO LATE

On Christmas Eve 1992 a couple noticed something at the end of their driveway.

It was a large object wrapped in plastic. Turns out, it was a wicker chair that had been stolen eighteen years earlier! Attached to it was a note which read:

"To whom it may concern: Approximately 13 to 17 years ago my husband stole this wicker chair from the porch of this house. I am ashamed of this behaviour and am returning this stolen item. I have since been divorced from my husband and have since been "born again." My life has completely changed and I want to undo any wrongdoing to the best of my ability... I realize the cowardly fashion in which I am returning this, but the reason is obvious. I will not bother you again. Please forgive us."[18]

This person had a burden on their heart for many, many years. But that didn't stop them from doing something about it. They still needed to put something right after all that time.

In Ephesians 4:32 (ESV) Paul tells his readers: "Be kind to one another, tenderhearted, forgiving one another, as God in Christ forgave you."

As I think about that passage I realize that sometimes you're the one who needs to give someone forgiveness. But sometimes you're actually the one who needs to *seek* it... no matter how much time has passed.

Do you have a burden on your soul? Do you need to put something right? Don't let the passage of time dissuade you.

It's never too late to right a wrong.

WEDNESDAY - THE GOLD IS IN THE GIVING

I was recently talking with someone about how we live in a "consumer culture," and about how deeply that kind of thinking has burrowed its way into our hearts and minds.

It's hard to escape. We consume. Products, plastics, food, ideas, even people sometimes. We spend our days being battered by advertisements and promotions which convincingly tell us what we need to buy and consume to make us healthier and happier.

Maybe it's just me but I think we can download this consumeristic mentality into our spiritual lives too.

We can consume church, as if it's a product to be accepted or rejected and whose sole purpose is to meet our felt needs. We can consume Christ's teachings, embracing what we already like and conveniently ignoring what makes us uncomfortable. And we can consume the spiritual blessings we receive, hogging every good thing in our lives as if we're the only one who truly needs it.

But in Acts 20:35 Jesus says: "It is more blessed to give than to receive."

Consumers take. Christians give. I know that's a simplistic way to say it. And I feel a bit convicted writing this. After all, I'm deeply ensconced in this consumeristic culture too and sometimes worry that I'm just playing into it as well.

So it's helpful for all of us—including me—to be aware of the consumerism around us, push back, and remember that the gold is in the giving.

So what spiritual blessings have you received in your life? And how can you share what you've received with others?

Speaking about this same theme, the Scottish teacher, preacher and World War One chaplain Oswald Chambers wrote: "God will never allow you to keep a spiritual blessing completely for yourself. It must be given back to Him so that He can make it a blessing to others."[19]

THURSDAY - DESPITE YOUR CIRCUMSTANCES

Viktor Frankl was a psychiatrist and Holocaust survivor. In World War Two he was in a concentration camp serving voluntarily as a doctor to his fellow prisoners.[20]

Some men approached him because they thought they found a way to escape. They wanted to know if he wanted in on the plan.

He thought about it, but ended up telling them no.

His reason was because he didn't want to leave his people without medical care. He had a daily purpose which was more important than even escaping a hellish concentration camp.

It's a story about being selfless. But it's also about having a daily purpose—even in difficult circumstances.

I realize that life can be tough. It's hard to get motivated sometimes. Maybe you're going through a rough patch or are dealing with the scars of the past.

But whoever you are, when you realize that God can use you to bless others and give him glory—no matter what your situation is—it motivates, challenges and energizes you for living a more purposeful life.

As it says in Romans 8:28 (ESV), "we know that for those who love God all things work together for good, for those who are called according to his purpose."

Parents, administrators, students, teachers, executives, janitors, consultants, labourers, and hairstylists, can live each day with meaningful purpose—in a way that blesses others and gives God glory.

Life isn't just about what your circumstances are, but who you become despite your circumstances.

FRIDAY - FOR THE PRAISE OF GOD, OR THE PRAISE OF OTHERS?

Would you rather praise God or be praised by others?

Let's be honest. Getting a pat on the back feels good. I'm not knocking that.

But we shouldn't be so obsessed by the praise and approval of others that it eclipses the priority of putting God first.

So here's something you and I can do in the financial realm which trains us and reminds us to keep it all about him:

When opportunities present themselves, *give generously anonymously*.

Maybe an opportunity presents itself to buy a meal for someone. Or maybe you get a chance to provide some much-needed financial assistance to a family who's going through a rough patch. Realistically speaking, sometimes it's hard to be anonymous. But what if, in the right situation, you were able to be anonymous in the help you gave.

The reason this can help our discipleship is because, even when we're generous with others, we can make it about us. We can either make a show of our generosity, or, if we're not careful, we can do it for the praise we receive—instead of doing it for God.

In 2 Corinthians 7:1 Paul reflects on the comforting assurance that God is with us. Because of that we should "purify ourselves from everything that contaminates body and spirit..."

I think that includes purifying ourselves from selfish motives. After all, if we have the assurance that God is with us, what else do we need?

Let's focus more on praising God than the praise of others. When opportunities present themselves, give generously anonymously.

SATURDAY - BYSTANDER SYNDROME

In 1964 in New York City, Kitty Genovese was attacked for thirty minutes outside her apartment building. She died as a result of the brutal assault.

A police investigation revealed that there were thirty-eight witnesses. These were people watching from their apartment windows. But not a single one called the police. Even as the attack continued for *thirty minutes.*

Why?

Two sociologists came up with a theory: No one did anything because they thought someone else was going to do something. It's called Bystander Syndrome.

The resurrection of Christ is central to the Christian faith. It compels and energizes us to be a people of hope. In 1st Peter 1:3 the apostle Peter calls it a "living hope." It's not dead, but living. In other words, the hope we have isn't something we just have to wait for—it's something we're invited to live out today.

And let me tell you, hope is water in the desert, especially in a society where a lot of people feel hopeless.

So live a living hope. Get out there and do it. It's not someone else's job. It's yours. If you are a follower of the resurrected Christ, and if you've been assured of God's powerful and hope-filled future, you are invited— no, summoned—to be a person of living hope... to speak hope, to show hope, and to offer hope to the people around you.

Don't succumb to Bystander Syndrome. The result of standing on the sidelines of discipleship is a life of grey. Instead, light it up.

Not only will the people around you benefit as a result, but you'll be a faithful witness to the resurrected Jesus.

Today, be hope.

SUNDAY...

MONDAY - THE HOPE OF TOMORROW TODAY

Remember the movie *Back to the Future?* I think it was so popular because people loved the idea of time travel and guessing what the future would be like.

Well, we don't know much about flying cars (yet), but we actually do know what the future is going to be like.

We know it because of the resurrection. The resurrection gives us insight not only into something that happened, but something that is *going* to happen.

Bible scholar Tom Wright says it like this: "Easter was when Hope in person surprised the whole world by coming forward from the future into the present."[21]

In other words, through the resurrection, God gave us a glimpse of what things will be like someday—for everyone who enlists in the cause of the resurrected Jesus. It's a future without fear or death; a future without mourning, or crying or pain; and a future with fullness of joy, peace, and celebration.

The apostle Peter says that the resurrection gives us a "living hope" (1 Peter 1:3). It's not a dead hope, but a living one. It's a way of life that shimmers and brims with the hope that, one day, God will re-make everything to as it should be.

Are there reasons to be concerned about our world? Yes. But none of them is bigger than the forward-looking power and hope of the empty tomb.

So although we don't know about flying cars (yet), we do know that God has a glorious future planned.

Because of that, the people who go by the name of the resurrected Jesus, are summoned to be the hope of tomorrow today.

TUESDAY - THE UNWELCOME RESIDENT BETWEEN YOUR EARS

Sometimes when I wake up in the middle of the night, I hear noises. Ninety-nine times out of one hundred, they're normal sounds. Things like the refrigerator or furnace.

On their own schedule, they go on, turn off, go on, and turn off again.

That's like worry.

Just when you think you've entered a place of mental quiet, they start to hum again.

For you, maybe it's a pile of bills, or a deteriorating relationship, or a job teetering on the brink, or a test result, or the fear that you'll make a big decision badly.

In response, some people try to control every detail of their lives, pretending they can manage every little situation. But that never works because control is always an illusion. As Max Lucado says, "We can't take control, because control is not ours to take."[22]

Other people over-medicate themselves. And others beat themselves up in a blame game that never ends.

But let me suggest another approach.

Rehearse the promises of God.

Promises like:

"I am with you always, to the very end of the age" (Matthew 28:20)

God "gives us the victory through our Lord Jesus Christ" (1 Corinthians 15:57)

"My grace is sufficient for you" (2 Corinthians 12:9)

"God works for the good of those who love him" (Romans 8:28)

When you continually remind yourself about the presence, power and promises of God, worry starts to get the picture and realizes he's not welcome for a long-term stay between your ears.

Is worry the recurring hum in your life? If so...

Rehearse the promises of God.

WEDNESDAY - SING THE TRUTH INTO YOUR HEARTS

The word "minister" isn't just a noun—it's a verb. To "minister" to someone is to serve someone, or to care for someone, especially in a spiritual context.

In the past month I've heard people say that someone "ministered" to them through a friendly conversation. Another person felt that someone "ministered" to them when they prayed for them after a worship service.

In a similar way, music can "minister" to you. It can feed your faith and help it flourish. Maybe that's why Paul says in Colossians 3:16 to "Let the message of Christ dwell among you richly as you teach and admonish one another with all wisdom through psalms, hymns, and songs from the Spirit..."

Behind a lyric or melody is a person; and behind the instruments are people; and behind a radio dial, digital download or compact disc are people... who may very well be *ministering* to your spirit.

Sometimes life can be overwhelming. And processing your own emotions can be overwhelming too. So take a deep breath, and let the great hymns and praise songs of the faith minister to you.

"In Christ alone, my hope is found..." "Then sings my soul, my Saviour God, to thee..." "Shine, Jesus, Shine..." "You're a good, good Father, it's who you are..."[23]

Many centuries ago, the great church father Augustine said, "We sing the truth into our hearts."

How true that is! Let music minister to your soul.

THURSDAY - GOOD FRIDAY AND A GRENADE

There's a marine training facility called Parris Island. A young man signed up who was a bit out of step with the others. He was nice enough—but he just didn't fit in. As a result he got picked on. A lot.

In his barracks there were guys who were particularly mean. One of them came up with an idea to drop a disarmed hand grenade on the floor pretending like it was about to go off. Everyone would be in on the joke and know it was disarmed—everyone except the new guy. They figure he'd freak out and totally embarrass himself.

So the next time they were all together someone out of view tossed in the disarmed grenade. "It's a live grenade, it's about to explode!"

But the young recruit, instead of running away, jumped on top of the grenade, hugged it to his stomach, and yelled, "Run for your lives! You'll be killed if you don't!"

They all stood there, frozen in their own shame, marvelling at what he was prepared to do for them without any regard for himself. What they thought would be that young man's moment of great embarrassment and humiliation turned out to be a moment of great self-sacrifice and glory.[24]

To me, that story sheds light on the meaning of the cross—except that for Jesus, the danger was real, and he knew it. Christ went to the cross, in an act of great self-sacrifice, for you and for me. Isaiah 53:5 says, "But he was pierced for *our* transgressions, he was crushed for *our* iniquities..." (emphasis added)

When you think about the cross, give thanks for the Saviour who takes upon himself the punishment and disaster that you deserve, and in return, by virtue of your faith and trust in him, gives you the gift of eternity and a healed relationship with God.

Every year there is a day set aside to specifically ponder the significance of the cross. It's called Good Friday. A few years ago a young person in our church said to me, "If that's the day when Jesus went to the cross, why is it called *good* Friday? Shouldn't it be called *sad* Friday?"

But Good Friday is "good" not because of what happened to Jesus, but because of what happened for you.

41

What many thought was a young man's moment of great embarrassment and humiliation turned out to be a moment of great self-sacrifice and glory—for you.

When you think of the cross, and what Jesus did, be thankful.

FRIDAY - "WELL, NOW YOU'RE SPECIAL TO ME"

In the popular TV series *Downton Abbey*, Daisy is a kitchen maid whose young husband William died in World War One. In one scene she visits William's father, Mr. Mason. Now that he has no children, he tells Daisy that she's all he's got. Let's listen in on their conversation:

Mr. Mason: "Without you, I'd have no one to pray for. I think William knew that. So will you be my daughter? Let me take you into my heart? Make you special? You'll have parents of your own of course..."

Daisy: "I haven't got any parents. Not like that. I've never been special to anyone."

Mr. Mason: "Except William."

Daisy: "That's right. I was only ever special to William. Never thought of it like that before."

Mr. Mason: "Well, now you're special to me."[25]

I love that scene. Mr. Mason seeks her out, "takes her into his heart" to make her his "special daughter." He's motivated by fatherly love and loyalty. It's one of the most touching moments in the whole series.

That's what your Heavenly Father's love is like for you.

You have a Loyal Champion in your corner—someone who will go to bat for you, advocate for you, sacrifice A, B and C for you... No. Matter. What.

Here is what we find in John 1:12: "Yet to all who did receive [Jesus], to those who believed in his name, he gave the right to become children of God..."

Today, remember this: Your life is exceptional, valuable, and firmly rooted in a love you can't lose.

SATURDAY - HUMILITY DEFINED

"Hey, follow me!" That's something you hear in a playground or park. One person leads, and everyone else follows.

In Christianity, the Leader is Jesus. The rest of us are followers. But if our understanding of Jesus is somehow distorted that means we can easily get off track.

One of the much-neglected traits of Jesus is humility. Philippians 2:8 (ESV) says that he "humbled himself by becoming obedient to the point of death, even death on a cross."

But if humility is so important, what exactly is it?

Here's a definition based on something C.S. Lewis wrote: "Humility isn't thinking less of yourself, but of yourself less."[26]

That means true humility isn't self-defeating or of the woe-is-me variety. It's about putting God's will and the interests of others first. In this way you "lose yourself" because you're not overly concerned with your reputation, your status, or looking good in the eyes of others. You just want to serve God and care for his people.

So, do you want to faithfully follow our everlasting Leader? If so, remember that humility should be a key ingredient in the cultivation of your character.

"Humility isn't thinking less of yourself, but of yourself less."

SUNDAY...

MONDAY - ANTI-HUMBLE

Two days ago, I shared a definition of humility inspired by C.S. Lewis: "Humility isn't thinking less of yourself, but of yourself less."

That means true humility isn't self-defeating or self-deprecating. It's about putting God's will and the interests of others first. In this way you "lose yourself" because you're not overly concerned with your reputation, your status, or looking good in the eyes of others. You just want to serve God and care for his people.

'Sounds nice, Matthew,' you might say, 'but how? *How* do I learn to be more humble?'

Here's one idea among many: When you need help, ask for it.

If you need help with something but don't ask for it, it might very well be a pride issue. It's anti-humble. It's being so stubborn that you would rather appear a certain way to someone else—"strong," "independent," or "self-reliant"—than reach out and actually improve your situation.

James 4:6 says, "God opposes the proud but gives grace to the humble." Pride is a me-first commitment to journey alone. But when you acknowledge that you're not 'all that and a bag of chips,' and when you care more about God's will and caring for others than you do your selfish me-first agenda, I think God breathes grace into your situation.

If you want to grow your humility, ask for help when you need to.

Pride is a me-first commitment to journey alone. Humility is a God-first commitment to journey together.

"God opposes the proud but gives grace to the humble."

TUESDAY - LIKE WATER OFF A DUCK'S BACK

"You never do it right."

"Your priorities are always messed up."

"You always say the wrong thing!"

How do you respond when people unduly judge and criticize you?

If you're like a lot of other people (including me), probably not very well!

So I stand in awe of the apostle Paul when he says, "I care very little if I am judged by you or by any human court; indeed, I do not even judge myself" (1 Corinthians 4:3).

Other people's judgments and criticisms roll off of him like water off a duck's back. Even his judgments and criticisms *of himself* roll off him like water off a duck's back!

But how?

In verse 4 he gives the answer: "It is the Lord who judges me."

He knows whose judgment ultimately counts—God's.

Today I want to tell you that what's true for Paul is also true for you: When you're confident that God alone is your judge, you're more confident that others aren't.

I think that many of us have a secret fear of somehow losing at life—of being judged as failures by other people. Because of that, we can think too highly of other people's judgments and criticisms, even when they're unfounded.

Today, rest securely in the liberating freedom that God alone is judge.

When you're confident that God alone is your judge, you're more confident that others aren't.

WEDNESDAY - ROYAL BLOOD

After World War Two, fifty men came out of a camp in Indochina with amnesia. They didn't know who they were. They simply didn't remember, and there were no records.

For those who were brought back to Paris, someone had the idea to advertise in the newspapers. The idea was to tell the public about the situation, and then promote a special evening at the opera house. The organizers would introduce the men one by one, and hopefully people in the crowd could identify them.

When the night came, one man walked out on stage and called out, "Does anybody out there know who I am?"[27]

That's a question many people are asking these days, perhaps if only to themselves. "Does anybody out there know who I am?" Quite often, perhaps because we live in confusing times, some people don't know what makes them unique, valuable, or important.

I'm here to tell you that if you are a follower of Jesus, you are a child of God. First and foremost. That's who you are. And as the dominant facet of your identity, it is more important than any other title related to your family, ethnicity, sex, or language.

It also eclipses those secret titles and lies that you say to yourself, or that other people have said about you: Dumb, Ugly, Weird, Poor, Unworthy, Insignificant, Lost, A fake.

Back at the opera house a man called out, "Does anybody out there know who I am?" If you ask that question about yourself, don't believe anything that undermines the beauty, truth and power of who you actually are. In Romans 8:14 Paul says that "those who are led by the Spirit of God are the children of God."

If you are a Christian, *that's* who you are.

You have royal blood. Live with humble confidence and bold faithfulness, knowing that this is true.

THURSDAY - JUST ONE PERSON

Recently a man in my congregation, Jeff Walther, delivered a sermon about making a difference in someone's life.

As a part of that, he told a well-known story about a man walking along a beach. He saw someone moving in the distance, almost like they were dancing.

As he got closer he realized that it was a young man. But he wasn't dancing. He was scurrying around, picking up small objects, and throwing them into the ocean.

The onlooker called out, "Good morning! May I ask what you're doing?" The young man replied, "I'm throwing starfish into the ocean."

"Why?"

"The sun is up and the tide is going out. If I don't throw them in, they'll die."

The man looked around and said, "But don't you realize there are miles and miles of beach and there are starfish all along every mile? You can't possibly make a difference!"

Hearing this, the young man bent down, picked up another starfish, and threw it into the ocean. As it met the water he replied, "It made a difference to that one."

In Ephesians 2:10 Paul writes, "For we are God's workmanship, created in Christ Jesus to do good works..."

That's true whether your good works impact the lives of a thousand people, a hundred people...

or just one.

In *The Power of If*, Mark Batterson writes that "if you do little things like they're big things, then God will do big things like they are little things!"[28]

You were made to make a difference. No matter how many lives you touch. So share an act of love. And trust God to take it from there.

FRIDAY - MORE THAN JUST ONE MOMENT

One of the ideas people have is that meaningful faith is formed and shaped in one big dramatic moment. Kind of like a spiritual "Big Bang" event. And in some cases, it is.

But what I've noticed is that most people's faith is formed and shaped over time—and as a result of *many* factors.

Here's why I think this should encourage you.

As you form and shape your faith, and as you try to positively impact the faith of others, know that it's not all up to you, and it's not always dependent on one moment. God is working behind the scenes and through other people and situations.

Faith forming and shaping is often a team effort. God composes and orchestrates the score, and the rest of us play our own little parts to help make the music.

The quiet conversation before bed, the experience at camp, a Bible story, the Sunday School teacher, the sincere friend in small group, that song on the radio, a humble godly example who lights the way...

It's like in 1 Corinthians 3:6 when Paul writes, "I planted the seed, Apollos watered it, but God has been making it grow." In other words, many people and factors are at play, but it is God who is making it all happen.

So as you form and shape your faith, and as you try to positively impact the faith of others, know that it's not all up to you, and it's not always dependent on one moment. God is working behind the scenes and through other people and situations.

You just have to be faithful in the daily things you say and do. Faithfulness is your job; effectiveness is God's.

SATURDAY - WHAT IS THE (REAL) REASON FOR YOUR HOPE?

"You don't actually believe in God, do you?"

"Why on earth would you read the Bible?"

"What reason would possibly make you want to go to church?"

Have you ever heard any of those questions? I'm guessing yes.

And unfortunately, many of you feel overwhelmed and unprepared to give a response when someone questions your faith.

But it doesn't need to be that way.

In 1 Peter 3:15 we read, "Always be prepared to give an answer to everyone who asks you to give the reason for the hope that you have."

Take note of a few things.

First, "be prepared." That means you need to think through a few things ahead of time.

Second, "give an answer to everyone who asks you to give the reasons for the hope that you have." That means you need to know the reason for the hope that is within you and be ready to share it.

So here's what I think you should do. In a sentence, write down the *real* reason for the Christian hope that is in you. Not someone else's reason, but the *real* reason to you.

For me, there are a tonne of reasons for my Christian hope. But the main one—ever since high school—has been that Jesus and his teachings offer the most hope for our world and for its future.

It feels natural for me to talk about *because it's true.*

So what's your reason? Think about it. Write it down. And prepared to respond graciously when someone questions you about your faith. Because they will. When you do, you'll feel less overwhelmed and more prepared.

What is the reason for the hope that you have?

SUNDAY...

MONDAY - WHEN WHAT YOU SAY ISN'T ALL THAT MATTERS

On Saturday, we talked about thinking very intentionally about coming up with the reason for the hope that you have within you.

The reason we did this is because of 1 Peter 3:15 that says, "Always be prepared to give an answer to everyone who asks you to give the reason for the hope that you have."

It's like our society is in the Yukon panning for something valuable. All people keep coming up with in their sifters is cynicism. Huge chunks of hope are coveted—but in short supply.

In light of that you should (a) be prepared for when others ask you about your faith, and (b) identify the reason for the Christian hope that is within you.

But when you identify the reason for the hope that is in you, and when you share it with someone else, it's important to do it in a way that increases the likelihood of it being noticed at all. Peter says to do it "with gentleness and respect" (1 Peter 3:15).

It's a warning against aggression and arrogance. Sometimes it's not just *what* you say, but *how* you say it.

When you speak about the reason for your hope, gently share your views while respecting the fact that others may disagree or think differently.

Arrogance and aggression close doors; gentleness and respect open them.

A lot of people are nervous about saying anything about their faith. They're worried about not being able to defend their views or that they need to turn someone into a full-fledged disciple of Jesus in a two-minute conversation.

But be at peace. Your job isn't to always hit a home run; it's simply to step up to the plate.

Know the reason for the hope that you have. Be prepared to share it when asked. And do it in a winsome way.

Arrogance and aggression close doors; gentleness and respect open them.

TUESDAY - EXPECT TO BE DIFFERENT

In the first century, the apostle Peter wrote a letter to encourage Christians who were feeling shunned and persecuted for their faith.

Since they didn't buy in to the dominant religions of the day, and would only worship the one true God of the Bible and order their lives according to his teachings, they were often considered radicals, subversives, and outsiders.

So Peter encouraged them to stand firm; to actually expect some suffering and marginalization; and to be prepared to explain their faith when asked.

In the midst of all this he said to "revere Christ as Lord" (1 Peter 3:15).

On the surface, this quite simply means what it says: To revere and honour Jesus as the Lord of their lives. But there's another implication too:

Expect to be different from other people.

Think about it. If Jesus is first in your life, that means you care more about being loyal to him than you do about what others think... and about fitting in... and about measuring up to the standards of popular culture.

The point is this. Don't be surprised when your faith makes you feel different. Expect it. Anticipate it. Consider it a blessing.

At first, this might make you feel alone. But that's part of the reason why your devotional life is so important; why worshiping with others Christians is so important; and why gathering and talking with others who share your faith is so important—either in a small group or some other setting.

In their book, *You And Me Forever*, Francis and Lisa Chan write: "If we are *not* making decisions in our lives that seem weird or radical to lukewarm people, we probably need to evaluate what's going on. Believers on a mission are going to look a little crazy to most of the world, just as the training regimen of an Olympic athlete looks a little crazy to us."[29]

So don't be surprised when your faith makes you feel different. Expect it. Anticipate it. Consider it a blessing.

And remember this: You are not alone. God is with you. And so are your fellow travellers in the footsteps of Jesus.

WEDNESDAY - THANK GOD FOR UN-ANSWERED PRAYERS

Can you imagine if God granted all your prayer requests?

In the movie *Bruce Almighty*, Bruce (played by Jim Carey) has the opportunity to do God's work for a while. In an effort to speed up the never-ending task of answering prayers, he simply says "Yes" to everyone's requests. Those who have seen the movie will know that it didn't turn out very well![30]

Truth is, God knows what's best for you more than you know what's best for you. Should we pray? Absolutely! But we just need to realize that we don't always see the big picture like God does.

There's a Garth Brooks song about this. It tells about how, at a football game, he and his wife ran into his "old high school flame." Back then he had prayed so hard that God "would make her mine."

But if God had granted that request, he wouldn't have met his current wife! He goes on to sing, "Some of God's greatest gifts are unanswered prayers."[31]

Sometimes prayers are answered in ways we expect. Sometimes they're not. But in and through it all we need to trust that God is sovereign and all-wise. As it says in Romans 11:33: "Oh, the depth of the riches of the wisdom and knowledge of God! How unsearchable his judgments, and his paths beyond tracing out!"

Have you ever thanked God for *un*-answered prayers? It's one of the ways you can open yourself to God's eternal and never-ending wisdom, and to whatever else he may have in store for you on your horizon.

THURSDAY - PROVING THAT YOU'RE SOMEBODY

"Keeping up with the Joneses" is an expression that has to do with how you think you're measuring up (and keeping up) with the people around you. It has to do with comparison.

And do you know what? It's an exhausting way to live.

In an incredibly honest interview with *Vogue Magazine*, pop singer Madonna said she feels mediocre and uninteresting unless she keeps doing new things to prove she's special. "Because even though I have become somebody," she said, "I still have to prove that I am somebody. My struggle has never ended and I guess it never will."[32]

I think it reveals an inner turmoil that a lot of people face.

We think we have to somehow prove that we're special and important and worthy in the eyes of others.

But that's a distracted way to live.

In Psalm 141:8 David said, "But my eyes are fixed on you, O Sovereign LORD..." I think that's a good idea for all of us! When our eyes are fixed on God, it means we're less fixated on how we measure up to others.

Today, as you go through your to-do list, make decisions, interact with others, and set priorities, try to fix your eyes on God, and try to focus your energy on being faithful him.

When you do that you'll feel less of a need to prove your importance and worth to other people.

Being faithful in the eyes of God is more important than being impressive in the eyes of others.

FRIDAY - TO MAKE LIFE RICHER

At a recent gathering for our small group, a friend named David Holloway shared something he had seen on a fridge magnet: "To make life richer, make life simpler."

We all nodded in agreement.

But *how* do you make life richer by making it simpler?

Here's a tip for those among us who resonate with this idea deep within our frantic souls.

Cultivate an appreciation for creation.

I could have said to "cultivate an appreciation for nature," but the word "creation" is better. It reminds us that we are living in a world that a good God has care-fully created. Genesis 1:31 says, "God saw all that he had made, and it was very good."

Has anyone ever regretted going for a walk in the woods? Has anyone ever said that watching a sunrise or sunset was a waste of time? Has anyone ever gone for a swim or had a picnic on the grass and felt worse as a result?

I'm guessing not.

I think that when we speed up our lives, never hit the brakes, and cut ourselves off from the beautiful world around us, we are somehow betraying a natural pace and place that keeps us in tune with God's deep shalom—his deep peace—which is woven into his creation... a creation that you and I are a part of.

If you want to make life richer by making it simpler, cultivate an appreciation for creation.

"God saw all that he had made, and it was very good."

SATURDAY - UNTIL WE ARE AWARE OF GOD'S MARCHING ORDERS

Life is full of decisions. Small ones, easy ones, tough ones, and over-sized.

But how do you make decisions in a faithful way? That is true to what God's purposes might be for your life?

Well, you're right. That's a big question. But here's some advice:

Consult God *first*.

Carl George writes, "Until we are aware of God's marching orders, our activities are vain and folly."[33] When he said that he was talking about the work and direction of churches. But it's a helpful word for our daily decision making too.

Consult God *before* you make a big decision. Don't just ask for his stamp of approval *after* you've already made up your mind.

This consultation includes prayer. It includes searching the Scriptures. It includes talking to a wise Christian who is a little further down the road than you are. It may even include some fasting.

Proverbs 3:5 says to "Trust in the LORD with all your heart..." For that to happen, you need to ensure he's the main player in the decision-making boardroom of your brain.

When you live like you're in charge, some good things can happen. But when you live knowing God's in charge, great things can.

Consult God *before* you make a big decision. Don't just ask for his stamp of approval *after* you've already made up your mind.

SUNDAY...

MONDAY - GRACE NOTES

You've heard the lie before: "Sticks and stones may break my bones but words will never hurt me."

The idea is that words—because they are invisible—cannot hurt us. But we know it isn't true. The put down, the threat, the lie that cuts deeper than a knife.

Words can have a negative power.

But they can have a positive power too. Let me give two examples.

First, it's true for God. Psalm 50:1 says, "The Mighty One, God, the LORD, speaks and summons the earth from the rising of the sun to the place where it sets." His word results in blessing.

Second, it's true for human speech as well. Our words can have a positive power which can result in blessing other people.

With all this in mind, I'd like to suggest an illustration. In the world of music there's this thing called a "grace note." It's an extra sound which is not "needed" for the melody but adds a touch of beauty. Just for the joy of it.

We can think of the sun, the rain, and the breeze, as God's grace notes—touches of beauty he gives to all of us. Just for the joy of it.

And we can also think of our own words in the same way—as grace notes —building up those around us in a crescendo of dignity and honour. Just for the joy of it.

Do you *have* to do it? Of course not. That's what makes it so meaningful. Grace notes: Immeasurable encouragement that surprise the soul. Just for the joy of it.

How will your words build someone up with dignity and honour today?

Remember: Your tongue just might be the most powerful muscle you have.

TUESDAY - GIVING TROUBLES OVER

Susanna Wesley lived a few hundred years ago. She gave birth to nineteen children. Ten survived infancy.

To say she was busy is an understatement. Plus, she had a difficult life— marital troubles, financial hardship, and illness were frequent visitors.

And that's not to mention the pain and difficulty of coping with the death of nine children.

Susanna is best remembered as the mother of John and Charles Wesley, influential Christian thinkers. Plus, Charles Wesley wrote thousands of hymns, including "Hark! The Herald Angels Sing," "And Can It Be," and "Come, Thou Long-Expected Jesus."

But what I love best about her legacy is her devotional life. As you can imagine, someone with that much hardship and that many children wouldn't have had a lot of spare time.

But she knew the importance of putting God first.

So, at a certain time every day, leaning back in her rocking chair, she would put her apron over her face. That was her agreed-upon signal to her kids that she was unavailable. Why?

Because she was talking to God.

I'm pretty sure she had a never-ending to do list. But she still did it because she knew it was important.

Giving your time to prayer is giving your troubles to God.

Psalm 34:17 (NLT) says, "The Lord hears his people when they call to him for help. He rescues them from all their troubles."

Do you have troubles? I thought so. So how can you *not* take time to pray?

Take the lead from Psalm 34:17 and from Susanna Wesley. Giving your time to prayer is giving your troubles to God.

WEDNESDAY - BLAME

Blaming. Other. People.

It's easy to do.

And to be honest, there are times when other people do in fact need to be called to account for having done something wrong or hurtful.

But what I'm talking about today is being quick to notice when *other* people have done something wrong... but being slow to notice when *we* have.

Here's my point:

Don't lay blame at someone else's feet when your own are standing still.

James 4:17 (NLT) says, "Remember, it is sin to know what you ought to do and then not do it." In its eternal wisdom, the book of James reminds us that it isn't just sinful to do something wrong, but to know the right thing to do and not do it.

Today, when you have a strong urge to blame someone else for something you think they've done wrong, be sure to ask yourself whether you've also been wrong in how you've spoken or acted. None of us are perfect. But people with integrity are continually on the move when it comes to wanting to say and do the right thing.

Make sure you don't just point out the problem, but are living in a way that makes you a part of the solution.

Don't lay blame at someone else's feet when your own are standing still.

THURSDAY - GOD FINISHES WHAT HE STARTS

We were talking in a restaurant on a Thursday afternoon while eating high-calorie French fries. My friend was telling me how down he was feeling about his spiritual progress.

He felt he should be further ahead... and that he often struggled with the sin of pride... and that his devotional life always felt like work.

Can you relate?

I certainly could. There are times when I feel like I should be further ahead too.

But as I look back on that conversation now, I wish I had pointed out to him how much progress he had *already* made. He had made a commitment to Jesus, and was volunteering in the music ministry in his church. Plus, other people sometimes sought him out for personal encouragement!

It's so easy to focus on the growth that still needs to happen, that we devalue the growth that's *already* happened.

So here's what I think you should do: Celebrate the ways that your faith has *already* improved your priorities and changed your life for the better.

Speaking to the Philippians in chapter 1, verse 6 (ESV), Paul writes, "he [God] who began a good work in you will bring it to completion at the day of Jesus Christ."

In other words, God finishes what he starts. Trust the process. Trust God's work. And celebrate all the ways that your faith has *already* improved your priorities and changed your life for the better.

Today, celebrate the good work of God that continues to take shape in you. It's there. You just need to look.

FRIDAY - STEP OUT OF THE TRAFFIC

A few years ago I was in Myrtle Beach—it was awesome!

Every time I go on vacation I learn something new. For example, on that trip to Florida I learned that cheap socks are never worth it, that the novelty of fast food wears off *very* quickly, and that America *still* doesn't have Ketchup Chips. Honestly, why is this still happening?

But seriously, one of the things I learned was the value of unplugging from the internet.

In Psalm 46:10 (NLT) it says "Be still, and know that I am God!" The Message version of the Bible paraphrases that line like this: "Step out of the traffic!" It makes me think not just about a highway, but the information super-highway.

When we got to the beach the sun was warm and the laughter was plentiful. I wanted to grab my smart phone and start taking a hundred pictures. But the problem is that as soon as you go to grab your phone for one thing, it sucks you in with ten others. Next thing you know you've read three emails from work and are trying to understand the rationale behind someone's weird Instagram comments.

So I put the phone down. And my mind more easily shifted gears into a more restful place.

I've never been dead so I can't fully confirm what I'm about to say. But I'm pretty sure that *none* of our pictures or social media feeds are coming with us to heaven.

This week, maybe exchange a bit of screen time for actual face time. Maybe for you it's about not checking the phone after (or before) a certain time of day. Whatever you do, just be aware that your smart phone and the internet can make you stressed out like you're driving through traffic even if you're relaxing on the couch, sipping a latte in *Starbucks*, or lounging on the beach.

Don't be so excited about capturing every single moment in life that you miss the beauty of actually living it.

SATURDAY - WHAT IS THE PURPOSE OF LIFE?

A question most people ask at some point in their lives is this: What is the purpose of life?

I'm not sure if you've noticed, but our society seems to have an answer: 'The purpose of life is to be healthy and happy.' That's certainly what the TV shows, talking heads, radio programs, advertisers, and writers of many curricula and books seem to think.

But that answer is seriously misguided.

Now don't get me wrong. I want to be healthy and happy. I want that for you and for my family too. But the problem is that none of us are always healthy and happy. Those things come and go. And they come and go for the people you care about too.

So if you think that the point of life is to be healthy and happy you're setting yourself up for a life of discontentment... because it never lasts.

So let's consider this. What if the point of life is to glorify and serve God? What if it is to get in on the ways he is renovating the world? What if it has to do with knowing God and making him known?

It shifts the focus from you to God. The result is deeper peace, improved perspective, more godly priorities, and a stronger sense of purpose.

In other words, a life focussed on *who* matters most is a life focussed on *what* matters most.

So how would you answer the question about the purpose of life? Is it all about your own personal health and happiness? Or is it about glorifying and serving God?

Psalm 34:3 says, "Glorify the LORD with me; let us exalt his name together." When we do that I truly believe the result is deeper peace, improved perspective, more godly priorities, and a stronger sense of purpose.

Sounds pretty amazing, doesn't it?

A life focussed on *who* matters most is a life focussed on *what* matters most.

SUNDAY...

MONDAY - FLOPPING AROUND LIKE A FISH

Three friends were walking along the beach and noticed a fish flopping around on the shore.

One person wondered if the fish was sad because it didn't seem to own anything nice. So he bought the fish a gold watch and set it beside him. But nope. It made no difference. It still just flopped around.

Another wondered if a nice place to live wouldn't do the trick. So she got a nice little castle from the toy store. But that didn't make a difference either.

A third person got a masseuse to come give it a massage. But the fish didn't seem impressed. It continued to flop around.

They just stood there scratching their heads. They were out of ideas.

You're right. It's a silly story. What did the fish need? Water![34]

But I think we often behave in a similar way. We try to satisfy our most important needs with less important things.

In John 7:37-38 Jesus said, "Let anyone who is thirsty come to me and drink. Whoever believes in me, as Scripture has said, rivers of living water will flow from within them."

The water was to that fish what the living waters of Jesus are to us: Essential.

Don't be duped by the false hope of shiny things. When we try to satisfy our deepest desires with anything other than Jesus, we're just flopping around on the beach.

"Let anyone who is thirsty come to me and drink," Jesus said, "Whoever believes in me... rivers of living water will flow from within them."

TUESDAY - AT THE START, NOT THE END

Many Christians end their prayers with something like this: "In Jesus' name, Amen."

The origins of that practice trace back to a few different Bible passages. One of them is Jesus' own words in John 14:14 where he said, "You may ask me for anything in my name, and I will do it."

But just because you pray in Jesus' name, that doesn't mean everything you pray about will magically happen like you want it to.

Praying in Jesus' name means not only that you believe in him and trust in his power, but that you're praying for things that are consistent with his character and which seek to glorify God.

But since it's easy to forget what praying in Jesus name means, why not put that statement at the *start* of your prayers instead of at the end? Let me show you what I mean.

"Dear God, in Jesus' name, help me be at peace with today's tests results, whatever they may be…"

"Dear God, in Jesus' name, as I go through my week, make me ready to help when someone needs me…"

"Dear God, in Jesus' name, give me love and courage as I confront so-and-so about…"

Saying "In Jesus' name" isn't a magic button that makes things happen like you want them to. It means not only that you believe in him and trust in his power, but that you're praying for things that are consistent with his character and which seek to glorify God.

If you need some help in that regard, trying saying "In Jesus' name" at the *start* of your prayers instead of at the *end*. Like the first sentence in the chapter of a book, it will set the tone for the words that come next…

And the actions that follow.

WEDNESDAY - OUT LOUD

The more you study prayer—and the more you pray—the more you realize there's a lot to know. It can actually be intimidating.

So I came up with a saying to help keep my brain on the right track:

Pray consistently, whole-heartedly, and expectantly in Jesus' name.

When it comes to praying "whole-heartedly" we often fall short. When we doubt that God can actually bring any real change to our situation or to our requests, it means we're being half-hearted (and not whole-hearted) in our prayers.

A symptom of this is when your mind continually wanders. I realize it happens sometimes. It happens to me too. But when your mind is *always* wandering, maybe it's because you're thinking of prayer like a religious box to tick instead of a profound opportunity to speak with the Creator and King of the universe.

So here's a helpful corrective. In Matthew 6:6 Jesus says, "when you pray, go into your room, close the door and pray to your Father..." When you do that, why not try praying out loud?

When you pray out loud, your words are more likely to be honest, conversational, and focused.

Will it be perfect? Probably not. But it sure can help. And it will most likely take you to the next level.

So if you're having trouble keeping your head in the game, find a place alone and pray out loud.

You're more likely to be honest, conversational, and focused as you meaningfully interact with the Creator and King of your soul.

THURSDAY - IT'S A WIN-WIN

In 2018 we learned that the great preacher Billy Graham passed away at the age of ninety-nine.

So for today's devotional, and as a testament to Graham's own teaching, let me share a story he once told, and which captures something about the hope that was deep within him.

There was a thirty year-old truck driver who had his whole future ahead of him. Life was smooth sailing.

But one day while driving he got pains in his chest. At the hospital he found out that a malignant tumor was wrapped around his heart.

It was complicated to say the least. But through the treatment and surgery his attitude amazed the doctors and nurses at the University of Michigan. In the midst of what would make many people crumple on the floor, he was incredibly positive.

Apparently the size of the hope *in* his heart was bigger than the tumour wrapped *around* his heart.

They asked him how he could have such a great attitude even though he was threatened with death. So he told them about his faith in Jesus.

Even still, they didn't hold out much hope and said that only a miracle could save him. He looked at them and said: "Docs, I'm in a win-win playoff. If I live I win. If I die I win."[35]

It makes me think of Romans 6:23 (ESV), that "the free gift of God is eternal life in Christ Jesus our Lord."

A short while later the truck driver died. But did he? Wasn't his death just his life getting a capital L?

Today, with whatever you're dealing with, just remember that everything you see isn't everything there is to see.

God is bigger than your problems. And although that doesn't make your problems go away, it does remind them that they're supposed to be in the trunk and not in the driver's seat.

Remember, you're in a win-win playoff. Live like it.

(With thanks to Billy Graham.)

FRIDAY - MOTIVES MATTER

You know a lot about your own body—probably more than anyone else (except God).

But you probably don't know this: That there is an average of seven octillion atoms in an adult's body; that half the population has eyelash mites (yikes); and that every tongue print is unique.

In other words, you know your body well—but there's always *more* to know.

That's like prayer.

Most of us think we know the basics of prayer. It's "talking to God," right? Well, yes. But it's helpful to remember that there's always *more* to know. If you want to grow in your faith, it's important to not only know *what* it is but *how* to do it.

So something I'd put in the "more to know" category is that *motives matter*.

Jesus' brother James taught about this when he wrote, "When you ask, you do not receive, because you ask with wrong motives, that you may spend what you get on your pleasures" (James 4:3).

If we always pray with selfish motives; are only ever asking God to make our lives easier or more pleasurable; and are never seeking God's will and how to glorify him, it's most likely going to negatively impact your prayer life.

As life goes on, you keep learning about yourself. (By the way, your blood apparently travels an average of 19,000 kilometres through your body each day!)

You also keep learning about prayer.

So check your motives, and align them as best you can with what the Bible teaches is pleasing to God. It will have an impact.

Motives matter.

SATURDAY - GET CONSISTENT

This week I'm sharing some thoughts about prayer. Like oxygen, prayer is a life-giving necessity for a vibrant spiritual life.

Yesterday, I talked about how motives matter. Today, let's talk about *consistency*.

In 1 Thessalonians 5:17 (ESV) Paul says to "pray without ceasing." But if you're like a lot of people, there's more ceasing than there is praying. Consistency is hard. Life gets busy. Your schedule fluctuates. Your mind wanders. You get tired.

That's why, if you struggle with consistency, it's helpful to set a specific time to pray every day.

Maybe it's first thing in the morning. Maybe it's during a pause in your school or workday. Maybe it's at night.

I once read that it takes six weeks of doing something consistently for it to become a habit. After six weeks, kids seem to get the picture that school is a part of their routine. When you go to church six weeks in a row is feels more natural. And when you pray consistently for six weeks, you develop a godly habit that will reap untold benefits in your life.

So if you struggle to be consistent in your prayer life, set a specific time to pray each day and stick to it.

Like oxygen, prayer is a life-giving necessity for a vibrant spiritual life. And it's totally within your reach to make it happen.

SUNDAY...

MONDAY - MISSED (OR SKIPPED?) OPPORTUNITIES

Every single day opportunities come our way. They are often disguised as hum-drum conversations, daily routines, or things people tell you.

A lot of these daily details are just that—details. But tucked into the conversation at the office, email with a friend, and random chunks of free time...

Are opportunities.

In 1987 Howard Schultz had to make a tough decision. Should he give up the security of his $75,000 salary to buy a small chain of coffee houses which was weirdly titled *Starbucks*? It was both a risk *and* an opportunity. He went for it. Five years later it went public and now has over 16,580 stories in forty countries with revenues in excess of 4.7 billion.

This week you may not get a chance to buy *Starbucks*. But you'll have conversations with people who need some support. You'll have some free time that you can either waste or invest in something renewing. Or you'll stumble upon a chance to take that next best step you've always wanted to take.

One of my favourite passages from Ephesians is this: "Be very careful, then, how you live—not as unwise but as wise, making the most of every opportunity..." (Ephesians 5:15-16)

What we call "missed opportunities" are usually skipped opportunities. We think we've missed something, when we've really just closed our eyes, arms and hearts to what's right in front of us.

There are 1784 "ifs" in the Bible. They're conditional conjunctions—which means that the outcome of a whole bunch of situations are conditional on someone making a choice. Someone like you.

This week, instead of trudging through life like it's a prison sentence, see each day for what it truly is:

An opportunity to see, discover and create something great.

TUESDAY - LOVE DEFINED

Today I'd like us think about what love actually means. And not just in the romantic sense, but in the wider love-your-neighbour sense.

I think that when we look at Jesus' example, love means acknowledging that other people are made in God's image, and pursuing God's best for them.

That's what Jesus did. So that's what we can do too. It's not based on our fluctuating feelings, or even on whether or not we want to.

It's based on the example of a steadfast Saviour.

I heard about a young girl named Ashley who started to date a boy. She gave him a picture of herself in her favourite sweater. On the back she wrote, "I love you more than life itself. I am yours forever. Love always, Ashley. P.S. If we ever break up, I want this picture back—it's the only one I have."[36]

Like this young romance, we can act like love is a powerful (yet unstable and uncertain) aspect of our lives!

But that's not biblical love.

1 John 4:8 says, "Whoever does not love does not know God, because God is love."

So love. But to do that in a biblical way, you need to know what it is.

Love is acknowledging that other people are made in God's image, and pursuing God's best for them.

WEDNESDAY - CHRONIC BUSYNESS

I talk a lot about love, mostly because Jesus commands us to do it! It involves acknowledging that other people are created in God's image and pursuing God's best for them.

But as a part of that life-long process, it's helpful to honestly name the things that hold us back from loving others more fully:

Busyness.

Yup. Chronic busyness can undermine your capacity to love others.

I realize that busyness is sometimes inevitable. Life happens. But I truly think that *chronic* busyness is the issue. If you *never* have any flexibility in your schedule it will be harder for you to respond to other people's hurts and needs when they arise.

Writing in Galatians 5:13 (ESV) Paul says, "through love serve one another." But that's very hard to do if you never have any time or energy to give.

If you're chronically busy, it may be hard to change overnight. But look for opportunities to lighten your load. Maybe it's less screen time or simplifying something in your schedule. Or maybe it's learning to say "No" to a request on your time and energy for something that just isn't a key priority in your life.

"Through love serve one another."

So proactively shape your schedule in a way that allows for it to happen.

THURSDAY - ZEROING IN ON THE KEY INGREDIENT

For centuries people chewed on the bark of Willow Trees to relieve pain.

As we entered the modern period, some people wanted to find out why. Did it have something to do with chewing on the rough bark itself? Or did it have something to do with the orange-ish resin?

They did some tests. Nope. Not the bark or resin.

Eventually they were able to find and isolate the key active pain-relieving ingredient. Our modern aspirin-type pills are the result.[37]

When it comes to faith, it's easy to get confused about what the key ingredient is (and what it isn't).

It's easy to think the most important thing is a specific moral issue that some politicians like to go on and on about. But no, that's not it. That's like the bark.

It's easy to think the most important thing is a specific denomination, or even a certain worship style. But no, that's not it either. That's like the orange-ish resin.

When it comes to how we act as followers of Jesus, 1 Corinthians 13:13

(ESV) says, "faith, hope, and love abide, these three; but the greatest of these is love."

So when it comes to how we act as followers of Jesus, the key ingredient is love. If you take that away, you end up with a weird orange taste in your mouth and sore gums. (Kind of. You know what I mean.)

I know you feel bamboozled some days. Or criticized. Or distracted.

But don't let go of love. It's the key ingredient.

Without love, your soul is sick. With love, your soul sings.

"So now faith, hope, and love abide, these three; but the greatest of these is love."

FRIDAY - LOVED PEOPLE LOVE PEOPLE

I was watching an interview with someone who worked with at-risk youth.

He said, "Hurt people hurt people." He meant that if someone has been deeply hurt in their past, they often hurt other people simply because it's what they know. Is that *always* the case? No. But in his experience it was often true.

As I thought about it, I realized you can apply the same logic to love.

Loved people love people.

If you've been really loved and guided throughout your life, it's probably more natural for you to share love and guidance with others. Why? Because it's what you know.

Plus, 1 John 4:10 says this: "This is love: not that we loved God, but that he loved us and sent his Son as an atoning sacrifice for our sins." When you take seriously the sacrificial love God showed for you on the cross, you're probably quicker to share mercy and love with others.

Here's one of the implications. Since God takes the initiative and is quick to love us, we too can take the initiative and be quick to love others.

Right now there are people around you. And if "loved people love people," then the love you show *them* will have a lasting impact down the line on the way they interact with others.

Your love is having an influence and is shaping the character of someone who was made to make a mark in this world. Does it seem grand? Like a high and noble calling? You better believe it!

Your love is an invisible investment in the life of someone who was born for a reason. God is preparing them for great things. And you can help.

Loved people love people.

SATURDAY - LOVE IS...

Everyone loves the idea of love. I'm not necessarily talking about romantic love (although what I'm about to say applies to that too), but love in general.

Who's ever heard of someone saying they don't like love, or that love is bad?

Since it's so widely venerated and used, it's a word that can easily be abused.

So here's one way to think about what love means: Love is sacrifice with a smile.

Love involves giving something up. In John 13:34 (ESV) Jesus told his disciples to "love one another: just as I have loved you, you also are to love one another." It's a sacrificial love. Not only did Jesus wash their feet, but he went to the cross for them—he sacrificed his life! But he didn't do it begrudgingly. He knew that the result would benefit them... and us!

In John 3:16 we're told that God so loved the world that he gave his one and only Son. There was a sacrifice, a cost. But again, it wasn't done begrudgingly. It was done out of love for his children. It was done to show us the way back to his heart.

You're right. Love is not always easy. Love is not always comfortable. But it's worth it.

Today, as you follow Jesus into your conversations, workplaces, schools, parenting, and decisions, think about love, sacrifice and joy as partners. Not because you're a perpetually-bouncy do-gooder—but because God is your true joy. He wants the best for you. And you want the best for others.

Love is sacrifice with a smile.

SUNDAY...

MONDAY - WHEN THEY SANG "HAPPY BIRTHDAY" SHE WEPT

Tony Campolo is a sociologist who traveled to Hawaii. Because of the time change he found himself wide awake in the middle of the night, wandering the streets, and looking for somewhere to eat.

He found a small diner and ordered a coffee and a donut. Soon, a bunch of loud, boisterous prostitutes came in.

He overheard a conversation between two of them. A woman named Agnes was turning thirty-nine the next day. With a series of brash responses, her "friend" shrugged off the news basically telling her that she could care less. "So what do you want from me? A birthday party?"

Agnes seemed to feel dejected. Soon they both left.

After talking with the owner, Campolo learned that this same group of women came in every night. So he decided to throw Agnes a birthday party! He went out and got some decorations, the owner made a cake, and the owner's wife spread the news.

Very early the next morning the place was decorated—and it was jam packed with prostitutes. Everyone was ready and in place by the time Agnes arrived.

"Happy Birthday!" they yelled. Never had Campolo seen anyone so astounded. She almost lost her balance. And when she heard them sing Happy Birthday, she broke down and wept. She was moved to the core.

After some time of stunned silence, Agnes said that she didn't want them to eat the cake—not yet, anyway. She just wanted to look at it. No one had ever done this for her before. In fact, she asked if she could take it down the street to show her mom who lived nearby. It was her first birthday cake.[38]

I think it's just a brutal fact of human nature that it's harder to love someone when we don't think we have anything in common with them. It seems *natural* to care about people who are somehow *like* us—perhaps someone in our family or who has similar hobbies or interests.

So it's easy to get apathetic to the plight of others. But Genesis 1:27 (NLT) says, "So God created human beings in his own image." And there's the thing. We all *do* have something in common—nurses, teachers, and postal workers, prostitutes, web designers, and C.E.O.s...

We are *all* made in the image of God.

Our care for others isn't based on how personally likeable they are to us, but on how personally loved they are by God.

TUESDAY - DO YOU MAKE DECISIONS... OR REACTIONS?

There was a woman who kept having her car vandalized. At first she discovered dents in the side. Then someone ran their car key down the length of the vehicle ruining her paint job. So she had it fixed.

And then it happened again!

After an all-night stakeout she discovered that the culprit was someone on her own street.

She was furious. She wanted to ring the guy's neck! But she knew that wasn't a good idea. She worshiped at a local church and had perhaps come to know the verse in Romans 12:21: "Do not be overcome by evil, but overcome evil with good."

So the next day she got up, took a few deep breaths, and baked an incredible double-decker chocolate cake. Then she delivered it to her guilty neighbour. "I baked this and thought you'd enjoy it, so here you go. God's been good to me and I just wanted to pass it on." Then she left.

When you study the biblical stories here's what you find: *Love is a decision; hostility is a reaction.* Too often we think loving someone is the same as liking them. But it's not. Loving someone has to do with recognizing that they are made in God's image and seeking God's best for them.

You may not like them, and you may not agree with every decision they've ever made, but you can still do your best to love them.

So when you're dealing with difficult people, what do you do? Do you make *decisions* about how to respond? Or do you make *reactions*?

When we humans are all charged up about something we're usually not thinking very clearly. So what I've found in those situations is that the most faithful way forward it to take some time, pray, and act in a way that honours God.

Love is a decision. Hostility is a reaction.

WEDNESDAY - BEING SPIRITUALLY "FED"

Do you want to be spiritually "fed"?

If so, here's a newsflash.

People today have more access to spiritually-enriching resources than at any other time in human history.

A hundred years ago, if you wanted to learn more about your faith, in addition to calling on God and engaging in the traditional spiritual disciplines, you have could read the Bible, gone to a worship service, or perhaps ordered a book through snail mail.

Today, not only can you do those things, but you can access thousands of studies, sermons, podcasts or blogs online; access any number of devotionals (like this one); listen to a wide range of stations on the radio or channels on T.V.; access an untold number of books about every single topic imaginable (either through the library, a bookstore, or the web). You don't even have to wait for a hard copy—you can just download the e-version. Plus, whatever your interests, there's probably an app for that.

Proverbs 18:15 (ESV) says, "An intelligent heart acquires knowledge, and the ear of the wise seeks knowledge." Did you see that? An intelligent heart *acquires* knowledge, it *seeks* wisdom.

In other words, it goes out and gets it.

Maybe you need inspiration to chase your dreams. If so, look up Mark Batterson's *Chase the Lion*. Maybe you want re-frame how you think about worry. If so, Max Lucado's *Anxious for Nothing* might be for you. Perhaps Tim Keller's *The Reason for God* will answer some of your itching questions. What if Margaret Feinberg's *Fight Back with Joy* which talks about her own battle with cancer were to offer some help? Or download the app about parenting from Parent Cue. Or... or... or...

Today, we have access to more spiritually-enriching resources than at any other time in human history.

Isn't it wonderful that you and I get to benefit?

Look, seek, acquire. And be stronger—and wiser—as a result.

THURSDAY - TALK IS... CHEAP?

"Talk is cheap."

Have you ever heard someone use that expression? It's the cousin to "Actions speak louder than words."

I get where it comes from. Quite often, we only know if someone means what they say if they back it up with their actions.

But *why*? *Why* do so many people think talk is cheap?

I think it's because many of us use, misuse and abuse words.

In Matthew 5:37 Jesus is speaking to his disciples about taking oaths. He says, "All you need to say is simply 'Yes' or 'No'; anything beyond this comes from the evil one." Although he was addressing a different situation 2000 years ago, he reminds us that the words we use should be honest and plain.

How often do we say we're going to do something, but don't follow through? How often do we insist something is true, even though we're not really sure? How often do we use flattery or eloquent words just to manipulate someone to agree with us?

So why not use sincerity and straightforwardness as your verbal guides?

To a lot of people, talk is cheap. But it doesn't have to be.

Your talk can be rich—full of value and integrity—revealing a heart that is true to the One who is true to you.

Today, use sincerity and straightforwardness as your verbal guides.

FRIDAY - WHOSE WORDS TO YOU WILL NEVER FAIL

A friend who doesn't share my beliefs was telling me his "bucket list"—things he wanted to do before he died, before he "kicked the bucket"!

In addition to things like snorkelling at the Great Barrier Reef was reading the Bible.

He told me that even though he wasn't a Christian, he realized that the Bible has huge cultural and historical significance. And since he respected many of Jesus' teachings he wanted to read it cover-to-cover.

In saying this, he gave me a gift: A reminder that the Bible has immense power. For all of us.

Today I want to give some advice to help those among us who are trying to read the Bible "cover-to-cover"—and struggling with it. Let's be honest, who among us hasn't laboured through sections, felt bad because it seemed like work, and wondered if they shouldn't just give up.

My advice is this: Keep returning to the Gospels like the light keeps returning to the dawn.

Read some of the early books, and then go to Matthew's Gospel. Then return to some of the prophets in the Old Testament, and then go to Mark's Gospel. Read through the Psalms, and then go to Luke. You get the picture.

Indulge in a regular diet of the Gospels, even while you're attempting to plow through cover-to-cover.

In Mark 13:31 Jesus says, "Heaven and earth will pass away, but my words will never pass away."

Keep returning to the Gospels like the light keeps returning to the dawn.

Not only will you give your Bible-reading new life, but you'll be drawn deeper into the wisdom of a Master whose words to you will never fail.

SATURDAY - FUZZY BELIEFS, FUZZY BEHAVIOURS

Writer Craig Groeschel coined the phrase "Christian Atheism."

Here's the idea behind it. If we say we believe in Jesus, are we actually living like it makes a difference? Or are we just blending in and living our lives as functional atheists?[39]

What do we say about prayer, verses how we actually pray? What do we say about loving our neighbours or the Bible or our priorities, verses how we actually live our lives?

The majority of people in my country (Canada) believe in God. But to be honest, I don't really know what that means. Is it a vague belief in a higher power, or in a universe that seems to be somehow sacred?

When your belief in God is vague, your life doesn't really change all that much. Fuzzy beliefs give birth to fuzzy behaviours. In other words, beliefs that aren't firmly rooted lead to lives and decisions that are usually more misguided than they would otherwise be.

That's why followers of Jesus can be confident. Why? Because when you know Jesus, you know God. Jesus provides clarity about who God is and what is most important. That's why in John 14:9, when referring to God the Father, he says, "Anyone who has seen me has seen the Father."

So if you want to know the character of God, look to Jesus. If you want to know the wisdom of God, look to Jesus. If you want to know the kind of justice and love that is important to God, look to Jesus.

Know Jesus, know God.

Fuzzy beliefs give birth to fuzzy behaviours. But confident beliefs give birth to confident behaviours. So be confident in Christ. And live in a way that reflects his truth, love and power.

SUNDAY...

MONDAY - CONFIDENT BELIEFS GIVE BIRTH

In 1932 the baseball World Series was between the New York Yankees and the Chicago Cubs.

The story goes that there were two outs, and who should step to the plate for the Yankees, but the famous big-hitting batter, Babe Ruth himself.

The first pitch hurled over the plate. Strike one! The second did the same. Strike two!

At that, Ruth apparently pointed his bat toward the centre field fence. That's a batter's way of saying he intends to hit a home run off the next pitch. What confidence!

The pitcher threw the ball, Ruth swung with gusto and made contact. The ball flew up and over the pitcher's head and out of the park. It was a home run!

Why would Babe Ruth make such a bold prediction? My guess is that he believed he could do it.

As I said two days ago, confident beliefs give birth to confident behaviours. Your (true) beliefs impact how you act. In John 14:12 Jesus says, "whoever believes in me will do the works I have been doing..." In other words, if we truly believe in Jesus, we will do the kinds of things he did: loving others unrelentingly, glorifying God fully, and speaking truth honestly.

As you give it a go, use this question as a guide: "How does the Lord Jesus influence what I'm going to say and do?"

Carry it into how you set your priorities and use your time. Carry it into the classroom or boardroom. Carry it into your home and relationships.

Confident beliefs give birth to confident behaviours. So ask yourself this: How does the Lord Jesus influence what I'm going to say and do? And then swing for the fence.

TUESDAY - INCOMPARABLE MAGNETISM

I firmly believe that apologetics will become increasingly important for Christians.

"Apologetics" is the art of defending and explaining the faith.

I'm not sure if you've noticed but Christianity is increasingly misunderstood. There's a lot of misinformation floating around. And, in general, as our society continues to be confused about morality, there is a lot of hostility toward those who claim to know something about God's truth, even when they share it in a loving and humble way.

But a lot of us feel unprepared to defend and explain our faith. When someone confronts and criticizes us, it's easy to feel defensive or get flustered. So today I'd like to give you some advice.

Make it about Jesus.

I don't want to dissuade you from becoming more intellectually robust in your faith or from thinking through the nuanced answers to A, B or C. I think that's a good thing. But at the same time, you don't need to have it all figured out.

Jesus, standing tall and radiating integrity, is a power unto himself of incomparable magnetism.

Maybe say something like, "You know, I don't have all the answers, but when Jesus said..." or "The reason this is important to me is because of Christ's example when he..."

You get the idea.

C.S. Lewis talked about a similar approach. He said that when it comes to Christianity you are not faced "with an argument which demands your assent, but with a Person who demands your confidence."[40]

Hebrews 12:2 (NLT) describes Jesus as "the champion who initiates and perfects our faith." It's about how awesome he is, not how bulletproof your arguments are.

Jesus, standing tall and radiating integrity, is a power unto himself of incomparable magnetism.

When you explain or defend your faith, keep bringing it back to him.

WEDNESDAY - THE MOMENTS YOU'LL NEVER GET BACK

One of my favourite vacation experiences was going on an overnight trip with my daughter. We loaded up the ATV and ventured out to a family cabin deeeeeep in the forest.

The trails we traveled have been in our family for generations. As we were riding along, I remembered something from my youth.

Our family had a wood stove. And every autumn my brothers and I would take turns helping my dad get the wood in. We'd jump in the tractor and wagon, head into the bush, and spend the evening slugging wood back to the house.

At the time I didn't really appreciate it. It was good exercise, fresh air, and valuable time spent with my dad (who has now passed away). Back then, I'm sure I couldn't wait to get it over with so I could go play road hockey or video games with my friends.

But how amazing would it be to have one of those evenings to do over again!

I can't blame myself. I was pretty young. But now I'm an adult. And so are many of you. My point is this:

Seize the moments you'll never get back.

Today, look around you. There are precious people. There are bonding moments. There are meaningful conversations and deep-belly laughs around every corner.

Psalm 143:5 (NLT) says: "I ponder all your great works and think about what you have done." I think that includes beautiful things like soothing sunsets and majestic mountains. But it also includes people, conversations and opportunities that can flavour your life with the goodness of God.

Today, seize the moments you'll never get back.

THURSDAY - WHAT A FLAME IS TO DYNAMITE

Pastor John Ortberg describes an internal question that a lot of people ask when approaching a challenge:

"When you face a difficult situation, do you approach it, take action, and face it head on, or do you avoid it, wimp out, and run and hide?"

When you face a difficult situation head on, he says, you feel good that you stepped up. Even if things don't turn out like you hoped, you have no regrets because you took on the challenge.

But if you play the avoidance game, you know you took the easy way out. Even if things somehow turn out well, you still feel deep within yourself that you wimped out.

So how can you rev up your engine to face the difficult situations of life regardless of how you feel?

You remember Psalm 145:18: "The Lord is near to all who call on him, to all who call on him in truth."

When you call on God in truth, he is near to you. You don't have to be scared to death when you're walking tall with the God of life.

"When you face a difficult situation, do you approach it, take action, and face it head on, or do you avoid it, wimp out, and run and hide?"

The presence of God is to fear what a flame is to dynamite. Explosive!

Never fear. Because the Lord is near.

FRIDAY - SOUL CINDERBLOCKS

I once heard about a church who created a website where people could anonymously confess sins and wrongdoings.

They did this because they believed in the healing power of confession. Plus, it was a chance to get other people to pray for them.

One young woman wanted to confess her promiscuous life and her feelings of shame. She also wanted to confess her concern that she was a horrible person and that no one would ever really love her.

Another person confessed a devious deed toward a sibling. Another to cheating on a spouse. Another to an addiction. Another to stealing.

The reason I bring this up is because there is power in confession.

It's not a popular topic. First, there's so much pseudo-positivity out there that a lot of people are in denial that certain thoughts and actions are sinful. And second, they doubt that being honest will make a difference.

Proverbs 28:13 says, "Whoever conceals their sins does not prosper, but the one who confesses and renounces them finds mercy."

People need a mechanism to confess their sins. Not only for forgiveness itself. And not only for personal accountability—and sometimes, for the healing of another person. But to invite God's help and renovating power into their ever-evolving life.

"Whoever conceals their sins does not prosper, but the one who confesses and renounces them finds mercy."

Unconfessed sins are soul cinderblocks.

Speak and seek forgiveness. And you'll be inviting God's help and renovating power into your ever-evolving life.

SATURDAY - ONE THING WE SHOULD EXPECT FROM OUR POLITICIANS

On a Sunday in 2018 I talked about Christian attitudes toward government.

To be honest, I was kind of nervous about it. After all, government and politics is a touchy subject these days. There are divisive and polarizing issues. And sometimes it seems that common sense and civility go out the window!

I think the congregation was a bit nervous too. That's why several people said it was good that I wore a black tie so that I didn't inadvertently identify with any one particular political party!

In light of that, I'm going to share some ancient bits of biblical wisdom from Romans 13 that still give us guidance today.

In verse 4, Paul writes that "the one in authority is God's servant for your good." Nowadays people balk at that idea because they think it puffs us politicians and paints them with a nobility they don't deserve.

But in the first century when Paul was writing, a lot of high officials thought they were divine and deserved worship. So Paul was actually providing a corrective: When government works properly, officials should go about their tasks with utter humility because they recognize they are *under* God—and are ultimately serving his interests (and not their own).

Here's the bridge to today.

You and I should expect *humility* from our politicians and government officials.

I don't know what country you live in or what political party you support. But think about your elected officials. I think we should expect certain things from our leaders—things like a heart for justice and honesty.

But one of the things I believe the Bible teaches is that we should also expect humility.

It should cause us to be very thankful when we see it; and it should cause us to be very concerned when we don't.

SUNDAY...

MONDAY - WRITING "THANK YOU" ON EVERY BILL?

Romans 13:1 says, "Let everyone be subject to the governing authorities, for there is no authority except that which God has established."

A lot of people discount this verse for a whole host of reasons. It makes them uncomfortable. But even though governments are made up of flawed humans who often miss the mark, I think that God values order and justice. And order and justice fall under the responsibility of our governing authorities.

There are many things that cause me concern when it comes to our governments—but I sure am glad that there are provisions for both order and justice. Yes, it's a work in progress. But without them a society descends into chaos and isn't able to help people flourish.

It makes me think of a man who wrote "thank you" on every bill he paid, including his tax bills. That didn't necessarily mean he agreed with every-thing about his government or that he loved paying money for things. He did it as a way of reminding himself to be grateful for what he had.[41]

When he paid his phone bill he wrote "thank you" on the bottom. He did the same with his water bill. He was thankful that he could vote, that his taxes helped pay for schools, and that his country was able to defend itself in times of conflict.

I think our countries are far from perfect, especially on this side of kingdom come. And I think we should advocate for change until the cows come home.

But in the midst, we can be grateful for the goodness we enjoy.

Veterans fought and died. Good people continue to serve and give. There is space to move and air to breathe.

And the flavour of the country you call home continues to be enriched by prayerful, hard-working, and honest people...

just like you.

TUESDAY - VALUED IN HIS SIGHT

In the Bible, God demonstrates an undeniable, loving concern for the poor and marginalized.

They are valued in his sight.

Psalm 140:12 (ESV) comes to mind: "I know that the Lord will maintain the cause of the afflicted, and will execute justice for the needy."

And since God cares about the poor and marginalized, he wants his people to do the same.

The way we do this is often through formal giving campaigns. Maybe you give money to a certain charity that helps the homeless. Maybe you support a food kitchen. Maybe you give to your local street centre. Even a portion of your tax dollars goes toward programs that help people who are suffering in some way.

Supporting these initiatives is good. But today I'd like to suggest something else as well.

Talk to someone.

Many times I've had the chance to talk to someone who would be considered "the poor and marginalized." The temptation is to rush past, or to give and run. And I realize that sometimes you're in a hurry.

But there are times when just slowing down and sharing some words injects compassion and dignity into your interaction.

Will it mean you can solve all their problems? Of course not. Will you occasionally stumble onto topics that you have no experience talking about or are uncomfortable with? Probably. And you certainly need to be sure you're in a safe situation and not at risk.

But caring for the poor and marginalized isn't always limited to physical needs.

There are times when just slowing down and sharing some words injects compassion and dignity into your interaction.

Not only will you be a blessing to someone else, but they just might be a blessing to you as well.

WEDNESDAY - YOU'VE NEVER FLED OR FALLEN TOO FAR

"God couldn't love me. Not after what I've done."

I hear this sometimes. Maybe not those exact words. But some form of them.

Sure, we know the words to "Jesus loves me" and, on some level, mentally agree that they're true. But then life goes on, things happen—sometimes terrible things—and we doubt God's love.

And there are consequences to that doubt.

When we doubt God's love, we are more self-deprecating. When we doubt God's love, we are less confident. When we doubt God's love, we put limiters on the amount of love we'll give. Maybe because we think it's a limited commodity.

Before I had kids, I remember a new father telling me that he loved his daughter so much that he'd do anything for her. He'd put his arm in a blender or jump in front of a train if that meant he'd make her safe.

Now that I have children of my own, I totally get it. It's a limitless love.

If my children do something bad, it would bother me. After all, I want the best for them. But there's nothing they could do that would make me love them less. I'm all in with love for those three little wonders.

And that's how God feels about you.

Writing to the Galatians, Paul said, "For you are all children of God through faith in Christ Jesus" (Galatians 3:26, NLT).

No matter what you've done, and no matter how far you've gone, fear not:

You've never fled or fallen too far for the welcoming embrace of God.

THURSDAY - TROLLS

For years, many people thought "trolls" were mythical, burly creatures who lived under bridges.

But in a book about living out your faith online, Toni Birdsong and Tami Heim offer another modern definition. Trolls are "people who repeatedly post negative comments on blogs and social networks."[42]

Like a burly creature under a bridge, their goal is to drag you down!

The reason I say this is because more and more of us are spending time online. And it's so easy to get sucked in to a word-war with trolls whose seedy purpose is to reach out from under their invisible bridge and instigate, annoy, enrage, and generally stir the proverbial pot.

Don't let them!

Last week it almost happened to me. A friend put out a spiritual question, and so I put in my two cents. An hour later some random guy was criticizing me and accusing me of saying things I didn't actually say.

My first instinct was to firmly defend myself and highlight his ignorance. And perhaps there's a time for that in certain situations.

But this was not one of those times. So I let it go. I realized there was no point. A troll doesn't want thoughtful conversation. He or she just wants to throw some mud, chuckle, and move on to the next victim.

When you allow trolls to impact your time online, you're letting them into your personal time, work time, family time, home, and brain. And that's exactly what they want.

In 1 Thessalonians 5:11 Paul says his readers should "encourage one another and build each other up." Why not bring that same attitude to who you are online (and to how you reply to others).

Some trolls are strangers. Some are people you know who just want to give you an invisible poke. No matter who they are, don't let them control you.

Life is short, and you only have a limited amount of time to glorify God and help Jesus renovate the world with his truth and love.

FRIDAY - FROM TROLLS TO GLORIFIERS

Yesterday I talked about "trolls" on the internet. According to Toni Birdsong and Tami Heim they are "people who repeatedly post negative comments on blogs and social networks."[43]

They also talk about "haters" (outspoken, anti-everything people), and "defrienders"—people who, if you hit a nerve, try to teach you some sort of lesson by clicking the de-friend button on Facebook.

But why aren't there any positive categories?

Social media is a complicated enterprise. It's where people post pictures, make comments, share information, bond over bizarre cat pictures, and connect to others. But it can also be a very negative place.

One study showed that excessive Facebook use made users feel sadder. Perhaps it's because we can compare ourselves to others. Or maybe we're just easily drawn into all the junk and complaints.

So in addition to "trolls," "haters" and "de-frienders," I'd like to add this category: *Glorifiers*.

A glorifier is someone who honours and glorifies God with their online presence. This doesn't mean you have to post graphics of John 3:16 all day long. But it means your words and activity honour God; it means you encourage and comfort; and it means you're thoughtful about how you click, tweet, or comment.

In Ephesians 4:29 (NLT) Paul writes, "Let everything you say be good and helpful, so that your words will be an encouragement to those who hear them." What if we slightly modified it for the internet? "Let everything you [type and post] be good and helpful, so that your words will be an encouragement to those who [see] them."

Don't be a troll, hater or de-friender. Be a glorifier. Because on the other end of a post, picture, blog or comment...

Is a person.

SATURDAY - ROCKEFELLER'S INSIGHT (AND WARNING)

The famous businessman John Rockefeller was asked, "How much money does it take to satisfy a man?" He replied, "Just a little bit more."

His answer was insightful—not only about how a lot of people think about money, but about how a lot of people think about life in general. 'If only I had better clothes, or a nicer house, or was more popular, or had better grades,' they think, 'then everything would be perfect.'

But more doesn't always mean better. And it certainly doesn't equate to faithfulness.

So how do you resist the sin of greed, especially in a culture of consumerism, excess and more?

Writing in 1 Corinthians 4:7 Paul said, "What do you have that you did not receive?" He was reminding them that all the good things they have in their lives are gifts from God.

The same is true for you. All the good things you have in your life are gifts from God.

And when you focus on being thankful for what you *already* have, you're less worried about what you *don't* have.

In short, the more grateful you are the less greedy you are.

So how do you increase your gratitude?

You intentionally say thank you to God for what you *already* have.

Maybe it's when you're driving, or lying in bed, or on a break between classes, or folding laundry. Start to thank him. A warm home, a friend to call, food in the fridge, a church family, singing birds...

Resist greed. It poisons your soul.

The more grateful you are the less greedy you are.

SUNDAY...

MONDAY - YOU: THE LIVING MEMORY

Siblings can become very close. That was certainly true for Theodore and Amity.

But as time went on, Amity contracted cancer. The doctors told her she could have surgery to try and remove the tumor. But since she was getting older and feeling weaker, there was a chance she either wouldn't survive or would go downhill more quickly afterward.

She decided not to have the operation.

Through it all, several times a week, Theodore would visit her. He noticed that in addition to dealing with cancer, she was losing her memory. She remembered something about the possibility of a surgery, but that was about it.

So every visit, Amity would ask her brother about the surgery, and why it wasn't happening. He would gently remind her about her own decision to not go through with it and why. Amity would thank Theodore for the explanation, and say that she agreed.

This happened every time he visited. Theodore served as Amity's memory.

It's a simple story. And a beautiful one. Two siblings. As one became forgetful, the other would serve as her living memory.

I sometimes think we live in a time of cultural amnesia. People can so easily forget what's important. About how to honour God. About how to care for each other. And about how to work hard for what is right.

That's why you and I—as followers of Jesus—are Theodore.

On our better days, we can be the living memory in our society of what it means to honour God, to care for each other, and to work hard for what is right.

Speaking to his followers in Matthew 5:14 Jesus said, "You are the light of the world."

Do you always get it right? Nope. Are you flawed? Yup. But you don't need to be perfect to have an impact.

Oh, one more thing. The name "Theodore" means God-given.

And you are.

TUESDAY - IF NOT YOU, WHO?

The thing that happens when people gather on Sunday is called a "worship service."

It's often at a building, but not always. Recently on vacation (in a very warm climate!) we gathered in a circle on the beach. Psalm 66:2 (ESV) says, "sing the glory of his name; give to him glorious praise!"

That's what we did as we prayed, read the Bible, and sang songs together. So that was a worship service too.

But another helpful way to think about the term "worship service" has to do with what it compels us to do afterward. With this in mind I like to think about it not only as a "worship service" but as "worship then service." After we gather to worship God we are dispersed into our communities as servants.

That's partly why worship is so important. It draws our idle hearts and distracted thoughts back to God, reminds us of what's what, and sends us back out into the world to be his hands and feet.

Matt Brough hosts a podcast called *Spirituality for Ordinary People*. In June 2017 he interviewed a hard-working and hope-filled Christian named Jennifer de Combe. Quoting Stanley Ott she said, "We have to be the people of God to do the work of God."[44] I like that because if you don't know who you are, it's easy to forget what you're supposed to do.

You *are* the people of God. And the people of God *do* the work of God.

Worship services remind us of that essential truth, and launch us back into God's world to be his hands and feet by the power of the Holy Spirit.

Many of the most powerful worship services are ones where you are compelled and propelled into service after worship. So think of it not only as a "worship service," but as "worship then service."

"We have to be the people of God to do the work of God."

And if not you, who?

WEDNESDAY - DON'T GET WORKED UP ABOUT $20

When I'm meeting with someone and we're about to pray, I often ask them what we should pray about.

One of the most common answers is to not sweat the small stuff.

I get that. Sometimes it's easy to let something small get blown out of proportion and take over our brain.

To help out in this regard, New York City pastor and author Tim Keller suggests an analogy.

Imagine two billionaires. They have cars, mansions, and dozens of staff. They're both walking down the street and see a twenty dollar bill on the sidewalk. Do you think they're going to run, dive, and battle each other for it? Of course not! They're probably not too concerned with a measly twenty bucks. After all, they're billionaires![45]

Here's where you and I come in.

If, as it says in Galatians 3:27 (ESV), you have "put on Christ," you "are Abraham's offspring, heirs according to the promise" (verse 29). In other words, you are a *spiritual billionaire*. It means that, because of God's promises, you have incredible riches...

You have forgiveness and purpose and love and truth and heaven... *forever!*

The more we're able to remember the amazing (big) things God has done for us, the less likely we are to obsess and worry about the (smaller) things which can contaminate our thinking and hijack our priorities.

I'm not saying you won't sweat the small stuff from time to time. But I think your stay in those boggy trenches will be shorter and less debilitating.

Remember, if you've placed your faith in Jesus, you are spiritual billionaire.

And billionaires don't get worked up about twenty bucks.

THURSDAY - WORTH THE RISK

When it comes to a worship service, I'm usually the one doing the talking.

So I was really looking forward to a service I attended at Knox Church in Midland in 2017. My friend and colleague Alton Ruff said that when Jesus calls us to do something, it quite often involves going out of our comfort zone.

Remember James and John, the fishermen? In Mark 1:20 we read, "Without delay [Jesus] called them, and they left their father Zebedee in the boat with the hired men and followed him."

They had probably saved up money for materials, spent time learning the craft, and been apprenticed under their father. But when Jesus invited them to follow him, they simply got up and left it all behind.

Including their father who was still in the boat!

His point was this: "Jesus is worth the risk."

First, it's good to acknowledge that following Jesus is in fact a risk. You give up being your own boss, you risk standing out, you risk going into situations that are outside your comfort zone because you sense God telling you to get in there and help.

And second, you come to realize that no one else can give what Jesus gives —salvation, eternity, purpose, forgiveness, truth, comfort, unending love...

Way back then, the disciples decided—almost, it seems, in an instant—that Jesus was worth the risk.

He still is.

As you think about your own walk through life, what is you holding back?

"Jesus is worth the risk."

FRIDAY - WHY OTHER PEOPLE'S STANDARDS ARE DISTRACTING

If you're spending a lot of your time and energy thinking about how you measure up to the people around you, not only are you sowing seeds for your own discontentment, but you're undercutting your own capacity to be faithful to God.

Why? Because you're more concerned with how you measure up to other people's standards than you are with focusing on God.

In 1 Corinthians 3:21 and 23 (ESV) Paul says that if you're a follower of Jesus, "all things are yours..." and "you are of Christ, and Christ is of God." One of the implications of this statement is that *when you're guaranteed important eternal things you should worry less about unimportant temporary things*.

It makes so much sense. If you are guaranteed salvation, eternity, a relationship with God, the knowledge that God has a plan for your life, and meaningful opportunities to serve God and others, there is no reason to scurry around worrying about trivial things that are ultimately unimportant and which don't last.

Compared to the gift of eternity, how big your house is, how many gadgets you have, and how popular you are, start to look pretty insignificant.

I get why people try to keep up with the Joneses. But it's a waste of time.

When you're guaranteed important eternal things you worry less about unimportant temporary things.

SATURDAY - OUR JOB (AND IT ISN'T MEASURING UP TO OTHERS)

Yesterday we talked about the fact that, as a follower of Jesus, when you're guaranteed important eternal things you worry less about unimportant temporary things.

Compared to the gift of eternity and a relationship with Almighty God, how big your house is, how many gadgets you have, and how popular you are, start to look pretty insignificant.

I don't think most people would disagree with what I've said so far. So why then is it so easy to continually compare ourselves to other people?

I think that if we look at the root issue we get some further insight.

Philippians 2:3 says, "Do nothing from rivalry or conceit..."

If we're conceited, and if our thoughts and actions are based on a sense of rivalry with others, we're operating out of a place of pride, of our egos being disproportionately puffed up.

And that's the root issue.

In *Mere Christianity*, C.S. Lewis writes: "Pride gets no pleasure out of having something, only out of having more of it than the next person. We say that people are proud of being rich, or clever, or good-looking, but they are not. They are proud of being richer, or cleverer, or better-looking than others. If everyone else became equally rich, or clever, or good-looking there would be nothing to be proud about."[46]

So what do we do?

Paul tells us. "Do nothing out of rivalry or conceit." It's about checking your motives and deflating your pride.

Our job isn't to measure up to others, compete with others, or be better than others. Our job is to bless others.

That's a part of what loving God and our neighbours is all about.

SUNDAY...

MONDAY - BEING A SORE... WINNER?

"Don't be a sore loser."

It's a way of saying you shouldn't sulk around when you lose. Don't be so sore about your loss that you draw attention to yourself and dampen the victory and accomplishment of somebody else.

But today I'd like to alter that phrase a bit: Don't be a sore *winner*.

A sore winner is someone who rubs their victories, good fortune and positive experiences in everyone else's face. Sure, it's good to be proud about some things and to share some of your successes with people you care about; but when you do it frequently and loudly—as if to remind other people that they're not as good as you—it doesn't do anyone any favours.

Think about your life online. Are you always subtly bragging about how awesome you are? Think about your conversations with your friends. Are you always subtly praising how good you are at such-and-such? Think about how you talk to people about your kids (if they're doing well), or your marks (if they're high), or your salary (if it's large). Are you always subtly dangling your happiness in front of everyone to, dare I say it, make them jealous?

Let me reiterate: I'm not saying you should never celebrate good things. The difference is that a sore winner frequently steps over a line to smoothly knock other people down a peg. And the last time I checked, it's neither humble nor loving to look down your nose at a fellow child of God.

Proverbs 27:2 says, "Let someone else praise you, and not your own mouth..."

Don't be a sore winner. Life is tough enough for people. So let's spend our time travelling with each other—not trampling each other—on the road of life.

TUESDAY - I'D RATHER BE ON THE RIGHT SIDE OF ETERNITY THAN HISTORY

"You can't stop progress."

Has anyone ever said that to you? It's the idea that society changes and moves "forward" in certain ways—in ways many people agree with. Therefore, they attach a positive value to that "forward" movement (called "progress"). Saying 'you can't stop it' is a way of saying 'don't even bother trying.'

As a pastor I sometimes hear it too. 'Well, the world seems to be doing such-and-such so we should just go along with it or else we'll be on the wrong side of history.'

But I'm okay with being on the wrong side of history if it means I'm on the right side of eternity.

Now don't get me wrong. I don't think we should dial back the clock one hundred years; that would be terrible. And there are many changes in society that are good—very good!

But we do ourselves a disservice when we naïvely think that all change is good, and that it's inevitable.

In 1 John 5:19 (NLT) the apostle John writes, "We know that we are children of God and that the world around us is under the control of the evil one." That's serious business. Even though the world God made was "very good" (Genesis 1:31) it has since come under various sources of pollution—and not just environmentally.

So why am I telling you all this?

Because when it comes to "progress," apathy or resignation undermines your willingness to pray and work for a world which honours God's ways. So with everything that comes along, see how it measures up to God's will as we find it in the Bible.

It's not about whether or not you can stop progress; but whether or not our lives and communities can better reflect the ways the God of grace and truth is making all things new.

I'd rather be on the right side of eternity than the right side of history.

WEDNESDAY - WHO IS AN EXPERT, REALLY?

Several years ago my wife and kids and I were up in Bracebridge, Ontario visiting some family. My daughter got a strange bug bite. And since it looked weird we went to the local walk-in clinic.

I was totally impressed by the doctor. First, he listened and didn't speak down to us. Second, he was very knowledgeable. And third, he said he needed to double check something he was unsure about. So he went down the hall and took a medical book off the shelf to confirm a possible diagnosis.

Everything turned out to be fine. But to me it was a demonstration about what an expert should be like. He was self-confident and humble enough to admit he wasn't sure about something; so he went and looked it up.

A general definition of an expert is someone who has gained a high level of competence in a specific field. But I'd like to add a bit more. Experts are people who have gained a high level of competence in a specific field... and are honest enough to know the limits of their own knowledge.

The Bible speaks about a partnership between humility and wisdom. Proverbs 11:2 says, "When pride comes, then comes disgrace, but with humility comes wisdom."

With humility comes wisdom.

If you're looking for some wisdom from someone, be cautious when you come across those who think they already know everything there is to know. They may be overplaying their hand because of their pride and desire to look impressive.

And if you're the one who other people seek out for counsel or knowledge, cultivate humility. The true experts aren't just the ones with a high level of competence in a specific field, but are honest enough to know the limits of their own knowledge.

"When pride comes, then comes disgrace, but with humility comes wisdom."

THURSDAY - USING GOD'S LOVE AS AN EXCUSE

Have you ever tried to go somewhere with only half a map? Have you ever tried to assemble a BBQ with basic picture prompts but instructions that were in a different language?

If so, you'll know that having *some* of the information isn't the same as having *all* of the information.

That's what I think happens with the statement "God loves and accepts you just as you are." It's true; but it's not the whole picture. Here's what I mean.

God does love and accept you just the way you are. It's like how a parent loves and accepts a child unconditionally. There's nothing my child could do to make me love them less. It isn't something they earn; they simply have it because they're mine.

But that doesn't mean I condone everything they do. Loving someone doesn't necessarily mean agreeing with every decision they make.

Well, that's like our relationship with God. Just because God loves us, that doesn't mean he condones everything we do.

Following Jesus involves transformation and life change. As he says in Luke 9:23, "Whoever wants to be my disciple must deny themselves and take up their cross daily and follow me." In other words, we need to go from being self-centred to Christ-centred. It involves taking biblical, God-honouring teaching and doing our best to sacrificially apply it to ourselves.

So yes, God loves you as you are. But God loves you too much to leave you as you are.

Don't use God's love as an excuse for stagnancy or disobedience. Accept it for the free gift that it is. Be thankful. But with the help of the Holy Spirit, grow and mature as you become less self-centred and more Christ-centred.

God loves you as you are. But God loves you too much to leave you as you are.

FRIDAY - THE CHAINS OF ENTITLEMENT

Having a sense of entitlement can be a huge problem for those of us who live in places like North America and Europe.

The more we have the more we seem to want. And the more we have the more we seem to think we have to have. And the more we have, the more we take it for granted!

That's why I think Psalm 73:26 is a powerful, sobering and liberating reminder of one of God's truths: "My flesh and my heart may fail, but God is the strength of my heart and my portion forever."

Think about that for a minute. If you apply it to yourself, it means that your *portion* is God. In other words, your portion isn't an achievement. It isn't a certain job. It isn't a plot of land. And it's definitely not a crash-and-burn from your past or a failed relationship.

Your *portion* is God.

This is a *powerful* truth because it reminds you that God himself is all you truly need. This is a *sobering* truth because it wakes you up from the intoxicating consumerism of our culture. This is a *liberating* truth because it frees you from thinking that your identity is based on your successes (or failures) in life.

Imagine you're dead—that your time on earth has come to an end. And imagine people you know talking about you. How awesome would it be if some of them said something like this: "Well, one thing's for sure: They sure had the Lord."

That's you. And if it isn't yet. It can be.

For whatever you're facing in life, God is more than enough.

"My flesh and my heart may fail, but God is the strength of my heart and my portion forever."

SATURDAY - DOES SOMEONE IN YOUR LIFE HAVE ISSUES?

Does someone in your life have issues? Someone in your family? A co-worker or classmate? Or maybe a friend? Perhaps it's just that their priorities are frazzled.

And you just don't know what to do. Maybe it's legitimate. Maybe it's not. Maybe you're just not sure. The point is that it can be complicated.

But you want to help because you care. So here's one thing you can do no matter what the situation is:

Be as healthy and as faithful as *you* can be.

I remember reading in a book—I think it was by Christian psychiatrist M. Scott Peck, but I can't be sure—that whenever he gets approached to help with a difficult person in a family situation, he tries to look around at the wider context, including what the surroundings are like and who the key people are. There is a greater chance of success if the person in the home who has the most emotional health gets even healthier. That's why he works with that person as well. Their strength impacts others' strength.

What if *you* were in a strong position to effect good change in someone's life? What if you could positively impact their well-being simply by being as healthy and as faithful as you can be... by showing what it's like to put God first, by showing how to live by key priorities, by taking care of yourself and showing genuine interest in the well-being of others?

"Love your neighbor as yourself" (Mark 12:31) is a passage that never stops renovating our hearts and attitudes. Doing a good job of loving others presumes a pattern of love and care that you first offer to yourself. That's why being as healthy and as faithful as you can be sends a ripple effect into your relationships.

Maybe this devo isn't for you. But if it is, be as healthy and as faithful as you can be. Either way, you won't be the only one who reaps the rewards.

SUNDAY...

MONDAY - OVER-COMMITTED PEOPLE

Let me start by throwing something out there that might rattle a few cages: Over-committed people are un-committed people.

Here's what I mean because I realize I'm going to have to put a few footnotes on that statement!

When you over-commit to the wrong things you can't deliver on the right things. In other words, if you say Yes to every request that comes your way —regardless of whether or not it's a good use of your time—you lessen your capacity to be effective at what matters most.

I realize that a lot of people who say Yes to things often mean well and simply want to help. I get that. But I think we need to seriously question whether that's the best way to live. It's easy to think that committing to every project or request is the right thing to do. But doesn't that water-down our effectiveness and make us less available when something comes up that really matters?

Micah 6:8 says, "And what does the Lord require of you? To act justly and to love mercy and to walk humbly with your God." Although it was said to Israel a long time ago, to me it endures as a reminder about what's what. Acting justly, loving mercy, and walking humbly with God are important.

But how can we do that if we're so over-committed that we never have the time or energy to do his will?

I need to be honest. This is hard for me too. In fact, one of the things I do each summer is re-think my routines so that when I hit September my life is more focused than it was the year before.

Over-committed people are un-committed people. So don't over-commit. Instead, know what's what, and commit to the things that honour the limited amount of time God has given to you while on earth.

TUESDAY - HE'S GOT YOU

Dr. J. Robertson McQuilkin used to be the president of Columbia Bible College and Seminary. But he gave up his presidency to care for his wife Muriel who was struggling with Alzheimer's disease.

Dr. McQuilkin wrote about a time when he was with his wife and their flight was delayed for several hours. Every few minutes Muriel would repeat the same questions about where they were, what they were doing, and when they were going home.

And every few minutes she would rush down the terminal, and back, and down the terminal again, trying to figure out what was happening. Dr. McQuilkin would follow her, calmly answering her repetitive questions.

Once after returning to their seats, a young woman who was working on her computer nearby muttered something. "Pardon?" Dr. McQuilkin asked. "Oh," she replied, "I was just asking myself, 'Will I ever find a man to love me like that?'"[47]

It's a story of love and fidelity.

And it's also a story that reminds us of the kind of love God has for you.

Maybe you take God's love for granted. Or maybe you wonder what difference it makes. But I think today's story teaches us something.

God's love means that when you're confused, he's got you. When you're frustrated, he's got you. When you're lost, he's got you. And when you're feeling worthless, worrisome or wrecked, he's got you.

God's love does for you what you can't do for yourself. Even when you don't know it.

First John 4:16 says, "And so we know and rely on the love God has for us." We *rely* on it. Muriel couldn't remember much about her surroundings and situation. But she could remember her husband and his love. And that is the peace that only true love can give. And it's a love that God gives *to you*.

Today, no matter what you're going through, trust the Saviour.

He's got you.

WEDNESDAY - EXCUSES OR PROGRESS?

Sometimes, I think we're our own worst enemy.

We want to be closer to God, but don't do anything to cultivate the relationship. Or we want to lose ten pounds but can't stay away from the high-fat snacks after 9pm. Or maybe we want to make a difference in our neighbourhood, but we jam our schedule so full that we don't have any time to think about others.

Recently, I read something by the super-motivated Craig Groeschel: "You can make excuses or you can make progress, but you can't make both."[48]

At first, I thought: 'Wow, that's awesome. I bet that's a helpful thought for a lot of people out there.'

Then I realized that it was a helpful thought for me too!

Proverbs 4:25 says, "Let your eyes look straight ahead, fix your gaze directly before you."

Look at the log jams in your life. Do you want to make progress? If so, maybe you've got to drop some dynamite into your excuses and blow up the fiction you've confused for fact.

I truly believe that Jesus wants you to live an abundant life.

"You can make excuses or you can make progress, but you can't make both."

THURSDAY - ARE FAITH AND REASON OPPOSITES?

Recently I was talking to someone who told me he was an atheist. "I'm just too rational to believe in God," he said. "That's interesting," I replied. "I'm a really rational person too. That's *why* I believe in God."

I felt it was important to say because there's a myth out there that reason is on one side and faith is on the other—as if they're opposites.

But they're not. It's a caricature.

When I first started making my faith my own, I was primarily propelled by the figure of Jesus—his teachings, his integrity, and his power. And the deeper I went into history, into science, and into philosophy, the more *reasons* I found to believe.

I say this because we need to acknowledge that putting invisible duct tape over your mouth when it comes to your questions about God never helps.

A thinking faith is a faith worth having.

Do you wonder if there is scientific evidence for God's existence? Good question, explore it. Do you wonder if Jesus actually came back to life? Good question, explore it. Do you wonder if God really cares about morality and how you live? Good question, explore it. Do you wonder if something bad in your life could be used for something good? Good question, explore it.

Albert Einstein said, "The important thing is not to stop questioning. Curiosity has its own reason for existing."[49] How awesome is that! I believe that curiosity exists to draw you closer to your Creator.

Asking honest, thoughtful questions often results in discovering honest, thoughtful answers.

So don't be afraid to explore. But you need to be committed to going deeper than some random blog post a friend sent you. As it says in Proverbs 18:15 (ESV): "An intelligent heart acquires knowledge..."

The Lord gave you a brain. I'm sure he didn't intend for you to turn it off. "Curiosity has its own reason for existing."

FRIDAY - PROTECT YOUR SOLDIERS

Why have many of us bought the lie that life is supposed to be easy?

Maybe it's tempting to believe all the shiny, happy people in the T.V. commercials. Or that if we're nice enough we'll be magically rewarded with a perpetual smile.

But no. Life is a *battle*.

In this country, one in four are "very stressed" at work. One in eight families struggle to put food on the table. Fifteen to twenty-five percent of people under nineteen experience mental health issues or illness. Plus, people die, gut-twisting diagnoses come, relationships struggle, rejection visits, faith falters. That's the tip of the iceberg. You know your battles best.

So here's one of the ways you can fight back: *Protect your soldiers.*

In her book *Fight Back With Joy*, Margaret Feinberg talks about the massive and refreshing importance of other people during her own battle with cancer. Wanting you and me to benefit from her own learning, she writes: "The Great Joy Giver is parachuting people into your life to remind you that you are not alone."[50]

I'm guessing that God has placed people in your life—right now—who are there by design. A part of their purpose is to help you through the battle. They have been parachuted in to the battlefield of your life to lift you, to refresh you, to encourage you, and to give you joy.

Those are the soldiers. *Your* soldiers.

In 1 Thessalonians 5:11 Paul tells his readers to "build each other up..." So when you think of your own soldiers, protect them; pray for them; reciprocate an act of kindness; encourage them back; build them up.

Yes, life is a battle. It's worth it, it's mind-blowing, and through it we come to know the unequaled power and beauty of God's eternity. But it's still a battle.

And one of the best ways to win a battle, is for the soldiers to be strong, and for the soldiers to know they're making a difference. "The Great Joy Giver is parachuting people into your life to remind you that you are not alone."

So protect your soldiers.

SATURDAY - GETTING OUT OF A RUT

A lot of people think that pastors never fall into the same ruts they do. Since we're always talking about prayer and community and love, many people think that we never have dry spells in our faith.

That's just untrue.

I will, however, say that I try my hardest to always keep learning and growing. And I think it's a part of my responsibility to share what works. And what I've found is that when I get down, I don't stay down as long as I used to. And here's why:

I've learned to keep coming back to Jesus.

The reason that's important is because it's all about him. It doesn't matter if you're a teacher, paramedic, stay-at-home mom, part-time custodian or financial guru. It's all about him.

Our lives tend to play out based on our strongest and most persistent thoughts. So when you continually come back to Jesus, he continually exerts greater influence on your thoughts and, therefore, your day-to-day activities.

So what do you do? You read the Gospels. And then you re-read them. And you don't stop until you die. As it says in Hebrews 12:2: "Let us fix our eyes on Jesus."

In his insightful and incredibly relevant book called *Making Sense of God*, author Tim Keller describes the majesty of this Redeemer who is worthy of our gaze: In Jesus we are "surprised to see tenderness without any weakness, boldness without harshness, humility without any uncertainty, indeed, accompanied by a towering confidence. Readers can discover for themselves his unbending convictions but complete approachability, his insistence on truth but always bathed in love, his power without insensitivity, integrity without rigidity, passion without prejudice."[51]

If you're in a rut—or if you ever happen to fall into a rut—remember that our lives tend to play out based on our strongest and most persistent thoughts. So make the Jesus you find in Matthew, Mark, Luke and John your regular, brain-feeding diet.

When you do, the ruts may still come to you, but they won't overcome you.

SUNDAY...

MONDAY - THE MIXED MESSAGES OF JESUS?

To be honest, I sometimes feel that living a life of faith is a contradiction.

On one hand, Jesus says, "If anyone would come after me, he must deny himself and take up his cross daily and follow me." (Luke 9:23). Taking up a cross is about living sacrificially and selflessly toward God and others. That's a pretty tall order and it can seem overwhelming.

And since I fail at it so much it can make me feel bad in the process!

Then, on the other hand, Jesus says, "Take my yoke upon you and learn from me, for I am gentle and humble in heart, and you will find rest for your souls. For my yoke is easy and my burden is light" (Matthew 11:29-30). Really? How is a daily cross and a life of continual self-sacrifice supposed to be restful, easy and not a burden!?

To fully understand what Jesus means it's important to look at the surrounding context. When we look at the first passage about taking up a cross, there are no loopholes. If we are serious about following Jesus it will involve replacing ourselves with God at the centre of our lives.

When you look at the second passage, Jesus has been talking about those who have been proud and arrogant, leaning on their own wisdom instead of God's. And then he talks about how God has revealed the true wisdom of his goodness to Jesus himself and "little children."

I think this helps. Yes we are to live sacrificially and selflessly. But at the same time, we are to receive Jesus' yoke and learn from him. There's the rub. The word that's used for yoke (*zygos*) is one meant for *two* animals, not one. The whole idea is that we are not alone. And that when we take the lead from Jesus and lean on him, the sacrifice and selflessness becomes lighter and more restful.

Maybe living a life of faith isn't so contradictory after all.

Jesus is the Saviour. Not you. And not me. As Jean Vanier so eloquently puts it: "We do not have to be saviours of the world! We are simply human beings, enfolded in weakness and hope, called together to change our world one heart at a time."[52]

TUESDAY - THE OPPOSITE OF FAITH ISN'T DOUBT

I've been a pastor for ten years. And one of the things that happens over time is that you start to see patterns. You start to see certain consistencies with the kinds of things people struggle with.

Although these things vary with people's age or upbringing or experiences or outlook, certain challenges seem to be deeply rooted in the human condition no matter who we are.

And do you want to know one of those things?

Control.

A few of your jaws just dropped. "How did he know?!" Lol!

On one hand I get it. Things just seem to go more smoothly when they're predictable and you're in your happy place, right? Plus, Galatians 5:23 talks about the importance of "self-control." So isn't that kind of the same?

No. "Self-control" in the Bible is different. It is the ability to know your priorities and live in line with them. It's not getting swept away by your feelings or impulses or desires. It's also not something that we all do wonderfully one hundred percent all the time. But followers of Jesus should be progressing in this area of their lives.

But capital-C Control is a different beast. It convinces you that you are smarter than God, that only you can solve problems, that you always have better answers than the people around you, and that if Plan A doesn't happen, the end of the world will soon follow.

Cue the sweat, worry, and non-stop babbling of anxious thoughts.

But faith is an invitation to enter a world that is bigger than you, and a plan that is better than anything you could ever pull off by yourself.

So today, trust God... and breathe.

The opposite of faith isn't doubt, it's control.

WEDNESDAY - A GREAT INVESTMENT OPPORTUNITY

Most of us probably have a role model. A role model is someone you look up to, someone who provides you with a good example—something to aspire to in life.

When storyteller Ace Collins was asked who his role model was he replied, "Lassie!" (The Rough Collie dog from T.V.) "Lassie loves unconditionally," he said. "Lassie is honest to a fault. Lassie will lay down her life for you. Lassie does not judge and is quick to forgive. Lassie always shares."[53] I love that.

For years I would have said my role model was Wayne Gretzky, the famous hockey player. But as we grow, most of our real role models are people we know.

For me—and for many of you—Jesus is our chief role model. It makes a lot of sense since we're supposed to grow in our faith and become more like him. And I don't want to underestimate that.

But we also can't underestimate the power of the flesh-and-blood role models around us. Parents are often big role models. So are friends or siblings. Teachers and coaches are often influential role models.

And so are you.

Up to this point, you've probably been thinking about your own role models. But what if, right now, *you were serving as a role model for someone else?* This isn't to put pressure on you. I just want you to know that you probably have more impact than you think.

I've met former addicts whose return to health was a source of inspiration to others. I've also met people struggling with depression or self-loathing or even "success," whose authenticity in the midst of struggle was a source of hope for a neighbour or young person. In Titus 2:7 Paul says this to Titus: "In everything set them an example by doing what is good." I think that's a good word for us too.

Role models often show up in the strangest places. Including the mirror.

Today, put your best foot forward. Every word of encouragement and good decision you make is an investment in somebody else's heart.

THURSDAY - WHEN CONDESCENSION STARTS

One of the things I've noticed in our modern society is that it's easy for civility to go out the window.

I realize that the internet has helped with a lot of things, but one of my concerns is that people do and say things online that they would never do and say in person.

If we're not careful, we can easily caricature people and opinions without respecting the complicated nuances of what's truly going on.

In his book *Uncommon Decency*, professor Richard Mouw offers a corrective that breathes a much-needed dose of decorum into how we interact with others. He says that you should "concentrate on your own sinfulness and on the other person's humanness."[54]

When you take your own sin, brokenness and misplaced priorities seriously, you're less likely to see yourself as perpetually superior. And when your default assumption about the person you're dealing with is that they're a human (just like you) who is also struggling through the complications of life, you're less likely to pounce on their every perceived misdeed.

One of the most famous—and most sobering—verses in the New Testament is that "all have sinned and fall short of the glory of God..." (Romans 3:23). That includes you. And me. Which is why we need God's mercy so much—and which is why other people need it too.

Will you still disagree with people? And will you still feel strongly about sharing your views? Probably. But you'll do it in a way that assumes a posture of humility instead of superiority. The one sure way to ensure no one ever listens to you is to talk down to them.

Real conversation stops when condescension starts.

There are a lot of things being said out there. And civility can seem endangered. So to buck the trend, "concentrate on your own sinfulness and the other person's humanness."

Real conversation stops when condescension starts.

FRIDAY - HONESTY IN A WORLD OF SPIN

Santa Clara University did a study of 2600 managers. They were trying to identify the top leadership quality.

Do you want to know what it was? It was honesty.

Honesty ranked higher than intelligence. Honesty ranked higher than competence. And it ranked higher than a leader's capacity to inspire others.

But why?

I think it's because we live in a world with so much marketing spin, fake news accusations, and people too proud and afraid to admit they're wrong that honesty is like water in the desert.

So my thought for you today is this. If you want to improve a relationship with someone, be honest. In a respectful way, be honest about your frustrations; be honest about your joys; be honest about your faith.

When you do that, it says to the other person—whether a friend, a partner, a spouse, a sibling, or whoever—that they can be honest with you too. It subconsciously communicates that the truth is welcome.

And what dishonesty weakens honesty strengthens.

In Psalm 25:21 when David said, "May integrity and honesty protect me, for I put my hope in you" (NLT), he was identifying the Lord as the source of his hope. With that focus, he was able to live with greater honesty because he was more concerned with his standing before God than his standing before others.

In today's society honesty is like water in the desert. So when it comes to your relationships, be honest.

What dishonesty weakens honesty strengthens.

SATURDAY - WHEN THE PAST HASN'T PASSED

Sometimes there's something holding you back—holding you back from moving forward in your life with a greater sense of mental freedom, peace of mind, and personal integrity before God.

Quite often that "something holding you back" is some unaddressed wrong from your past. But just because something is *in* the past that doesn't mean it *has* passed. It can exert a continuing influence in your life and on your brain.

That's why forgiveness is so important.

Usually when we think about forgiveness we think about *giving* forgiveness. But do you know what? Sometimes we need to *seek* it too.

1st John 1:8 speaks very directly. It says, "If we claim to be without sin, we deceive ourselves and the truth is not in us."

All of us sin. All of us have wronged someone—and that's true no matter how much you pray, worship God, volunteer, or serve the poor. It's also true no matter how much money you make, how popular you are, or how many achievements you've stacked up.

That's why I think it can be helpful to think of someone you've wronged... and apologize.

I'm not saying it will change the world. But I think it will make you more free, and give you more peace of mind and personal integrity as you stand before a God who has also forgiven you.

Just because something is in the past that doesn't mean it has passed. So think of someone you've wronged...

And apologize.

SUNDAY...

MONDAY - THE POISONOUS ROOT OF BITTERNESS

Two days ago, I said that there can be unaddressed wrongs in our past which continue to exert an influence on us. Just because something is *in* the past that doesn't mean it *has* passed. That's why forgiveness is so important.

Usually when we think about forgiveness we think about giving forgiveness. But on Saturday we talked about seeking it. So I encouraged you to think about someone you may have wronged and apologize.

When you do that there can be a benefit to you personally: you can move forward in your life with greater mental freedom, greater peace of mind, and more personal integrity before God.

But today let me focus on another benefit: You can bring healing to someone else's life.

Think of a time when someone apologized to you. Do you remember how much better you felt? Do you remember how it gave you more peace knowing that someone was trying to right a wrong against you?

You could give that to someone else.

Hebrews 12:15 (NLT) is part of a wider passage with different reminders about how to keep the faith. It says, "Watch out that no poisonous root of bitterness grows up to trouble you, corrupting many." I don't know about you but according to my line of thinking I'm pretty sure that unaddressed wrongs from the past can qualify as a "poisonous root of bitterness"!

Just because something is in the past that doesn't mean it has passed.

So when you identify someone you may have wronged, and when you apologize, you may bring some unexpected healing into someone else's life.

TUESDAY - WHAT A 4-YEAR-OLD SAW CHANGED HER LIFE

Ann Voskamp's earliest memory is when she was four years old. She witnessed her eighteen-month old sister being run over by a truck in their farmyard.

Horror.

Ever since she's struggled in her relationship with God.

With this memory seared in her mind, Ann became accustomed to seeing suffering everywhere in the world. But in her book *One Thousand Gifts* she describes an email she received from a friend. It was a challenge:

Could she write a list of one-thousand things she loved? It was a challenge to name one thousand blessings, one thousand gifts. Not gifts she wants; but gifts she's already been given. So she started her list which included morning shadows across old floors, jam piled high on her toast, the cry of a blue jay from high in the spruce...[55]

One of the silent messages of our society is "not enough." Not enough love, not enough beauty, not enough money, not enough energy, not enough time. But what if we were looking at things with one eye closed?

Ann was challenged to write a list of one thousand blessings.

In 1 Thessalonians 5:18 (ESV) Paul urges his readers to "Give thanks in all circumstances..." Could you?

This week, it's easy to see all the problems. So to tip the scales a bit, just start listing the gifts you've been given. I'm not even asking you to write them down. Just name them... in the car, doing laundry, during a slow stretch at work.

What would they be? A sister who cares, a good night's rest, a car that starts, barbecue sauce, a singing bird?

It won't solve all of your problems. But it will help you remember that, in the midst of life's bruises, a good God has already been giving you more than you even know what to do with.

WEDNESDAY - AMAZING GRACE FOR A TELEMARKETER?

Amazing Grace is one of the best-known hymns. And for a lot of us it conjures up special memories.

When I hear it on the bagpipes I think of my Grandpa Ruttan. He was the pipe major in the Bracebridge Legion Band for years. When I was young and would come home from school, I remember hearing his pipes echoing that powerful melody through the trees and over the hill as he played outside his log home before evening practice.

As a pastor, I often invite people to sing the first verse *a capella* when we're gathered around the grave of a loved one:

> *Amazing grace, how sweet the sound*
> *That saved a wretch like me!*
> *I once was lost, but now am found,*
> *Was blind, but now I see.*[56]

That kind of grace is... amazing! And of course, it's biblical. In John 1:16 (ESV) we read, "And from his fullness we have all received, grace upon grace."

But when you get used to something it becomes predictable. When that happens, you need to do something to remind yourself that God's goodness is always... surprising.

While speaking in Toronto, Philip Yancey asked if anyone wanted to tell about their experience of sharing grace with others. A lady stood up and said:

"I feel called to minister to telephone marketers. You know, the kind who call at inconvenient hours and deliver their spiel before you can say a word... I try to respond kindly, though I almost never buy what they're selling. Instead, I ask about their personal life and whether they have any concerns I can pray for. Often they ask me to pray with them over the phone, and sometimes they are in tears. They're people, after all, probably underpaid, and they're surprised when someone treats them with common courtesy."[57]

When I heard that I immediately thought of all the times I simply cut them off and said I wasn't interested!

My point is this: God continually overflows our lives with a grace that is surprising. If you've started to take it for granted, maybe what you need to do is show some surprising grace to somebody else.

> *I once was lost, but now am found,*
> *Was blind, but now I see.*

THURSDAY - YOUR LITMUS TEST

The purpose of a "litmus test" is to see what something is really made of, to see what it really is on the inside.

This happens in science with different substances, of course. But it can also happen with people. Here's what I mean.

I'm always looking for litmus tests for my faith. I know, I know—I'm kind of weird like that. But the idea is a good one: Am I really a follower of Jesus? Or am I just talking the talk? 2 Corinthians 5:17 (NRSV) says, "So if anyone is in Christ, there is a new creation." When it comes to my own life, is that true?

Over the past few years I've had a little question that I ask myself. It's a litmus test. I want to share it with you in case it's helpful for you as well. Here it is:

"When was the last time I said or did something *differently* because of Jesus' teachings?"

If we really believe that Jesus is the Lord of our lives (that's a key Christian statement of faith), we can't live like he doesn't make a difference. Well, I guess we can; but if so, we fail the litmus test!

Jesus impacts. Jesus makes new. Jesus seeps (and sometimes explodes) into our relationships and decisions and priorities. Maybe it's in how you approach a problem at school or work. Maybe it's in the kind of person you are when you're with your friends. Maybe it's a life decision that you know you have to make.

I'm not saying we're all perfect—we're far from it. But Jesus is the eternal King who impacts your daily living.

So take the litmus test. The last I checked, integrity was pretty high God's wish list for his kids.

"When was the last time I said or did something *differently* because of Jesus' teachings?"

FRIDAY - THEY BROUGHT IN PETS. AND EVERYTHING CHANGED.

Maybe it's because we're so used to shopping through all the stores at the mall or picking and choosing whatever we want from restaurant menus. Whatever the reason, in today's society, it's hard not to be...

Consumers.

Even when it comes to worship.

Believe it or not we are actually made to worship God. That makes worship primarily about God... and not primarily about us.

In his book *Being Mortal*, physician Atul Gawande tells a story about a doctor in a nursing home who brought in pets to be cared for by the residents.

This had a massive and positive impact. The residents "began to wake up and come to life. People who we had believed weren't able to speak started speaking... People who had been completely withdrawn and non-ambulatory started coming to the nurses' station and saying, 'I'll take the dog for a walk.' All the parakeets were adopted and named by the residents."

The doctor concluded, "I believe that the difference in [lower] death rates can be traced to the fundamental human need for a reason to live." Then Gawande himself observes that "we all seek a cause beyond ourselves."[58]

For those of us who are Christians, a part of this great "cause beyond ourselves" is to glorify God. As it says in Psalm 96:9, "Worship the LORD in the splendor of his holiness..." Worship is to so honour and praise the Lord, that he replaces you at the centre of your life.

So when you worship, don't just think about what you consume and get out of it—but what it means to give honour and thanks to the One who calls you by name, floods your life with purpose, and who deserves every morsel of respect you can throw his way.

"We all seek a cause beyond ourselves," Gawande says. For us, a part of that cause is to glorify God. In a world with so much darkness and death, it's what keeps bringing us back to life.

SATURDAY - SPIRITUAL FERTILIZER

When you have an amazing and tasty experience at a new restaurant, what do you do? You tell someone about it. And when you beat the odds and win the hockey pool at work, what do you do? You tell someone about it.

So when God shows up and does something significant in your life, what do you do?

You tell someone about it.

In today's society it might be hard to do. Maybe you even get the cold shoulder from some people for believing different things than they do. Plus, talking about God can mix a little bit of Awkward into the conversation!

So here's some motivation for you to be a little more open about what God is doing in your life.

When you talk about your faith you bring about faith.

When God does something good in your life—whether you think it's big or small—and when you tell someone about it, it becomes fertilizer for their own spiritual growth. That just doesn't happen if you keep it to yourself.

A little while ago I delivered a Sunday message about angels. Afterward, several people came forward with moving stories about God's presence and power in their own lives at very difficult times. So during another service, we shared two of them.

As a result, people were really encouraged. Why? Because when you talk about your faith you bring about faith. God can use the good in your life to cultivate spiritual growth in somebody else's.

So this is what you do: When God has been active in your life, tell someone, and give God the credit. That's it. You don't have to be a Bible scholar or know how to explain the Trinity. You just have to tell someone and give God the credit.

I think the Bible encourages us to share. In Psalm 78:4 we read: "we will tell the next generation the praiseworthy deeds of the Lord, his power, and the wonders he has done." As a result, others become more confident in their convictions.

So when God has been active in your life, tell someone, and give God the credit.

Then leave the rest up to him.

SUNDAY...

MONDAY - MORAL THERAPEUTIC DEISM?

In the book *Soul Searching* by Christian Smith and Melinda Lundquist Denton we learn about research done with 3000 young people. What they found was that many shared these basic beliefs about God:

- God wants us to be nice and fair
- The purpose of life is to be happy and feel good about yourself
- God only really needs to be involved in your life when needed to solve a problem
- Good people go to heaven when they die

The book calls this view "Moral Therapeutic Deism." But it doesn't totally jive with the Bible.

Now before I sound like a Bible-thumping hard rear, I want to say it's awesome when people sincerely seek God. And I actually think these beliefs apply to a lot of people, not just youth.

But it makes life about us instead of God. Watch the shift that happens when I compare it to a more biblical perspective:

"God wants us to be nice and fair." Kind of. The Bible gives us a vision of mercy, justice and love. If we leave what is "nice and fair" up to each society or individual, it's easy for our understanding to get twisted from God's intent.

"The purpose of life is to be happy and feel good about yourself." Not really. Happiness comes and goes. Life's goal is to glorify God, to experience the joy that comes from knowing him, and to follow Jesus as he renovates our relationships, communities and world.

"God only really needs to be involved in your life when needed to solve a problem." Actually, God wants in one hundred percent.

"Good people go to heaven when they die." While some good people certainly go to heaven, the New Testament teaches that heaven is for those who place their faith in Jesus.

So why am I telling you this?

Because living for Moral Therapeutic Deism is selling yourself short. I realize that today's devotional is a bit heavy. But it's vital. A god who just confirms what you want is just a bigger version of yourself with the same problems.

Instead, believe big and believe bold.

In John 17:3 (ESV) Jesus prays, "And this is eternal life, that they know you the only true God, and Jesus Christ whom you have sent." The holy, wise and loving God of heaven and earth wants real estate in our souls for the healing of the world.

TUESDAY - WHEN DO WE WANT IT? NOW!

Have you ever been to a public protest? If so, you've probably heard some chanting.

Usually the leader is equipped with a bullhorn and yells out, "What do we want?!" Then the people respond with their demand. Then the leader says, "When do we want it?" And the people reply, "Now!"

I think this is slowly becoming the mantra of our society. Whatever we want, we want it...

Now!

It's as if we've become ridiculously bad at saying No. Maybe we just don't want to hurt anyone's feelings. Including our own!

I forget where I heard it, but I recall a story from a Halloween several years ago. A man's doorbell rang and he went to answer it expecting some kids. But instead, he found a full-grown woman. "It's for my daughter," she said, as if offering an apology and explanation.

Apparently, it was cold that night. So the mom—not wanting to deprive her daughter of the unbearable suffering that would surely come with trick-or-treating in the chilly weather—drove the daughter around in her car. The daughter didn't even get dressed up. Instead, the girl just sat there in the car while her mom got a costume on and went door-to-door on her behalf! To top it all off, the daughter fell asleep! When she woke up, she would have a bag full of candy and an exhausted mommy.

I have a theory: *The more instantly gratified you are the less permanently satisfied you are.*

Truth is, it's so easy to buy into instant gratification these days. Credit cards give us the impression that we can afford things (which we can't), social media gives us the impression that everyone is having a good time every single day (which they're not), and commercials give us the impression that life is all about satisfying our various appetites (which it's not).

But the more we cave to instant gratification, the more we feed a life of ingratitude.

I'm not saying you shouldn't indulge yourself sometimes. In fact, I probably do it a bit more than I should! But when instant gratification becomes a daily habit, we become less thankful, less disciplined, and start to feel entitled to more than our share.

The more instantly gratified you are the less permanently satisfied you are.

Psalm 118:24 (ESV) says, "This is the day that the Lord has made; let us rejoice and be glad in it." Today, be content. Be thankful. What if it was already enough?

WEDNESDAY - YOU'RE POROUS

When I was young I remember learning about "porous" materials. Things that are porous have tiny holes or spaces so that liquid or air can pass through.

A sponge is porous. Cork is porous.

And so are you.

Well, kind of. If I were to pour water over your skin it wouldn't run through right away. That's not what I mean. When I say you're porous, what I'm saying is that what's on the outside of you effects what's on the inside of you.

When you're in the sun (something on the outside of you) if often changes how you feel (on the inside). And when you're around thoughtful people (something on the outside of you) if often changes how you feel (on the inside).

In other words, you're porous.

All of this is my way of saying that you should remember you're porous when making significant decisions.

Too often we make significant decisions when we're in a bad state of mind —when we've just let a bunch of junk into our souls. When we've just had a bad day, sat through traffic, or listened to some crazy talking head on the news, we need to create some distance between us and the junk if we're going to make healthy, faithful decisions.

In Matthew 5:13 Jesus says, "You are the salt of the earth, but if salt has lost its taste, how shall its saltiness be restored?"

One of my own personal rules is that I never make a big decision in front of a screen. Instead, I go for a walk, pray, or just relax for a bit. Since I'm porous, I let out the dark to make room for the light.

No matter who you are, I want the best for you. So be sure to make those big decisions when you're at your best.

THURSDAY - WHAT WORKING AT MCDONALDS CAN TEACH YOU ABOUT GOD

I know I shouldn't start with a negative, but I'm going to do it anyway:

Don't retaliate or take revenge. That's God's job, not yours. Let me explain.

The summer after grade nine I worked as a cashier at McDonalds. I was glad to get a job. But I was also... *petrified!*

As soon I started the reality set in. I had just finished the ninth grade so everyone knew me as a "minor niner." And how would it go down when one of the cute girls came in? Or even worse, what about my hockey friends?

One of the things you have to realize is that the McDonalds uniforms that people wear now are like Oscar-worthy designer clothes compared to what was being used in 1992. To make it worse, I remember a quarter pounder with cheese stain that... Would. Not. Come. Out.

Okay, breathe.

One of the things you learn at McDonalds is that everyone has a specific job to do. If you do what you're supposed to do, then you do well. But if you try to do what someone else is supposed to do, you fail.

For example, say a cashier tried to do the manager's job. Instead of pouring shakes they try to order supplies, study health regulations, and tamper with the employee schedule. If that happened everything would go off the rails.

Maybe it's a strange way of putting it, but in life our job is to do our job and not God's. Our job is to glorify God, and to love and serve him and the people around us as we try to continue Jesus' healing mission to the world. It's not to retaliate or take revenge when things don't go our way. That would be like a cashier playing manager at the golden arches.

Isn't that liberating?

Focus on glorifying God, and loving and serving him and the people around you as you try to continue Jesus' healing mission to the world.

The apostle Paul quotes God's wisdom in Romans 12:19 to make the point: "It is mine to avenge; I will repay," says the Lord."

In other words, don't retaliate or take revenge. That's God's job, not yours.

FRIDAY - WHEN THEY SHOOK SHE GOT JABBED WITH THE PIN

In 1911 a psychologist named Edouard Claparede was treating a woman with no short-term memory. As you can imagine, her life was drastically altered because of this condition.

One day Claparede tried an experiment. At the start of every session they would shake hands. But this time, he hid a small pin inside his hand. When they shook, she got jabbed with the pin. A few minutes later, she didn't even remember what had happened.

But from that moment on, even though she had no short-term memory, she never again felt comfortable shaking the doctor's hand.

Somewhere deep within, she had a memory of pain.

Sound familiar?

You've been hurt. I've been hurt. We've all been hurt. Maybe to varying degrees, but it's true. And sometimes these hurts have a way of defining how we live today. Just like that pin-pricked patient, you may not even know why you're hesitant when it comes to other people or God, but you still make a habit of pulling back—of being less confident because of something that happened in the past.

I don't think the answer is to pretend past hurts didn't happen. But I do think a part of the answer is to name them for what they are, and to move into tomorrow with a steadfast confidence that the God who lifts you up is stronger than the hurts that weigh you down.

What if God's promise to Joshua many years ago was also God's promise to you? "Be strong and courageous. Do not be frightened, and do not be dismayed, for the Lord your God is with you wherever you go" (Joshua 1:9, ESV).

Think about whatever you're facing in life. As you consider how you're going to handle it, don't let past problems define your current life. They're a part of you. But they're not all of you.

Instead, be strong and courageous. For the Lord your God is with you wherever you go.

SATURDAY - YOUR CRAZY BUTTON

The band *Family Force 5* has a song called "Cray Button." They're talking about a "Crazy Button"—something you push and, well, go crazy! Here are some of the lyrics:

> *A lunatic, a time bomb just got dropped*
> *I get cray all day, it's my full time job.*
> *Wild like a wolfpack, howlin' at the moon.*
> *Attack, attack, you've been bitten by the wolf.*[59]

They're just talking about having a good time and letting loose. (FYI, they're a Christian rock band from Georgia.)

But the song reminds me that all of us have a Cray Button, a "Crazy Button." You can't see it. But it's there. Here's how it works.

Someone says or does something annoying or frustrating that really gets under your skin. Shivers go up your spine. You feel your heart start to beat faster. Instinctively you know something just happened, and you realize you are no longer your formerly calm self.

'What just happened?' you wonder. Well, someone hit your Crazy Button.

Sometimes it's not even *what* someone says but *who* says it! And trust me, it happens to all of us.

The reason it can be a menace in our lives is because Jesus calls us to love one another. And that's hard to do when you're pulsating with fury or annoyance or an otherwise debilitating lack of judgment. So here's what you do.

You take some time before you speak or act.

Nine times out of ten, the first thing you say or do after your Crazy Button has been pushed is not something you'd faithfully do in one of your better moments. As John Ortberg writes, "Never try to choose the right course of action in the wrong frame of mind."[60]

I don't think that time heals all wounds. But I do think that time and prayer helps restore some godly perspective. In 2 Timothy 1:7 (ESV), Paul says this: "God gave us a spirit not of fear but of power and love and self-control." Back then he was writing to a young man named Timothy. But it's just as true for us today.

Today, you can't control what people say or do. But when someone hits your Crazy Button, you can take some time before you speak or act, pray, and decide how to respond in a way that honours Christ.

"Never try to choose the right course of action in the wrong frame of mind."

SUNDAY...

MONDAY - THE CLIFFS JUST STARTED MOVING CLOSER

When I was young we would go back to the cliffs behind our house. There was a tall cliff on this side, and a tall cliff on that side. In the middle was a vast expanse. We'd try to throw rocks from one side to the other.

It was a long distance.

In the same way, there is often a distance between people.

Sometimes it's easy to know why this happens. There was a fight or disagreement or general parting of ways. Other times, it's just hard to be sure. Life decisions, circumstance, busyness and apathy have a drifting effect.

This week, I'm going to offer some super-practical ideas to connect with people and bridge the gap so that you can love them. After all, Jesus calls us to love one another. That's easy when we feel connected, close, and have similar interests and time on our hands.

But what about when someone is on that side of the cliff and you're on this side? How do you bridge the gap? What do you do?

You make an effort to learn about their life.

Maybe you ask them a question about where they're from or what their interests are. Maybe you inquire about their hobbies or what they did on the weekend.

When you do that, two things happen. First, you learn that you probably have some common ground in life. Second, the other person gets the sense that you actually care about them. Oh, and I should also say this. Don't use it as an opportunity to just talk about yourself or make a thousand comments or judgments about what is going on in their life. Just listen and learn. As we read in James 1:19 (ESV), "let every person be quick to hear, slow to speak, slow to anger…"

Feel that? The cliffs just started moving closer. Attentive conversation can move mountains.

When someone is on that side of the cliff and you're on this side, and you want to connect and bridge the gap so that you can be a loving, caring presence in their life, make an effort to learn more about them.

Sometimes your next best step as a loving person doesn't have to be rocket science. But it does have to be made by you.

TUESDAY - LOVING PEOPLE YOU JUST DON'T LIKE

Some people put their foot in their mouth, but seem to enjoy the taste. Some people rub you the wrong way, but act like it's the right way. Some people know how to push your buttons, and you detest that they can have so much negative impact on you!

It's true: Some people just drive you crazy. They're people at school or work or church or in your family or at the arena.

But as people of faith, this doesn't sit well with us. Why? Because Jesus' words to "love one another" (John 13:34) echo in our ears. So how can we be at our best when some people put us at our worst?

Today let me suggest just one thing to un-stick your thinking and propel it toward a more loving place.

When you pray, think of the people you don't like, and then *thank God that Jesus died for them too.*

Here's the thing. Jesus loved you so much that he died for you. But guess what? He died for other people too. And not just the ones who make you feel hunky-dory, but the ones who make you scream, tear out your hair and run for the hills.

So many things start with prayer, including this. Do you want to be at your best even when some people put you at your worst? If so, when you pray, think of the people you don't like, and then thank God that Jesus died for them too.

I'm guessing that God will use that prayer to un-stick your thinking and propel it toward a more loving place.

Start today.

You may not *like* everyone, but there are things you can do to start *loving* them.

WEDNESDAY - THESE GROW UP INTO OAK TREES

Imagine a child trying to put together a barbecue from scratch. All seven hundred and thirty-nine pieces laying out on the back lawn... and a four-year-old scratching their head.

That's actually how many of us feel when it comes to loving people we just don't like. It seems like an overwhelming task that we don't want to do. Like a kid looking at the seven hundred and thirty-nine pieces of a yet-to-be assembled barbecue, we don't even know where to begin!

So today, let me suggest this: *Respond to a practical need they have.*

Everyone has needs. Including you. And including every single person around you. Keeping in mind that love isn't a feeling we have but a decision we make, one of the ways we can be loving followers of Jesus is to respond to a practical need they have.

Maybe they're upset because a family member died and they just need a meal brought over. Maybe they could benefit from some help on the computer or with their car. Or maybe you just want to do something nice because they have a cloud over their head.

When I worked at the Ontario Legislature one guy in our office always brought another guy a coffee on Monday or Friday. They certainly weren't best friends. In fact, they often disagreed. But it was one way to connect on the level of caffeinated kindness.

In Philippians 2:4 (ESV) Paul writes, "Let each of you look not only to his own interests, but also to the interests of others."

Do you want to do be more loving, even toward someone you don't even like? Then respond to a practical need they have.

Never underestimate the acorns of respect and care that end up being oak trees.

THURSDAY - YOU GO NOWHERE BY ACCIDENT

I've been offering super-practical ideas about how to love and connect with people, even people you just don't like.

But if you're going to be a person of love, I think you need to *want* to be that person. And even more importantly, I think you need to trust that *God* wants you to be that person.

For twenty-three years, Richard Halverson pastored Fourth Presbyterian Church in Bethesda, Maryland. Halverson believed that one of the most important things he did at the end of the service was pronounce the benediction. That's the moment in a worship service before everyone leaves when the pastor lifts his or her hands and not only blesses God's people, but gives them a charge for the coming week.

Today, the benediction he gave to his congregation for twenty-three years is the one I give to you:

> *You go nowhere by accident.*
> *Wherever you go, God is sending you.*
> *Wherever you are, God has put you there;*
> *He has a purpose in your being there.*
> *Christ who indwells you has something He wants to do through*
>   *where you are.*
> *Believe this and go in His grace and love and power.*[61]

I love the powerful sentiment David expressed in Psalm 139:16 that God is fully in charge of every chapter in his life, even before David knew anything about what was going on: "all the days ordained for me were written in your book before one of them came to be."

Friends, remember that you made on purpose and for a purpose—and that purpose is most fully understood and realized when you come to know, follow, and share in the mission of Jesus.

Right where you are.

You go nowhere by accident.

FRIDAY - YOUR CARE FOR SOMEONE ELSE CAN'T BE BIG IF

Sometimes the most significant thing you can to do care for someone else is staring you right in the face.

Here's what I mean. "Love your neighbour as yourself" (Romans 13:9). Remember that one? Yeah, it's pretty huge. But most of us read that principle like this: LOVE YOUR NEIGHBOUR as yourself. But what if we read it like this: Love your neighbour AS YOURSELF?

That statement—which occurs multiple times in the Bible, including on the lips of Jesus himself—presupposes that you actually love yourself. So if you're not spiritually caring for yourself, the care you give others is going to be *seriously* compromised. In other words, *your care for someone else can't be big if your spiritual care for yourself is small.*

So what do you do?

I think you need to attack spiritual inconsistency in your life. Why? Because inconsistency equals inconsistency. If you are inconsistent with homework you're going to be inconsistent in getting good grades. And if you are inconsistent with exercise and a good diet you are going to be inconsistent in reaping health benefits. I think the same ideas applies to your faith.

The way you spiritually care for yourself is to be consistent in the fundamental practices of Bible reading, of worship, of giving, of serving, of rest, and of prayer.

When you're consistent in those areas you have more capacity for compassion, more margin for mercy, and more get-up-and-go for sharing God's goodness with the world.

Your care for someone else can't be big if your spiritual care for yourself is small.

So take your next best step toward consistency. By this point I'm guessing you already know what you need to do.

You can't fill someone else's gas tank when you're running on empty.

SATURDAY - SOMETHING CHOKING YOU FROM THE INSIDE

Protestant Christians like myself don't really go into confessional booths to confess our sins to a priest. It just seems like a strange thing—kind of like something from another culture that I don't know much about. (No offence to any of the Roman Catholics out there. It's just not a part of my own tradition.)

For the most part, Protestants don't confess to priests. They may talk about their concerns, secrets or moral failures to a pastor, small group leader or friend, but they mostly confess directly to God.

But recently I came across something that has made me rethink the power of other people in the whole confession process. It was a study that said confessing your sins to another person helps reduce stress and also lessen anxiety and depression.

Huh?

When we get together with others, rolling out the personal sin list isn't usually number one on the fun agenda.

But this study makes me rethink things a bit. What if confessing your sins to another person actually helps you reduce stress and also lessen anxiety and depression?

Maybe it's because each sin weighs a thousand pounds. You can't "feel" it, but you can *feel* it. And there's no feeling like something choking you from the inside.

So today, I wonder: Is something choking you from the inside? From your past? Or even from your present? If so, maybe you need to find someone you trust and spill your guts with an all-out honesty that maybe even kind of scares you.

They won't be able to forgive you like God can. But they may be able to offer a skylight for your conscience.

Consider Proverbs 28:13: "Whoever conceals their sins does not prosper, but the one who confesses and renounces them finds mercy." If you conceal your sin you will not prosper. But if you confess and renounce it, you will find mercy.

Sounds good to me!

You may never go in and out of a confessional booth. But you may go into an honest conversation with someone you trust, and come out with less stress and more peace.

SUNDAY...

MONDAY - STARING AT A LOADED GUN SHE STILL SAID YES

Is your belief in God rooted in how good God is to you, or in the goodness of God?

One of the most inspiring biblical stories is of Shadrach, Meshach and

Abednego. Because of their unswerving loyalty to God they refuse to worship the false gods of King Nebuchadnezzar.

So they're threatened. Either bow down to them or be thrown into a fiery furnace. Here's how they reply in Daniel 3:16-18:

> "King Nebuchadnezzar... If we are thrown into the blazing furnace, the God we serve is able to deliver us from it, and he will deliver us... But even if he does not, we want you to know, Your Majesty, that we will not serve your gods or worship the image of gold you have set up."

Did you see it?

They said that God was able to rescue them. *But even if he did not*, they would *still* not bow down and serve his "gods." Their loyalty was not contingent on God acting in a way that made them happy.

Regardless of what happened, God was still God, God was still good, and he deserved their praise.

It makes me think of a story I heard about the horrendous Columbine High School shooting. One of the attackers shot a victim named Valerie thirty-four times. Still alive, he asked her, "Do you believe in God?" Here's how she replied:

"Yes."[62]

We often think that the only evidence for the goodness of God is the immediate goodness in our lives—in other words, things turning out like we want. And although incredibly gut-wrenching experiences may cause us to question, challenge God, or be angry, God is still God; God is still good; and God is still worthy of praise.

So again I ask: Is your belief in God rooted in how good God is to you, or in the goodness of God?

I'm not saying I have all the answers. But I do have one. God is God. God is good. God is worthy of praise. And no hardship in this life will change that. No. Matter. What.

It was true for Shadrach, Meshach, Abednego and Valerie. And it's true for you too.

TUESDAY - THE MORE SERIOUSLY YOU TAKE YOUR DEATH...

There are certain things we just don't like to think about. Things like taxes. Things like flooded basements. Things like that embarrassing picture of you in grade eleven going up on Facebook!

And things like death.

But there's no way around it. That's why Genesis 3:19 (ESV) is spoken at many graveside services across the land: "...for you are dust, and to dust you shall return."

But do you know what I've found? *The more seriously you take your death the more abundantly you live your life.* Or, as Las Vegas writer Jud Wilhite says it, "The people who are most aware of their mortality tend to spend their lives most richly."[63]

I think taking your own death seriously involves a couple of key things.

First, taking your own death seriously means ensuring you're in a right relationship with God through Jesus. That's the biggie.

Second, it's an awareness that your time on this planet is limited. It could literally end any moment. All of us are one heartbeat away from meeting our Maker. Because of that, you start to cherish relationships; you start to serve others; you start to do the things you were put on this earth to do.

And third, it's confident hope. Life is a one-hundred metre race. Are you running it timidly like there's a brick wall at the end, or boldly like it's a runway?

Today, take stock. And ask yourself this: "Am I being smart with the time I've been given?"

The more seriously you take your death the more abundantly you live your life.

WEDNESDAY - WHEN CONFORMITY AND SELF-DISCOVERY FALL FLAT

In the movie *Witness*, a young Amish woman named Rachel falls in love with a police officer who is clearly not Amish. Her father Eli tells her it's forbidden and that the community elders could have her punished for her actions which, he says, are childish.

"I'll be the judge of that!" she says. "No, *they* will be the judge of that," Eli replies. "And so will I... if you shame me."

Rachel is visibly upset. "You shame yourself," she replies.

The interchange reveals two different approaches to life. The one represented by Eli is the way of conformity. It's the choice to live based on what tradition or certain people expect of you.

The second way is represented by Rachel. Let's call it self-discovery. In today's society it's certainly the more celebrated of the two. It's a choice to make yourself the sole judge of right and wrong in your life. But are these the only two options?

In reality, they're both partial. While Christians certainly honour many traditions, and while it's certainly important to discover things about ourselves, tradition alone is insufficient to direct us, and we are definitely not the sole judge of right and wrong.[64]

In Rio de Janeiro there is a statue of Christ that stands thirty metres tall and twenty-eight metres wide. It *towers* over the city from the top of a massive hill. From most places in that city of 6.3 million people, you can see Jesus. In fact, it's hard to get lost because of it. Why? Because Jesus—with arms outstretched—is the unmoving reference point.

That's the kind of power he should have in our lives no matter where we live. Jesus is our unmoving reference point so that we don't lose our way.

You aren't totally defined by tradition. And you aren't totally defined by you. If you are a follower of Jesus, you are defined by him.

So live confidently.

He loves you. He challenges you. He changes you. He forgives you. He grows you. He heals you. He teaches you. He surprises you. He commands you. He blesses you. He embraces you. He changes you. Again.

Stand firm and trust him. Jesus is "the way, and the truth, and the life" (John 14:6). He's the only Compass in a topsy-turvy the world that will make sure you're headed in the right direction.

THURSDAY - WHAT'S THE POINT?

What's the point?

Have you ever asked yourself that question? I have. It's a question we ask when we're feeling overwhelmed or alone or frustrated.

But it's also a question we ask as life goes on and we haven't figured out how our daily purpose fits into God's eternal plans.

Harry Addison and Lee McGlone tell a story that makes the point.[65] "A young man was about to graduate from high school. With a 4.0 grade-point average he had been selected to be the valedictorian. He was called into the principal's office.

"Well, you've done it; you made valedictorian. Congratulations. So what are your plans for the future?" The young man replied, "Well, I plan to go on to college and get my bachelor's degree."

"Great," said the principal, "what then?"

"I guess then I'll go on to med school and become a doctor." "What then?" said the principal.

"Well, then I plan on getting married, having children, and pursuing my career." "What then?"

"I guess I'll retire." "What then?"

"I would like to travel the world." "What then?"

And the young man thought for a few seconds and said, "Well... I guess then I'll die." And the principal said, "And what then?"

Maybe it's because life rushes by so fast, but many people simply don't stop to ask how their daily purpose links up with God's eternal plans.

Here's part of the reason why asking and answering that question is so significant, as expressed by pastor Rick Warren: "Purpose always produces passion."[66]

If you know the bigger things God is doing in the world, and if you're a follower of Jesus, you're going to be motivated to get in on the action on a day-to-day basis. Here is what he says to his disciples in John 15:16: "You

131

did not choose me, but I chose you and appointed you so that you might go and bear fruit—fruit that will last…"

Purpose produces passion. And motivation. And fruit. That lasts.

Today, take a few moments to think about it. How does your daily purpose link up with God's eternal plans? If you have a good grip on the answer, great. If not, what are you going to do to find out more?

FRIDAY - YOUR MAGIC TOESHOES

Alongside literary giants like Shakespeare and Tolstoy are the Berenstain Bears. (Maybe that's a stretch, but just go with me on this one.)

In one of their timeless classics we learn about *The Magic Toeshoes*. Basically, a young bear wants to be a ballerina. But her toes are wobbly. So an old ballet master takes pity and gives her some "Magic Toeshoes," saying that with these shoes she'll be steady and confident.

Convinced of their power, she tries them on and is amazed at the result. As the year goes on, and as the big recital approaches, everything is set for her performance. But then, on the night of the show, she forgets her magic toeshoes at home!

Upset and anxious, she tells the old ballet master, who then discloses that they were never magic in the first place. They were just ordinary shoes.

So out onto the stage she goes and does an amazing job—as steady as ever!

The reason I like this story is because we are quick to doubt God's power and presence in our lives unless he swoops to our aid in a dramatic, miraculous, over-the-top intervention. Like the Berenstain Bear ballerina, we think that if someone could only give us some kind of magical guarantee, *then* we could surely face our giants.

Well, what if I were to tell you right now that with whatever you're facing today, the Holy Spirit is with you and within you, guiding you in God's way and providing a strength that only he can give?

Wouldn't that make you more confident?

Well guess what? It's true! If you have placed your faith in Christ, you've been given the gift of the Holy Spirit. He is with you and within you, guiding you in God's way and providing a strength that only he can give.

As we read in 1 Corinthians 3:16 (ESV): "Do you not know that you are God's temple and that God's Spirit dwells in you?"

So no wobbling.

Today, dance with giant, godly confidence. You are not alone.

SATURDAY - CO-RENOVATORS

In Christian teaching over the past seventy or eighty years there has been an emphasis on heaven and life after death.

In a sense, I get that. It's huge! But I sometimes worry it has overshadowed (to an unhealthy degree) what we're summoned to do in this life *before* we die.

One of the thinkers I've come to really admire is C.S. Lewis. He writes: "If you read history you will find that the Christians who did most for the present world were precisely those who thought most of the next."

What he means is that the Christians who take heaven seriously are the ones who do the most to transform their present world to look more like it. They are motivated to bring heaven to earth.

In 2 Corinthians 6:1 the apostle Paul says, "As God's co-workers we urge you not to receive God's grace in vain." It's a way of saying that as God's co-workers the Corinthians shouldn't receive the gift of God's goodness and generosity without purpose. They should get off their duffs and live differently as a result!

He uses the phrase "co-workers," but I like the term "co-renovators." Because if you're a follower of Jesus, and if you take seriously the prayer he taught us for God's will to be done "on earth as it is in heaven" (Matthew 6:10), that's what you are.

A co-renovator.

Friends, you were made on purpose and for a purpose: To be a co-renovator with Jesus as he brings heaven to earth... in yourself, in your relationships, in your homes, in your communities, and in the world. Living for this purpose brings God glory and you joy.

Today, think through the kinds of things you pray about, talk about, and act on. God cares about his people and this troubled world. I think you should too.

Are you just waiting on earth for heaven, or are you working for heaven on earth?

SUNDAY...

MONDAY - INFLATED WITH PURPOSE

Hebrews 13:1 (NRSV) says "Let mutual love continue." Sounds simple enough. But it can take a lifetime to refine. Let me explain.

These days I'm thinking a lot about purpose. I just think that knowing your purpose has the potential to inflate your days with meaning, energy, zest and faith.

And if you don't ever think about how your daily purpose connects up to God's bigger plans, I think you risk spiraling into some sort of abyss... mental or spiritual.

That's what happened to Leo Tolstoy. He was the great Russian author who wrote *War and Peace* and *Anna Karenina*. Here's what was going on in his mind when he had his own personal crisis:

"My question—that which at the age of fifty brought me to the verge of suicide—was the simplest of questions, lying in the soul of every man... a question without an answer to which one cannot live. It was: "What will come of what I am doing today or tomorrow? What will come of my whole life? Why should I live, why wish for anything, or do anything?" It can also be expressed thus: Is there any meaning in my life that the inevitable death awaiting me does not destroy?"[67]

Ponder that last question and apply it to yourself: "Is there any meaning in my life that the inevitable death awaiting me does not destroy?"

In other words, when you think about how you spend your time and energy, are you investing in things that will last beyond death?

You're right. There's no way a one-minute devotional can help you fully answer that question. But today I just want to help you forward with one suggestion:

Are you spending more of your time and energy on things... *or on people?*

Many of the people reading this are from affluent countries. And we are exceptionally skilled at putting work, things and money ahead of the people God has placed in our lives. I realize there are bills to pay and jobs to do. But those things shouldn't define you.

Along with Tolstoy, ask: "Is there any meaning in my life that the inevitable death awaiting me does not destroy?" As you search for the answer, think about the (actual) priority you place on the people around you.

Investing grace, truth, help and respect in people is one God-honouring way to live a life inflated with purpose.

Are you spending more of your time and energy on things... or on people?

TUESDAY - A VERSE WE READ WITH ONE EYE CLOSED

I don't know about you, but when I read the Bible there's a silent conversation happening in my head. With a lot of stories and verses I'm saying things like 'Yeah, that's awesome, that's good too, oh yup..."

But then I run into passages like this one and yup turns into gulp:

"If any of you wants to be my follower, you must turn from your selfish ways, take up your cross daily, and follow me." (Luke 9:23, NLT)

It can be one of those passages we read with one eye closed. We mentally agree, but know in our soul that it's a hard thing to do. (So we bounce along to the next story.)

While talking about his own suffering, self-giving love and sacrificial death, Jesus says that the cross (an ancient way to execute people which included a public shaming and torture ritual)—is a necessary part of the lives of those who want to follow him. He doesn't mean you'll have to carry an actual cross. But he does mean you'll have to make serious and love-based sacrifices as you put God's will before your own.

What *he* wants is more important than what *you* want. And that's when the metaphorical ground beneath us starts to shake. Because it's hard. And risky.

(And worth it.)

With his next breath Jesus says, "If you try to hang on to your life, you will lose it. But if you give up your life for my sake, you will save it" (Luke 9:24, NLT). You may lose what you once knew. But what you gain will be infinitely more.

I wish I could say I was perfect at living this out. I'm not. I struggle with it all the time. A few years ago I started a blog called "Why I'm a sinner in 100 words." But I haven't published it yet because those 100 words have turned into 100,000 words!

But the question I'm always trying to ask myself as I go about my day and make decisions—and the question that might be helpful to you too —is this:

"Is this just what I want, or is it what God wants?"

How we answer tells us whether we're carrying our cross... or not.

WEDNESDAY - THE PABLUM OF THE WEAK

Have you seen the *Zootopia* movie? It came out from Disney in 2016. In one scene, police officer Judy Hopps (a bunny) and Nick Wilde (a fox) go into the Department of Motor Vehicles.

And all the clerks are sloths! So of course, it takes *forever* for anything to get done. They move at a snail's pace and even talk at a snail's pace. Watching them *slowwwllllyyy* tell a knock knock joke is painful... and hilarious!

And although we laugh at sloths and how long it takes them to do anything, isn't that kind of like us?

We run and rush and scurry and scatter. But when it comes to those big priorities in life, we're just so good at going slowly, and delaying, and making excuses.

What big priority are you still waiting to act on?

Maybe it's a spiritual goal you've set for yourself like reading the New Testament or finding a church. Maybe it's scheduling a weekly family activity so you deepen your relationships. Maybe it's looking into that new job. Or maybe it's chipping off the invisible glue that seems to have your backside stuck to the couch so you can get on with establishing an exercise routine.

Well, today I'm here to tell you this:

Procrastination is the pablum of the weak.

Consider Proverbs 15:19: "The way of the sluggard is blocked with thorns, but the path of the upright is a highway."

So friend, get to it. Today is the best day to change.

THURSDAY - THE BOOMERANG OF YOUR SOUL

Human pride is the boomerang of your soul.

Just when you think you're done with selfishness and ego they come hurling back to their home within your heart. Pride is like that.

Now don't get me wrong: There are two kinds of pride. Good pride is the way you feel when someone you love scores the winning goal or makes a tough-but-great decision. You're proud of them, and rightly so.

But bad pride is when you're invisibly puffed up like a peacock. It's when you live and talk like your way is the only way. Unfortunately, it's a naturally occurring phenomena.

That said, I'm pretty sure none of us would describe ourselves as a puffed-up peacock. But when we live and talk like our way is the only way, that's basically what we're doing.

Are you right sometimes? Probably. But are you right all the time? Probably not.

Here's the thing.

The more narrowly focused we are on our own little plans, the harder it is to welcome and receive God's bigger plan for our lives.

Even if our own puffed-up plans seem grand, when compared to the majesty of God they're teeny-weeny.

Our vision is limited, but God's is unlimited. Our wisdom barely gets us out the door, but God's wisdom is broader than the sky. And yet, it's so easy to think we have a better handle on things than the Maker of heaven and earth.

So today, remember that "Pride brings a person low..." (Proverbs 29:23). If you think you have all the answers and can do it all yourself, you're not only wrong, but you're also deluded.

Don't overestimate what you can do, but don't underestimate what God can do through you.

FRIDAY - WORRY OVER A WORRY WORTH WORRYING ABOUT

Does worrying serve a purpose?

I actually think it does. To a point.

For me, worrying brings into focus something I need to act on. The key is to then do something about it, give it to God, and let it go.

Unfortunately, there are times when worry starts to escalate and dominate us. This can happen when we (a) worry about things we can't do anything about, and (b) keep worrying after we've done what we can.

Another dimension of worry—whether it's about a relationship, a bill, a child, an illness (the list goes on!)—is that it tricks you into thinking you're God. As if just thinking about a problem could make it go away.

Now, I don't want to minimize things. I realize worry can be a deep darkness that keeps us up at night. I also know from experience that worry has the blurrying effect of mixing up what we *can* do something about and what we *can't*. So here's some insight from Dr. Kennon Callahan to help us out:

"When you worry, worry over a worry worth worrying about."[68]

Say that three times fast! Lol He goes on to say, "ask yourself, 'Is this a worry I can do something about? Then, relax and go to sleep.'" Having done that he also suggests we give it over to God. As it says in 1 Peter 5:7, "Give all your worries and cares to God, for he cares about you."

Today, I'm guessing you're worried about something. Ask yourself, "Is this a worry worth worrying about?" If so, do something about it, give it to God, and let it go.

When you pick up a hitchhiker named Worry, and if he tries to muscle his way into the driver's seat of your brain, remind him that it's not his place. If he has something worthwhile to say, give him respectful attention, and then drop him off as fast as you can.

SATURDAY - ARE YOU (DIS)QUALIFIED?

"I'm just too messed up to be a part of something significant."

"I'll serve after I get my life together."

"I'm too imperfect for God to use me."

I've heard some variation of these sentences before. For some reason, many of us think that our imperfections disqualify us from being used by God for great things.

I think it's because we've heard stories about godly people who were so noble that they probably had actual halos around their heads. But we just need to chuck those mental images in the trash.

I'm not knocking people who appear to have it all together. But when you look at the biblical stories, so many of the big heroes were incredibly flawed. For example, King David hid his adultery with Bathsheba by murdering her husband Uriah. As it says in 2 Samuel 11: 26 and 27 (NKJV), "When the wife of Uriah heard that Uriah her husband was dead, she mourned for her husband... But the thing that David had done displeased the Lord." And he's one of the most widely celebrated biblical figures of all time!

Whoever you are, know this: *When it comes to serving God, your faith is more important than your flaws.*

You're not the only one with shadows in your closet.

You're not the only one with a weakness you're afraid to even whisper.

You're not the only one with a dozen bad decisions in your back pocket.

And you're not the only one with a few hurts that colour your outlook on life with a shade of grey.

When it comes down it, if you say that your imperfections disqualify you from being used by God for great things, that's the same as saying that God is weak.

Humbug.

Today, remember that you're not qualified to serve God because you're so good; you're called to serve God because he's so great.

When it comes to serving God, your faith is more important than your flaws.

SUNDAY...

MONDAY - YOUR FIRST MINUTE

When I first started pastoring Westminster Church, I remember visiting a man in a nursing home. He told me that before he got up each morning—before his feet even hit the floor—he would pray for me. He would also pray for his church family, for his biological family, for God's will to be done, and that the Lord would be merciful to him as he struggled through his day.

It made me think of Psalm 46:10: "Be still, and know that I am God!" Every morning, he would wake up in stillness, open his eyes, and close them again to start the day right.

So today I'd like to suggest a spiritual practice that is inspired by that conversation: *Give your first minute to God.*

Before you even get out of bed, say a one minute prayer. Ask God to set your priorities, to keep you focused, to guard you against the distractions that can take a wise, focused and Christ-centred way of life and turn it into hair-pulling rush.

What you'll find is that the character, content and quality of your day will go through the roof.

Spend the first minute of your day with God.

TUESDAY - WHAT IF IT WASN'T A COINCIDENCE?

When you look up "coincidence" at dictionary.com here's what you find:

Coincidence. Noun. a striking occurrence of two or more events at one time apparently by mere chance.

It's like being in New York, saying to your friend that you miss so-and-so from back home, then bumping into that person you just mentioned ten seconds later. Then you say, "Oh, I was just thinking about you, what a coincidence!"

Some kind of coincidence has happened to all of us. Maybe you've even experienced one this week.

But look closely at the definition. It says "a striking occurrence of two or more events at one time apparently by mere chance." The key is the word "apparently." It only *seems* like "mere chance."

I realize that there are legitimate coincidences. But what if coincidences weren't always just chance? What if some of them were orchestrated by God?

God is omnipresent, which means he is always present wherever you go. That's the thinking behind the words in Ephesians 4:6 that God is "over all and through all and in all."

What if you randomly keep bumping into someone because one of you is supposed to somehow encourage the other? What if a certain message keeps surfacing in your life like a broken record because you are supposed to pay attention to it? What if you keep hearing talk shows or songs about similar topics because you are being prepared for something that's coming in your life?

What we call *coincidence* is often *providence*. It's God's guiding and directing hand, leading us into a future he already occupies.

Today, as you go about your life, pay attention. Our God guides and directs you, leading you into a future he already occupies. A part of what that means is that, through people, places and events, God is preparing you, seeking the best for you, and using you to bless the world.

What we call coincidence is often providence. So pay attention. God may be directing you, leading you, preparing you, and using you way more than you think.

WEDNESDAY - WHEN BETTER ISN'T EASIER

Our culture promotes convenience, comfort, and things being quick and easy.

One hundred years ago it would have been virtually inconceivable to drive up to a restaurant window, order your meal, and get it back almost instantaneously. Today, fast food drive-thrus are incredibly common.

Twenty years ago it would have been virtually inconceivable to pick up a smart phone or iPad and video call someone on the other side of the planet in real time... for free. Now it's taken for granted.

Yup, convenience and comfort are king.

But when it comes to faith, here's my question: Does God always make your life better by making it easier?

Let's look at Luke 9:23. Jesus says, "Whoever wants to be my disciple must deny themselves and take up their cross daily and follow me."

A cross was a way to torture and kill political criminals. So when Jesus says to take up a cross daily and follow him, he doesn't mean we need to physically experience death every day. (Because you can only die once.)

What he means is that we need to crucify our egos and selfish ways every day if we truly want to be his disciples. Only then can we put him first, be a part of the change *he* is doing in the world, and experience the abundant life he wants for us.

So, does God always make your life better by making it easier? No.

Granted, some things are in fact better and easier at the same time. Like an illness being cured or an acute stress coming to an end. But when you think about the big picture decisions you make, the tough choices, and the ways you cultivate your character to be more like Jesus, God doesn't always make your life better by making it easier.

The way of Christ—the way of self-sacrificial love—isn't always easy. But it's better. And more meaningful. And more joyful. Your life will also start to be less heavy and more light.

Think for a moment about your next twelve months. What big decision do you have to make? Don't just do what is easy. Do what is right.

Approach life with wisdom and a big heart for self-sacrificial love. Easier isn't always better.

THURSDAY - REPEAT IT OUT LOUD TO STOP THE CYCLE

Did you realize that ninety-five percent of the ocean is still unexplored? That's right. Ninety-five percent!

That statistic just blows me away. Imagine all the beauty yet to be seen. Imagine all the cures for diseases that are simply undiscovered!

That's like the Bible.

Most of us can recall a few key passages like "love your neighbour as yourself" (Mark 12:31) or "The LORD is my shepherd" (Psalm 23:1). But the incredible depths of the Bible often remain unexplored, and therefore, undiscovered. We miss out on its vastness and power.

So here's what I think you should do.

I think you should be honest with yourself about the areas of temptation in your life. Maybe you're tempted to overspend, or possibly overeat. Maybe some of you are tempted with lust. Maybe some of you are tempted to overwork. Think about it for a second: What is your greatest temptation?

When you answer that question, look up what the Bible says about resisting that temptation. You can use Google. Or if you have a study Bible with a word index at the back, go there.

Then here's what you do: Memorize the verse that talks about your specific temptation. And then, whenever you feel tempted, repeat that verse to yourself out loud.

The more you get into God's word, the more God's word gets into you.

In Luke 11:4 (ESV) Jesus teaches his disciples to pray and includes the words, "And lead us not into temptation." You don't have to be pushed around by it. In fact, most of the time, the reason we get pushed around by our temptations is because we let them do the pushing, and close ourselves to God's wisdom in the process.

But it doesn't have to be that way. Today, memorize the verse that talks about your specific temptation. And then, whenever you feel tempted, repeat that verse to yourself out loud.

The more scientists explore the ocean, the more they discover its beauty and life-giving gifts. The same is true for the Bible.

The more you get into God's word, the more God's word gets into you.

FRIDAY - SERVING PEOPLE YOU DON'T EVEN LIKE

In John 13:34-35, Jesus says, "A new command I give you: Love one another. As I have loved you, so you must love one another. By this everyone will know that you are my disciples, if you love one another."

When you read this story in the book of John, it becomes powerfully clear that Jesus doesn't just say things—he lives them out. He demonstrates what he means. I think that's a part of the reason why he's so captivating to so many people all around the world. There's a oneness to his words and actions. For example, just before he gave this command to love one another, he washed his disciples' feet.

Think of that for a second. The Son of God—the Saviour of the world— stooped down and washed the dirty feet of his friends. Feet that had just walked through filthy city streets which were surely covered in all kinds of things, including animal excrement.

So he washed their feet. Including the feet of Judas Iscariot. The man who betrayed him. The man who Jesus *knew* would betray him.

There's a lot I could say about this, but let me just offer this one thought: If Jesus can love Judas and wash his feet, you can love and serve people you don't even like. It's not always fun. And it's not always easy. It's life in the foot washing footsteps of Jesus.

Regardless of how you feel about the people you meet today, "Love one another."

SATURDAY - A PERSON WHO DEMANDS YOUR CONFIDENCE

The resurrection of Jesus from the dead is at the heart of the Christian faith. And because we celebrate that mind-blowing fact Sunday by Sunday, we can easily forget to think through the implications for our own lives.

Bible scholar Luke Timothy Johnson says the most important question about Jesus is whether he is dead or alive.[69] If you think he's a great teacher who simply came to an untimely end on the cross, you're living like he's dead. But if you believe he's God-in-person, raised and ruling, then you should be living like he's alive. That perspective should make a colossal difference in your life. That's why you need to keep coming back to this soul-searching question: *I am open to the resurrecting power of God in my life and in the world?*

Friends, if God did it then, he can do it again. The resurrecting power of God wasn't a one-time thing. It's an *ongoing* thing. Because of that, your life can be different. It can be bold and courageous because you are open to God's ongoing resurrecting power.

Pliny the Younger was a ruler in the early second century in Bythynia. He led trials of Christians. If they didn't renounce Christ he would kill them. He even gave them three chances! And time after time, many of them chose to die for their faith rather than renounce their Master.

The resurrection changes things. It turned the disciples from cowards into lions of courage. Back then. And now. You may not be on trial for your faith. But you can live a transformed life because after the resurrection all things are actually possible.

Are you open to the resurrecting power of God in your life and in the world? Do you believe that? (Or do you just say it?)

Having been confronted with the resurrection, in Matthew 28:8 we read that "the women hurried away from the tomb, afraid yet filled with joy..." Why? Because Jesus was alive. And do you know what? He still is.

So live like the resurrecting power of God isn't just something that happened, but that continues to happen...

In you.

SUNDAY...

MONDAY - WHEN MANY THINGS ARE IMPORTANT NONE OF THEM ARE

Fifteen years ago one of my co-workers had a habit of writing important things on sticky notes and pasting them around his computer screen.

He soon ran out of space. So he started sticking them on his desk, and then on the wall.

But when you have that many "important" sticky-note reminders, how do you know which is the *most* important? You don't!

When that many things are important, none of them are.

That's like how we think. We make little mental sticky notes about important things to remember. We see or hear things like "Seize the day" or "Stay positive" and think to ourselves, 'Yeah, I gotta remember that one.'

But like my co-worker's office, you accumulate so many mental sticky-note reminders that they all start to fade in importance.

That's why I think you should focus and do this: Write down your God-centred purpose.

I know it sounds weird, but I still think you should do it. Literally write it down. Take a scrap piece of paper, grab a pen, or open your note-taking app on your phone, and do it.

"Today I'm going to respectfully stand up to my boss because I'm made in God's image." "Today I'm going to turn off my phone and be emotionally available for my kids." "Today I'm going to finally go for a run because my body is a temple of the Holy Spirit." "Today I'm going to _____."

Attention-deficit disorder used to be someone else's diagnosis. Now it's a part of your D.N.A.

When you write down your God-centred purpose, you are pulling yourself back from the thousand possible flight paths before you and are training yourself to come back to your God-centred ground zero. The result is a less scattered you.

Proverbs 16:3 says, "Commit to the Lord whatever you do, and he will establish your plans." So ask for God's guidance, commit to living for

God's glory, write down your purpose, and lean on him as he leads you forward.

When you live like everything is important, nothing is. So make a choice.

TUESDAY - SPEAK LIFE

A few words can alter someone's life: "You got the job!" "It's a boy!"

When we think about life-altering words, we usually think about big events with photo-ops and months of planning.

But you can also have a positive, life-altering impact in your everyday conversations with the people around you. "I'm proud of you." "You got this!" "I'll pray for you."

Proverbs 18:21 says, "The tongue has the power of life and death..." Think about that for a second. Your words can wield more life—or more death—in someone else's existence.

Singer Toby Mac has a great way of framing it in his song "Speak Life":

> *Some days the tongue gets twisted;*
> *Other days my thoughts just fall apart.*
> *I do, I don't, I will, I won't,*
> *It's like I'm drowning in the deep.*
> *Well, it's crazy to imagine,*
> *Words from our lips as the arms of compassion,*
> *Mountains crumble with every syllable.*
> *Hope can live or die.*
> *So speak Life! Speak Life!*
> *To the deadest darkest night!*[70]

Your words have the power of life. And that's true whether you give speeches or wipe noses, and whether you're twelve, fifty or ninety-nine years old.

Choose life. And speak it. Today.

WEDNESDAY - THE SILVER BULLET

We humans often make things more complicated than they are.

A few days ago I saw someone having a really hard time raking their lawn. They had a phone in one hand. And with the other, they were raking a pile of dead leaves leftover from the fall... with a shovel.

That's right. They were trying to rake old leaves. With a shovel. With one hand!

We sometimes just make things more complicated than they need to be.

So today I'd like to give you some advice. And if you do it, I think it will make you a better person. It will help you be at your best. You'll be less grumpy and more giving. You'll be less impatient and more positive. It may be a silver bullet. Are you ready? Here it is.

Go to bed earlier.

I know what you're thinking. 'Matthew, I went to all this trouble to read this devotional and the "advice" you give me is to just go to bed earlier?

Yup.

When your car runs out of gas, do you scratch your head and wonder what's wrong? Do you blame the engine? Do you complain about the seats or compare it to another perfectly running car that just so happens to be full of gas?

No you don't. You put gas in your car.

When King David was panicked and fleeing from his rebellious son Absalom, even though he perceived danger all around him, he said this: "I lie down and sleep; I wake again, because the LORD sustains me" (Psalm 3:5).

Things were coming apart. So he trusted God... and went to bed!

In my own life, when I'm feeling swamped, what I've discovered is that I can do more in twenty minutes with a full tank of gas than I can in two hours if I'm running on empty.

If you're feeling spent, dazed, and overwhelmed, maybe a better you is easier than you think. Get some more sleep.

Your gas tank doesn't fill itself.

THURSDAY - BEST FRIENDS WITH THE ENEMY

When you think about your worst enemy, who you do think about?

A betraying friend? Someone who has abused you? Satan?

How many of you answered, 'Me'?

I'm guessing not very many. But I'm also guessing that many of us act that way.

Let's consider Hall of Fame baseball pitcher Gaylord Perry. He was known for his pitching—not for his batting. So when he stepped into the batter's box in 1963 he is reported to have said, "They'll put a man on the moon before I hit a home run."

Maybe he was being modest or realistic. But wasn't he also being self-defeating?

Turns out he did hit his first and only home run... six years later! And get this. He did it a few hours after Neil Armstrong made history and walked on the moon!

I'm not saying your words will automatically turn into reality. You're not God. But the things you say to yourself have a powerful impact on the kind of life you live.

So you need to remind yourself—daily—about who you actually are. You are a victorious child of God. If you are a follower of Jesus, you are the redeemed, the light, a champion. This is what Paul says in Romans 8:37: "No, in all these things we are more than conquerors through him who loved us."

That's you!

Word has it that before Canadian swimming champion Mark Tewksbury won gold in the 100-metre backstroke in 1992 he visualized winning the race and being on the Gold Medal podium hundreds of times. He trained himself to think like a conqueror.

And that made it more natural for him to act like one.

Today, don't be your own worst enemy. Stop putting yourself down when God is lifting you up.

"No, in all these things we are more than conquerors through him who loved us."

Live like it.

FRIDAY - WHAT DO YOU PRAY FOR IN A SITUATION LIKE THAT?

During a healing service at a church in Ethiopia, a boy came forward with no fingers. What do you pray for in a situation like that?

Inner peace? Strength?

Pastor Mesfin of Kolfe Kale Hiwot Church decided to boldly pray for healing. After he did so, everyone who was gathered could hear a popping sound, then another, then another, and another, and another. Five fingers appeared on his hand![71]

As modern, scientifically-minded people, what do we make of a story like that?

At first, maybe we respond with cynicism. But where we start isn't where we should end. Why? Because Jesus performed miracles. He restored sight to the blind and even walked on water. And he rose from the dead after three days!

I'm not saying I fully understand the mind of God, or that healing prayers are magic tricks. They're not. But when you read many of the biblical stories, what you often find is that people who believe Jesus can do powerful things, experience God doing powerful things!

What situation in your life needs God's dramatic healing power? An illness? A toxic relationship? An injustice?

This week, pray bold prayers!

And expect God to act.

God is wise. God is just. God is powerful. We don't always know how he answers our prayers; but we know that he does.

Bring your big concerns to Jesus first. Trust in his power. Be open to the incredible. Pray the biggest prayers you've ever prayed.

When you believe Jesus can do powerful things, God does powerful things.

"Now to him who is able to do immeasurably more than all we ask or imagine..." (Ephesians 3:20)

SATURDAY - POUR YOURSELF INTO WHAT'S IN FRONT OF YOU

In World War Two, Viktor Frankl found himself in a Nazi concentration camp. His book *Man's Search for Meaning* recounts many of the terrible things he endured.

He also talked about how you can find meaning in horrible situations. Here's an example.

Some of Frankl's fellow prisoners had figured out a way to escape. So they approached Frankl to see if he wanted to be included in the plan. But by that time, Frankl was serving as a doctor to other sick people in the camp.

So he told them no. He didn't want to be a part of the escape plan. But why? Because he had a personal purpose that was more important than escape: To help those who would be left behind—to help those who still needed care.[72]

If you're reading this, you're not in a concentration camp. And I'm not doubting there are hard things in your life. And I know it would be good to be in a different situation sometimes.

But what if you took a lead from Viktor Frankl and poured yourself into what's in front of you, even though it's tough?

What if a difficult relationship you're already in is the one you're supposed to enrich? What if a challenge you can't seem to get around is the one you're supposed to overcome? What if a problem in your neighbourhood that makes you want to move is the reason you should stay?

Having a godly purpose can redefine your experience of hardship.

Proverbs 24:10 says: "If you falter in a time of trouble, how small is your strength!" Sometimes a time of trouble does in fact mean that something needs to change. But sometimes, a time of trouble means you need to pull up your socks, lean on God, and flex the muscle he gave you to expand his light in a place that is otherwise dark.

Sometimes you just have to pour yourself into what's already in front of you. For light. For the good of the world. And usually, for the benefit of somebody else.

More often than not, that's what it means to be alive.

SUNDAY...

MONDAY - ALREADY HEALED

When Tom Long was in training to be a pastor, his supervisor sent him to visit some families in the Carolinas. One of them was a mother with a bunch of children.

But one of the children—whom we'll call Robert—wasn't included in the activities in the same way as the other children. He was born with cerebral palsy and always stood at a distance, watching others having fun from the outside.

One day on a subsequent visit, Long was there alone with the mother. She needed to tell him something. A few days before, she was home alone with Robert. She was sitting in the living room while Robert stood at the end of the hallway, watching her from a distance.

She felt a shift in the room that caused her to look down the hallway toward Robert. This is what she said next: "I saw Jesus with his arm around Robert's shoulder."

She looked away, and then quickly back. But this time she only saw Robert.

"For the first time since he was born," she said, "I saw my son as already healed in the power of God."[73]

I share that story with you because it's surrounded in mystery and magnitude. There's a beauty that I don't totally understand. A power that resists exact explanation.

Kind of like God.

But I share it with you today in case you need the reassurance that our God is a God who heals. Speaking about this very thing, inspirational writer and pastor Max Lucado says that God heals you either instantly, gradually, or ultimately. What he means is that God heals you right away, or through time, or ultimately in heaven.[74]

Instantly. Gradually. Or ultimately.

Revelation 21:4 gives us a glimpse of what things will be like one day in the new Jerusalem: "He will wipe every tear from their eyes."

Take courage. Fear not. All pain and worry is temporary. You may not see it yet. But in Christ, you are healed.

TUESDAY - TEACHING FROM A TWO-YEAR OLD

I have three children, two girls and a boy. Several years ago I was wrestling with the older two. We do that a lot. Imagine screams mixed with laughter and the occasional head bonk.

They charge at me and I grab them, swing them around and toss them on the couch. They giggle with delight and then body-check me at full speed. (My wife cringes while all of this is going on—but hey, this is some of what we dads do best!)

But off to the side, my youngest daughter watches. She's not sure if it's serious or not. But she thinks I might be hurt and yells, "No, this my daddy!"

She wants to defend me. But all she can do is run over and give me a hug. She buries her head deep in my chest and tightens her tiny arms around my neck. "No, this my daddy!" I tell her it's okay and that her brother and sister and I are just playing. But still she clings.

That's how she stands up for me. Maybe she doesn't know enough to hit out at her brother or sister, or devise some other clever strategy to offer rescue. The only thing she knows how to do is run to me and hug me.

When someone is hurting we often search for the right words or explanations. Or we busy ourselves with a hundred clever rescue strategies.

When all we need to do is *be there*.

In John 15:12 Jesus says, "This is my commandment, that you love one another as I have loved you." Sometimes that's simpler than we make it out to be.

Is there someone in your life right now who needs some support? Maybe you don't know what to say. Maybe you don't have the right strategy. That's okay. Take some teaching from a two-year old: Just be there. And maybe even give a hug.

Sometimes the best way to stand up for someone, is simply to stand beside them.

WEDNESDAY - SAY IT BEFORE IT'S TOO LATE

One of the profound privileges of being a pastor is being with people who are in their last stages of life on earth.

I've been a pastor for ten years and I've held many people's hands as they've passed from this world to the next.

What does it teach me? A lot of things. But today, let me share this one thought with you.

Say what you need to say to someone you care about before it's too late.

One of the most gut-wrenching sentences I hear is this: "I just wish I had taken the time to say..."

For some reason we delay saying what needs to be said. Maybe it's "I love you" or "I forgive you." Maybe it's a question about a dark chapter from the past. Maybe it's sharing your hope-soaked faith in Jesus. Maybe it's "Thank you so much for helping to make me into who I am today."

I don't want to alarm you, but every single person in your life is one heartbeat away from death. I hope that everyone lives long, robust, faithful lives. But what if that one chapter-closing heartbeat was closer than you think?

As we're reminded in Ecclesiastes 3:2, there is "a time to be born and a time to die..." If you have something important to say to someone you love, say what you need to say before it's too late.

It may be the source of immeasurable peace, not only for them, but for you.

THURSDAY - IMPERFECT PEOPLE

What I'm about to tell you is terrible. But I'm going to tell you anyway!

I forget where I heard it, but someone told me about a Bible study group. They called it "Owl." At first, people thought the name was based on the bird. Since owls are symbols of wisdom, it made sense.

But it came to light that the name wasn't based on the bird. It was an acronym. O.W.L. stood for "ones we like." Basically, the organizers only wanted to include in their Bible study people they liked!

How terrible!

Fortunately, the people were reprimanded and the group was disbanded.

I tell this story because it's easy to assume that people we don't like or disagree with or who are different than us have no real role to play in our faith.

But they do.

Life is a team sport. And so is faith. It's more like baseball than it is like a 100-metre sprint. We need other people—including "imperfect" people— along the way.

In fact, *imperfect people are perfect opportunities for you to grow in godliness.*

When it comes to your brothers and sisters in faith, if you only interacted with people who thought the same things as you, and who you liked, you'd never be pushed and challenged to grow and mature in the same way.

So whenever we interact with people who think or do things differently than us, it's a chance for us to grow in godliness. We can ask ourselves, 'What am I going to do in this situation? If Jesus were here with us now, what kind of person would I be?'

In Ephesians 4:29 we read that words should be used that are "helpful for building others up according to their needs." I think that's good wisdom for you and me, and for whoever we interact with.

If you're going to really mature in your faith, you actually *need* imperfect people. They are perfect opportunities for you to grow in godliness.

Wouldn't that be a better way to approach "imperfect people"? I hope you agree with me. After all, it might help other people know how to deal with you.

Why? Because you're one of the imperfect people too.

FRIDAY - WHY IT'S EASY TO BE JUDGMENTAL

Being judgmental is about as attractive as a racist proudly gallivanting around your living room on a high horse.

But what does it mean to be "judgmental," anyway?

If someone says you're being judgmental, what they usually mean is that you're acting morally superior—as if you're always right, others are always wrong, and you're a better person because of it.

It's not the same as simply using judgment. Using judgment is good. That's thinking through a situation, weighing the facts, and humbly sharing your wisdom, even if it puts you at odds with someone else.

Judgmentalism is different. It's the person on the moral high horse who likes to look down their nose at you.

But do you know what? It's easy for *all* of us to be judgmental from time to time. We may not always say judgmental things out loud, but we can certainly think them!

Here's why it's easy to slip into that mode of thought.

Always being "right" is easy. Always being thoughtful is not.

Basically, being judgmental means you never have to grow your thinking.

When you think you already know everything about someone else's situation, and when you think you're already an expert on most topics, and when you think you've never made any mistakes, you never have to look in the mirror.

Self-examination is hard. It means being honest about how much we don't know. It means owning up to our own issues and mistakes. It also means taking that next best step to become a more mature, wise, loving, and humble human being.

I think that's why Jesus said, "Why do you look at the speck of sawdust in your brother's eye and pay no attention to the plank in your own eye?" (Matthew 7:3)

Planks have a way of obscuring vision. And self-examination. And maturity.

Remember the expression "Err on the side of caution"? I think we should modify it to this: "Err on the side of grace."

With each new day, including today, let's continue to grow as we take that next best step toward being the mature, wise, loving and humble human beings we were created to be.

SATURDAY - MAKE YOURSELF UNCOMFORTABLE

I'm sitting here in a comfortable chair. I'm drinking a flavoured coffee in comfortable clothes. I'm comfortable.

Then I open my Bible and read about the apostles being persecuted for their faith.

In Acts 5 they get brought before a tribunal called the Sanhedrin and are ordered to stop teaching in Jesus' name.

The apostles refuse. So the Sanhedrin threatens to kill them. But a wise rabbi named Gamaliel diffuses the situation. Instead of killing them, they decide to severely beat and whip them—something called flogging.

I wonder how the apostles felt. Sad?

Here's the answer: "The apostles left the Sanhedrin, rejoicing because they had been counted worthy of suffering disgrace for the Name" (Acts 5:41).

They were *rejoicing* because they had been counted *worthy* enough to suffer for Jesus!

That blows my mind. When something bad happens to me I wonder, 'Oh Lord, am I being punished? Why are you not helping me? Where are you?'

In contrast, they *rejoice* because they were *worthy* enough to suffer for Jesus!

I realize we live in a different time. Although there is Christian persecution in our world, many of us in the West are pretty comfortable.

So maybe it's time to do something for Jesus that makes you UNcomfortable. Like taking a stand on an issue that puts you at odds with the majority view. Like sharing something about your faith with someone. Like reorganizing your schedule so that God's priority in your life is actually reflected in how you spend your time. Like serving the poor or giving to the point where it really stretches you.

And yes, it will involve sacrifice. It may make you different...

And alive.

Jesus didn't live and die to make you more comfortable. Jesus lived and died for the forgiveness of sins, and so that you could also die and come back to life by his resurrection power for the healing of the world.

Maybe it's time to do something for Jesus that makes you UNcomfortable. Don't let the comfort in your life get in the way of Christ in your life. He himself is all the comfort we really need.

SUNDAY...

MONDAY - DEAR YOU

Recently I was reading Psalm 139:14 where it says, "I praise you because I am fearfully and wonderfully made..."

I've read a lot about this verse. Different scholars say different things.

But in and through it all are a few firm facts of modern life: That sometimes you need to acknowledge the dark difficulty of the world. And that sometimes the ugliness of that world latches on to your soul and sinks in a few claws.

Because of that, everyone needs help rising above the grime by being reminded of a truer truth—a piece of Real that is un-threatened by the clawing paws of a bruised and bruising world.

Everyone needs to be reminded that they are beautiful to someone.

So today, know this: You are beautiful to God.

TUESDAY - RECYCLE YOUR PAIN

I don't think I've met a single person who hasn't had challenges in their life.

Sure, some challenges seem bigger than others. Some people have had children die or been sexually abused or experienced other kids of trauma. But any kind of difficulty—no matter the "size"—can change your life forever.

When we've gone through something hard, we often want to tuck it away and not talk about it. And I get that. But what if that experience could somehow improve the life of someone else?

Mark Batterson doesn't think we should waste our difficulties. He says that if you let God do his work, "He'll recycle your pain for someone else's gain."[75]

He doesn't mean that bad things are good (they're not), or that you should re-live your past, or that you should be forced into talking about something if you don't want to. He's talking about being open to the idea that your experience could somehow improve the life of someone else.

In Romans 8:28 (NRSV) we read: "We know that all things work together for good for those who love God, who are called according to his purpose." That doesn't mean that all things are good—but that for those who love God and are called according to his purpose, good can come out of all things, including hardship.

What if you could lend an ear of support to someone who no one else understands because you've "been there"?

What if you have some wisdom that only you can give because you've been through that dark valley?

What if a mistake in your own life has grown you as a person, and you can be a better leader to those around you in a way you could never have imagined before?

Your most painful moments don't have to be your defining moments.

Maybe over the next few days you just need to keep your ears open. Someone will ask a question or need some support, and you'll be able to provide wisdom or encouragement that only you can give.

Why?

Because, by the power of God, you've got an invisible scar that may be able to help heal someone else's wound.

WEDNESDAY - YOU ARE SOMEONE'S MISSING PIECE

In 1 Corinthians 12:27 the apostle Paul says, "Now you are the body of Christ, and each one of you is a part of it."

This idea that the church is the "body of Christ" is pretty well-known. In fact, when people say that Jesus is the "head" (boss and brains) of the church, and that you and I are his "hands and feet," this is where it comes from.

But there's another implication we often miss.

If "each of you" is a part of the body of Christ, it means that each of you is also connected to other people in that same body. Just as our own bodies are effective because they benefit from eyes and ears and hands and knees, if you take one of those parts out of the mix, the rest of the body suffers.

In the same way, other people in the church *need* you to be mature and effective. And you *need* them.

We downplay the role of other people in the church—the body of Christ —because we are so dramatically influenced by the highly individualistic society around us. That society focuses on the importance of "me, myself and I," but not really other people. But get this:

Your presence can be someone else's medicine.

Your insights can fill in someone else's blind spots.

What you have to offer can be someone else's answered prayer.

Because faith isn't about being independent; it's about inter-dependency.

As Paul says, each of you is a part of the body of Christ. Yes, you are the hands and feet of Jesus. But you are those hands and feet *together*. Remove yourself from the body and everyone suffers... including you.

Take the local church seriously. And your role within it.

You are someone's missing piece. (And they are yours.)

THURSDAY - BASEBALL, BULLFIGHTS OR BOTH?

Someone told me about two groups of people who participated in an experiment.

The first was a bunch of Americans who had never been to Mexico. The second was a group of Mexicans who had never been to America.

The researchers asked everyone to look into some binoculars. But they weren't normal binoculars. At the end of one lens was a picture of a baseball game. At the end of the other was a picture of a bullfight.

(Baseball is common in America, and bullfights are common in Mexico.)

Both groups were asked to look into the binoculars—but only for a moment—and report what they saw. The Americans said they saw a baseball game. And the Mexicans said they saw a bullfight.

But why?

The researchers speculated that we often see what we're used to seeing. If you're used to seeing a baseball game, your brain will pick up on that first. If you're used to seeing bullfights, your brain will pick up on that first.

When it comes to God, I think our brains often operate in the same way. We think that God only works in our lives in ways that are consistent with how we've experienced him in the past.

When Jesus is talking to the disciples about the difficult but life-saving journey of faith he says that "with God all things are possible" (Matthew 19:26). He doesn't say that with God all things are possible insofar as they're consistent with how you've experienced him in the past with your limited vision.

No. He says that with God all things are possible.

That includes things you haven't thought of before. If those things are faithful to what we learn about God's character in the Bible, and if your heart is prayerfully set on learning and doing his will before your own, those things will start to materialize around you, in you, and because of you.

The possibilities of God are not limited by your limited perspective.

Look bigger. There may be more God-inspired prospects staring you in the face than what first meets the eye.

FRIDAY - WHEN STRIKEOUTS AREN'T STRIKEOUTS

I've been thinking about baseball lately. Maybe it's because two of my kids are in little league.

Consider this.

A decent batting average in the major leagues is .250. That means you consistently get a hit one out of every four times you go to the plate.

If you get a hit one out of every three times your average goes up to .333. That's considered exceptional.

No one has *ever* had a perfect 1.000 batting average. Not Babe Ruth. Not anybody.

That means that most major league professionals—including the greats—*don't* get a hit more times than they do.

When it comes to faith, it's easy to get down on ourselves if we don't always "feel" connected to God. We want to *feel* his closeness, his power, his goodness.

But isn't that just like expecting to get a hit every time you go to the plate?

It's just not realistic. We won't always "feel" connected. But that's okay.

If your faith is driven by your fluctuating feelings, your fluctuating feelings are driving away a stronger faith. So what do you do?

First, you remind yourself that it's normal to not always "feel" connected to God. You're going to have dry spells. You're human.

Second, make decisions based on what Jesus teaches and not on how you feel. As I've said before, what God's Son says goes.

I realize there are ups and downs. But don't let a rough patch make you feel like a strike-out king just because you can't *feel* the connection.

Instead, go out of your way to remember what Jesus teaches, and act accordingly.

When you do, you'll be building a stronger faith.

As it says in 1 John 3:20: "If our hearts condemn us, we know that God is greater than our hearts, and he knows everything."

Your feelings can be helpful, like a friend. But they're not the Lord.

SATURDAY - DEEPER AND MORE DESTRUCTIVE WITH TIME

When I lived in Toronto I marvelled at how many statues there were. They were things like warriors riding on horses or heroes from a previous age.

From a distance they always looked impressive.

But the closer you got, the more cracks you saw. There were fault lines and chips and discoloration.

Isn't that like you and me?

I'm not talking about physical cracks, but invisible ones. They're cracks in our character that threaten our integrity as people. And the closer you look, the more you find!

Envy is a crack: eyes and hearts always lusting for what other people have and never being content.

Control is a crack: an insatiable need to manipulate people and conversations.

Smoldering anger is a crack: a quiet anger you just can't shake that destructively seeps into your relationships.

I'm currently reading a dynamite book that offers some help. It's called *Home Run: Learn God's Game Plan for Life and Leadership* by Kevin Myers and leadership guru John C. Maxwell. In it, Maxwell says, "Unaddressed cracks in character only get deeper and more destructive with time."[76]

It makes me think of Proverbs 11:3: "The integrity of the upright guides them, but the unfaithful are destroyed by their duplicity."

It's a question of integrity. If we don't address the invisible cracks in our character, they'll get worse with each passing day. And they won't just threaten your own foundation, but the foundations of the people around you.

So what do you do?

MATTHEW RUTTAN

Start with your thoughts. What thoughts do you have that dishonour God? That somehow smear his image within you?

Seal that crack before it spreads. When you do, you'll be honouring your Maker, growing your integrity, and protecting the people you care about most.

SUNDAY...

MONDAY - IN PUBLIC

Psalm 63:3 says, "Because your steadfast love is better than life, my lips will praise you."

Being aware of God's love and then praising him for it is easy enough when you're by yourself or when you go to a worship service. But verbally honoring God when you're talking to friends or family who don't share your beliefs can be a different story. It makes you *different*.

But when you do it, a few things happen: First, it gives God the glory he deserves. Second, it strengthens your own faith. And third, it encourages others. To show you what I mean let me offer you one very practical suggestion.

Before you eat a meal, you probably say grace, right? But what about when you're in public?

One of the very down-to-earth ways to glorify God with your lips is to say grace when you're in a restaurant. Don't hide it. It doesn't matter if it's a dive, a diner, or McDonalds.

When my family says grace publicly, we know it makes us stand out. Not many people seem to say grace in restaurants these days. Our prayer may only last for ten seconds, but it can still draw looks of puzzlement. But when we do it, it gives God the glory he deserves, it strengthens our own faith, and it encourages others. One time a lady came up to us as we were leaving a restaurant and said, "I just want to say how nice it is to see people say grace together—to see people thank the Lord. It's good to know there are others."

Camouflage is good for hunting. Just not for faith.

Maybe you should stand out a little bit more. Sure, some people will see you. But don't worry; it's not about them. It's about God. "Because your steadfast love is better than life, my lips will praise you."

Amen. And *bon appetit!*

TUESDAY - THEY'RE STANDING ON YOUR SHOULDERS

It's an expression that many of us have used: "Standing on the shoulders of giants."

It means that someone has benefited from the knowledge or strength of someone who has gone before. And they are simply building on that.

With that in mind, I think you and I are standing on the shoulders of giants.

People before us have spent time and energy on us, set an example, taught us, and prayed for us. Not all of them have been perfect, of course. But some of them have most likely been spiritual giants who have somehow sought the best for us.

One of the places we see this at work in the Bible is when the apostle Paul mentioned the "sincere faith" of his young co-worker Timothy. It's a faith "which first lived in your grandmother Lois and in your mother Eunice" (1 Timothy 1:5). It's something they nurtured in him. We don't know much about Lois and Eunice, but Timothy is certainly standing on their shoulders!

But when we think about this idea of standing on people's shoulders, here's what we often miss.

If you are standing on the shoulders of giants, *future giants are also standing on yours!*

Friends, children, nieces, nephews, co-workers, classmates and more, are currently being impacted by you. You may not always see the result. But it's happening. Year after year.

You have the potential to be a spiritual giant in someone else's life!

You don't need to have all the answers or have a perfect track record. (None of us do.) Just try to grow the sincerity of your faith and invest your time, energy and prayer into those God has placed in your life on a daily basis. In fact, that's how Tim Kimmel, co-founder of *Family Matters*, defines success: "the conscientious stewarding of future generations."[77]

God grows what you sow into the next generation.

You are standing on the shoulders of giants. And future giants are standing on yours.

WEDNESDAY - TEACHABLENESS

Have you ever noticed that people who think they're really smart also think you're not?

I don't know about you, but I've noticed something about the people who are *truly* wise in my life. Those who are truly wise (a) aren't threatened by the wisdom of others, and (b) are always open to learning more.

Recently I came across Psalm 50:17. Speaking to a wicked person, God said, "You hate my instruction and cast my words behind you." To get the full gist you need to read the whole Psalm. I find it illuminating that the wicked person *hates* instruction—they *hate* being taught God's words; they *hate* guidance.

(Maybe they think they already know everything.)

Don't get me wrong. Wise people aren't wishy-washy or vacant. They also know things. They know *lots* of things about life and love, about knowing right from wrong, about knowing when to speak and when to put a sock in it.

But they also know that the world is a big ole place, and that the Maker of heaven and earth has a bigger brain than they do.

Let's call it *teachableness*.

Today, as you venture into conversations, relationships and decisions, do you already know everything? I hope not; that's a lonely existence.

Be open to the Lord's instruction—through him directly, and through others.

The more you learn the more there is to learn.

THURSDAY - THE DEVIL

In 1 Peter 5:8 we read this: "Your enemy the devil prowls around like a roaring lion looking for someone to devour."

This may be the shortest devotional yet, but here goes: The Devil wants you to *not* pray...

FRIDAY - THE ART OF SLOWING DOWN

When you drive through a construction zone you're bound to see this sign: "Slow Down"

But what if instead of referring to the speed of your vehicle it was referring to the speed of your life?

What if it was a message from God? 'Hey you, yes *you*: Slow Down.'

The problem with speed, hyper-busyness and bustling through life is that you miss things because you're rushing past them. Beauty turns to blur.

As I write this I'm mentally agreeing with this idea of slowing down, doing less, and smelling the proverbial roses. But to be honest, I really struggle with it. I'm a part of a very active church, have a growing family, and have a bunch of things that I like (and need) to do. How can I slow down when my to-do list is so long!

Since I'm a very practical person, let me suggest something very practical: *Slowly recite biblical wisdom to beat back your mental craziness.*

Here's what I mean.

Last week I had a frantic day, and in the afternoon I had to walk to my kids' school to pick them up. I was feeling frazzled. So I left three minutes earlier... but walked slower.

As I walked, I repeated a verse of the Bible to myself. "He must increase, but I must decrease." It's John the Baptist talking about Jesus in John 3:30 (ESV).

I said one word for every four steps. "He... must... increase... but... I... must... decrease..."

It totally turned my brain space around. It slowed me down, even as I worked my way through a crazy day. The reason it worked is because (a) it's biblical, (b) it reminded me to prioritize Jesus over my own selfish pursuits, and (c) it physically calmed me down.

Why don't you give it a try? Maybe on a walk. Or maybe while driving. Maybe folding laundry, or maybe just lying on the couch.

"He... must... increase... but... I... must... decrease..."

Slowly recite biblical wisdom to beat back your mental craziness.

SATURDAY - THE NEXT COURAGEOUS STEP

I've been talking to a lot of people about prayer lately. Maybe that's because after a Sunday message I delivered about miracles, I encouraged people to "pray boldy."

So people have been telling me how it's going. And one of the things they've found is that God answers prayers—but not always in ways they expect... and not always in ways they understand.

There's a story about a woman who locked her keys in her car in a bad neighbourhood. So she prayed, "God, send me somebody to help me."

A few minutes later a rough-looking guy approached. She decided to tell him about the situation and asked if he could break into her car to get the keys out. He said he could. And in a few seconds it was open.

"You're a very nice man," she said. "I'm not a nice man," he replied. "I just got out of prison today. I served two years for auto theft."

She hugged him again, smiled big, looked up to the heavens and shouted, "Thank you, God, for sending me a professional!"[78]

Maybe you're praying for healing. But what if God was healing your life... just in a way you didn't expect? Maybe you're praying for wisdom. But what if God was making you wise... just in a way you didn't expect? Maybe you're praying for someone you love. But what if God was working in their life... just in a way you didn't expect?

For some reason, God works in and through people and situations we don't expect. Maybe it's his way of making sure we keep our eyes open and hearts humble.

There are hard things. Life can be dark. But remember that our vision is always limited. There is more than what meets the eye. And God is bigger than you and me.

As we read in Job 37:5: "God's voice thunders in marvellous ways; he does great things beyond our understanding."

So keep your eyes open and heart humble. And keep praying boldly.

When you start to understand that God's goodness extends beyond your understanding, you are taking the next courageous step along the road we call Trust.

SUNDAY...

MONDAY - RETALIATE

Recently I heard that approximately 215 million Christians experience significant persecution because of their faith. For many, this includes the risk of torture or death.

Because of this I sometimes get asked, "Do you think overt persecution is coming to Canada?"

I honestly think certain kinds of persecution are starting. That may sound crazy to some of you, but just hear me out.

It's not as harsh as in other parts of the world, but people and organizations are going to face increased marginalization and hostility because of their faith. Medical professionals will be asked to do more and more things they can't agree to. So will Christian schools, churches, and other organizations.

Persecution may not be physical or obvious—but people and groups will get sued, and therefore have to defend themselves in courts with money they don't have. I'm also guessing that more of us will be criticized, made fun of, or excluded from job opportunities and friendships because we believe in Jesus and scriptural teachings.

So what do you do?

First, you need to get used to being different. Second, you need to thank

God for the privilege of bearing Jesus' name. Third, you need to humbly yet confidently trust in God's wisdom and power along with other Christians all over the world.

And last, you need to do this: *Retaliate with grace.*

In sports, when someone hits or trips you, you're not supposed to retaliate. Why? Because nine times out of ten the retaliation is what the referee sees!

The same is true with life and faith. When you respond in kind to those who treat you poorly it may feel good, but it doesn't help them, it doesn't help the team, and it doesn't jive with Jesus' teachings. As the apostle Peter says, "those who suffer according to God's will should commit themselves to their faithful Creator and continue to do good." (1 Peter 4:19)

Continue. To. Do. Good.

Today I want to encourage you, especially when it's hard. And even when you deal with hostility or marginalization...

Retaliate with grace.

TUESDAY - MAKE SURE THEY KNOW

In 1894 the United States mint in San Francisco made twenty-four coins. That's not many.

The superintendent, John Dagget, knew how valuable they would be some day. So he gave three of the dimes to his daughter, Hallie. "Hold on to these, my dear," he said, "and they'll be worth much more than ten cents someday."

Hallie skipped home. But on the way she stopped in for some ice cream— and used one of the dimes her father had just given her.

In 1981 one of the 1894 coins surfaced. It sold for $34,100! Little Hallie didn't realize the value of what she had been given.[79]

Do you?

The people in your life are sacred gifts from God. They might not seem like much. After all, they get bad breath, speeding tickets, and mediocre work evaluations just like everybody else. Like a dime in a pile of dimes, nothing appears to make them stand out.

But they have a value beyond anything you can ever imagine. James 1:17 says that "Every good and perfect gift is from above..." The people around you are gifts from God. And they enrich your life beyond anything you can ever imagine.

So today, it's simple. Don't squander the amazing gifts God has placed in your life.

Make sure someone who matters to God knows how much they matter to you.

WEDNESDAY - WAIT, WAIT, WAIT... BOOM!

The Chinese Bamboo Tree takes a long time to grow above the soil. You need to water it and ensure it gets enough sun... for *four* years.

It's not until the fifth year that you actually see anything. But when you do, something awesome happens:

It grows eighty feet in just six weeks!

To the casual observer nothing was happening for those first four years. But not so. It was doing everything it needed to do, including developing roots that sank deep into the earth to support the massive tree that was soon to come.

You probably want something awesome for your life, or for someone you care about, or for the world at large. So do I.

You pray and wait and wait and pray. But in the process you can get discouraged because you don't see progress.

Well I'm here to tell you to keep your chin up. Don't let discouragement put a stranglehold on your hope. As Paul writes in Romans 8:25: "...if we have hope for what we do not yet have, we wait for it patiently."

Think of the Chinese Bamboo Tree. Even though you couln't see progress for four whole years, critical things were still happening. Roots were sinking deep into the earth, soil was giving nourishment, and the sun was doing its thang.

And then... Boom!

The same thing happens with you. Prayer deepens the root structure of your soul. The Bible and other people nourish and guide you. And daily acts of faith ready you for eternal upward glory.

Don't let a lack of evidence shake your confidence.

Don't give up hope.

Since God sees things through, so can you.

THURSDAY - SMALL AWESOME GOALS

If I asked you about some of the big goals in your life, what would you say? Something about making a difference... or nurturing a certain kind of family... or sharing God's love in a powerful way... or a professional achievement?

A lot of us have goals. But we don't always achieve them.

One of the reasons we fail is because we're not sure how to get from here to there. It's too big a leap. So we stumble, and bumble, and get frustrated.

That's why it can help to make *small awesome goals*.

Small awesome goals are stepping stones in the direction of something great. Even if they don't get you from here to there in one day, they set you on the right trajectory and start to quench those incessant feelings of frustration.

Do you want to be a prayer warrior? Decide to pray three times a day. Set an alarm if you have to.

Do you want to have a strong marriage? Decide to do three things daily to bless your spouse. Maybe it's picking up junk around the house or doing the dishes or being the taxi on Saturday morning so they can get a bit more rest.

Do you want to start that new business venture that you keep putting off? Choose three evenings in the next four weeks to do some research and answer some ground-level business questions.

Every gold medal moment, every joyous faithful home, every "overnight" success story, is the result of small awesome goals that are set and met day by day by day.

I'm reminded of Proverbs 21:5 (ESV): "The plans of the diligent lead surely to abundance…"

If you're frustrated because you're not sure how to get from here to there, make some small awesome goals and start now.

"Rome wasn't built in a day." And neither were you. And neither are your dreams.

You don't need to arrive before the sun goes down, but you do need to lay some bricks.

FRIDAY - WHAT WE VALUE MOST DEEPLY

For a long time I kind of skipped over those parts in the Bible about "idolatry." Those old stories about misguided people bowing down to golden calves or statues just seemed so irrelevant.

'These days,' I thought, 'not many of us are bowing down to that stuff anymore.'

Or are we?

An idol can be anything you love more than God. Think about that for a moment.

Your wardrobe can be an idol.

Your body can be an idol.

Your career can be an idol.

Your bank account can be an idol.

Your "likes" can be an idol.

Your reputation can be an idol.

Your friends can be an idol.

Your grades can be an idol.

Your home can be an idol.

Your family can be an idol.

We may not bow down visibly, but invisibly?

Maybe it's tempting to disproportionately devote ourselves to these things because we think our lives will somehow be better. But loving things or people more than God actually brings us harm. It skews how life is supposed to be. It distorts all it *can* be.

The reason God keeps warning our wayward selves about idolatry is because he wants the best for us. And a Father grieves when his sons and daughters keep inflicting themselves with pain.

Think of idolatry like addiction—to wardrobes or bodies or careers or bank accounts or "likes" or reputations or friends or grades or homes or families. None of these things are bad. In fact, they can be very good! But just not when they start to pull your eyes away from God.

With that in mind, 1 Corinthians 10:14 is wildly current: "flee from idolatry"!

Today, enjoy the good things in life. And take a moment to honestly ask yourself, "Is God the source of my hope, or is it something else?

SATURDAY - CONSISTENT, NOT CASUAL

"Dear God, please make me stronger." I think that's probably the number one prayer for a lot of people. I've certainly said it. Maybe you have too.

Stronger to do what we need to do.

Or to deal with health problems.

Or stress at work.

Or a family issue.

Or challenging friends.

Or to follow Jesus.

Or to be the right kind of parent.

Or to choose the direction to take or decision to make.

Being stronger would be awesome. So how do you do it?

You get consistent.

Too often we're reactive instead of being proactive about our spiritual depth. We reach out to God, pray, read the Bible, and go to church when we feel desperate or when things aren't going our way. I'm not saying that's wrong. But if we're *only* reactive—and not proactive—we're severely limiting our potential for strength.

Strong people are consistent—not casual—about their spiritual depth.

I like the word "depth" because it makes you think of roots. When you make a regular effort to worship, pray, read the Bible, and get together with other Christians, your root structure grows deeper and deeper. The result is a stronger you, standing above the ground, and withstanding the winds that blow.

When Paul says to "be strong in the Lord and in his mighty power" (Ephesians 6:10) and tells the Ephesians to put on the armour of God, he's not casting a metaphor about licking lollipops and going for a stroll. He's talking about battle. Every day.

Do you want to be stronger? Me too. It's a battle, folks. So treat it like one.

Strong people are consistent—not casual—about their spiritual depth.

SUNDAY...

MONDAY - ONE VERSE MEDICINE

When I say "medicine" you probably think about being sick or going to the doctor.

But it can also be a way to think about the power of God in our lives.

In the fourth century, a church father named Ambrose of Milan composed a prayer that pulled from this same idea: "You are medicine for me when I am sick..."

Then in the fifth century, the great thinker Augustine compared the church to a hospital that was full of wounded people recovering under the care of the Good Physician and his medicine.

When you take medicine orally, it goes into your stomach and into your digestive system. Soon enough, it has an effect on your body—and sometimes, on your mind.

That's how you should think about what happens when you memorize one Bible verse and repeat it to yourself. It's medicine—something from the Good Physician, internally digested, and radiating outward through your veins, mind, words and actions.

Medicine does something for you that you can't do for yourself. This week, take one verse, memorize it, and keep repeating it. When you do that, something from the Good Physician—his medicinal power—will work in you and through you.

Psalm 27:1 is a great one: "The LORD is my light and my salvation—whom shall I fear?" Another is Joshua 1:9: "Be strong and courageous. Do not be afraid; do not be discouraged, for the Lord your God will be with you wherever you go." Or Philippians 4:13: "I can do all things through him who gives me strength."

Memorize one verse from the Bible and keep repeating it to yourself. It's your daily dose of divine medicine.

It will do something powerful for you that you can't do for yourself. Trust the Good Physician. He knows what he's doing.

TUESDAY - FAILURE BELIEVES IN YOU

This is going to sound weird, but failure believes in you. Let me explain.

We often think of failure as the outcome of something we've done (or haven't done). For example, if we don't get the answers right, we fail the test. Or if we never keep our promises, we fail our family. I get that line of thinking.

But failure can start to develop its own personality in your brain. And the more you listen to what it has told you about your past, the more you start to believe what it tells you about your future. It's like a loud whisper you can't turn off, and it believes it can weigh you down by taking up real estate in your ear. Pretty soon you start to think of failure not as something that has happened in your past, but as someone you are.

But if you belong to God (and you do), and if you trust and follow Jesus (and I hope you do), the whispering reverberations of failure shouldn't be the governing voice in your mind. The reason you are (and will be) victorious in this life is because of what *Jesus* has done for you—not because of what *you* have (or haven't) done for you.

In 2016 I enjoyed watching the Rio Olympics. The sprints were probably my favourite. Do you think the judges cared about what the runners had done in previous races? Nope. It was all about the race they were presently in. As the writer of the book of Hebrews says, "let us run with endurance the race that is set before us" (Hebrews 12:1)—not the race that is *behind* us.

In life, and in Christian faith, each day is new, and the winds of the Holy Spirit are at your back—and in your heart.

Today, check your state of mind. Failure believes in you. You don't have to reciprocate.

WEDNESDAY - LET THE MUSIC CARRY YOU

"Matthew, I just feel so spiritually dry."

Every once in a while someone says some version of this statement to me. What they mean is that they don't "feel" close to God, or that they are missing something and need some divine jumper cables hooked up to their heart.

They want and need some help to kick-start their spiritual selves.

Lately I've been thinking about something that helps me, and which I know has helped others too. So let me share it with you.

Let the music carry you.

Think of a piece of godly music and sing it. For me, I like to use this from the Taize community:

> *Jesus, remember me when you come into your kingdom.*
> *Jesus, remember me when you come into your kingdom...*[80]

When your battery is dead, you need a shock from an outside source. Melody and lyrics can be that shock in the best possible way.

Psalm 104:33 (ESV) says, "I will sing to the Lord as long as I live..." Why not put it into action?

Do you like the chorus to "How Great Thou Art"? What about the modern praise anthem "In Christ Alone" or "10,000 Reasons"? What about "Good, Good Father," "Just as I Am," or "Be Thou My Vision"?

When you're feeling a bit depleted, let the music carry you.

Turn on your speakers or put in your earbuds. When you do, spiritual dryness can quickly turn into a downpour from heaven.

THURSDAY - HONEST ABOUT NEEDING HELP

Honesty is a virtue. I'm not sure anyone would argue with that. It's good to be honest about how we deal with our neighbours and about answering people's questions.

But we're not always honest about needing help.

Maybe that's because we think "being strong" is the same as being independent. 'If I'm honest about needing help,' we think, 'maybe people will think I'm weak.'

Well, guess what. Strength isn't about pretending to have it all together, knowing all the answers, and lying about how perfect your life is.

That's just stubborn foolishness.

In fact, it's the strong ones who are honest about needing help. And it's also the strong ones who are serious about getting that help.

Are you in a spiritual dry spell? Do you need to unburden your soul? Do you need to talk to a Christian counselor? Are you in over your head with something? Are you stressed beyond what you've experienced before?

It's okay to ask for help. In fact, it can be a sign of strength (not weakness).

I think that's what Paul is getting at when he says this in 2 Corinthians 12:10: "For when I am weak, then I am strong." Being honest about our weaknesses compels us to call on God with greater rigor, and opens us up to receiving his wisdom and strength from other godly people in our lives.

Strong people are honest about needing help and serious about getting help.

If you need help with something, that's okay. Be honest, be strong, and reach out.

FRIDAY - WHEN YOU'VE GOT SOMETHING TO LOSE

When I think of the word "courage" it makes me think of taking a stand on a difficult issue, or doing the right thing when it's hard, or facing an illness or accusation with steely resolve.

Courage is also word people invoke when preparing for battle.

But I'd like to throw a different nuance into the mix:

Courage is admitting you're wrong, especially when you've got something to lose.

It's hard to admit when you're wrong. In fact, I think that's why a lot of people have so many bitter arguments. It's not because they want to uncover the truth—it's because they want to "win"! And they certainly don't want to admit they're wrong!

So the key question for you and me is this: Are you willing to lose an argument—or are you willing to let go of what you thought you knew—to put the truth first?

Psalm 145:18 says that "The Lord is near to all who call on him, to all who call on him in truth."

The truth, love and presence of God trumps the presence of foes.

The truth, love and presence of God trumps the presence of fear.

The truth, love and presence of God trumps—or should trump—our egotistical craving to be right one hundred percent of the time.

I'm not sure what you're dealing with today. But when and if you're wrong, just admit it. A life following Jesus isn't designed to glorify your own reputation or win/loss record in the argument department. It's to glorify God. He's the audience who matters most. And I'm pretty sure he cares more about the integrity of your heart than your ability to stubbornly defend an untruth.

Courage is admitting you're wrong, especially when you've got something to lose.

SATURDAY - MORE THAN YOU TAKE

Several years ago Kevin Myers was meeting with his mentor, leadership guru John C. Maxwell. In response to a relationship problem, Myers shared some simple-but-solid advice:

"Always give more than you take."[81]

If something sounds familiar it's probably because Jesus' words from Acts 20:35 are ringing in your ears: "It is more blessed to give than to receive."

So carry that thought into your relationships with your friends. Carry it into your relationship with your spouse or partner. Carry it into your relationship with your kids. Carry it into your relationship with your parents. Carry it into your relationships with people at work or at church or at the gym.

I know it's good to receive sometimes too. And if you *only* give (and never receive) you'll end up spent and passed out on the sidewalk of emotional and physical fatigue. #bummer

But as a general rule, give more than you take. And the footprint of your life will be a legacy of greater joy.

Not only will you be *giving* joy to other people, but you'll be *getting* it too.

SUNDAY...

MONDAY - WHEN YOU DISAGREE

It's easy to have a good time when everyone agrees about everything. You laugh at the same jokes and see eye to eye about what's right (or wrong) with the world.

In fact, when we grow up, it's often the people who agree with us most who become our friends.

But times goes on. And you discover that life is more complicated than you once thought it was. With each passing year, you start to realize that more and more people think differently than you. Maybe not about everything, but certainly about some things.

This makes some people frustrated and drives them to distance themselves from anyone who thinks differently.

But it can make other people more humble, driving them to learn more, and to love more.

Here's what I've come to find. That disagreement and friendship don't have to be allergic to one another. In fact, as the years go on, and as you become wiser, expecting disagreement—and even welcoming disagreement—can actually enrich friendships to a new level of respect and intimacy.

As David Kinnaman and Gabe Lyons say, "By making room for disagreement, you make space for friendship."[82]

It's okay to disagree with someone. It'll probably happen to you today! But when you disagree in a way that is humble, respectful and loving, friendships can go from cheap to deep.

First Peter 2:17 (ESV) gives us some motivation: "Honor everyone." (Even when you disagree.)

Show humility, respect and love. And go from cheap to deep.

"By making room for disagreement, you make space for friendship."

TUESDAY - BRAINWASHING

Mark Clark was getting a lot of criticism from people.

They said that because he consistently read his kids the Bible and explained who Jesus was (and is), and because he explained God's hope for the world, that he was "brainwashing" them.

If you're a person of faith, have you ever been criticized like that?

I love how Mark replied. He said that *he* wasn't the one doing the brainwashing. *Our culture was doing that!*

TV shows are doing it! he replied. Some music is doing it! A hundred other things are doing it![83]

(By now I've hopefully got you thinking. Your blood might even be starting to boil.)

So what do you do?

1. Be suspicious and proactive about the one thousand cultural messages—about things like values, power, sex and the meaning of life—that are bombarding you and your family every single day.

2. Be confident about what the Bible teaches.

Recently I was reading Philippians 2:15 where Paul encourages his readers to be "blameless and pure" as children of God in the midst of a "warped and crooked generation." They are to shine "like stars in the sky."

That wisdom still stands.

So shine. And don't be bullied into snuffing out your candle.

If you are humbly, lovingly and consistently learning and teaching God's word... you're not the one who's doing the brainwashing.

WEDNESDAY - IF IT'S SO OBVIOUS, WHY DON'T WE DO IT?

If you run out of gas your car will stop working. It's so obvious, right?

Well, if it's so obvious, why does it happen to so many people?

It's because we don't always pay attention to what we're supposed to pay attention to, even when it's important.

With that in mind, I'm hoping we can re-frame our thinking about our physical health. Here goes.

In some cultures, people think that since you can't see your soul, prayer or God, that they must be more "spiritual" than things you *can* see. It follows that since you can see your body, physical health, and day-to-day activities, then they must be somehow *less* spiritual.

I get where that comes from. But when God created humans he made them in his image and called everything he had made "very good." Then in 1 Corinthians 6:19 Paul says that "your body is a temple of the Holy Spirit, who is in you, whom you have received from God..."

If you're a follower of Jesus, you—the invisible parts of you *and* the visible flesh-and-blood parts of you—are a temple of the Holy Spirit. You're not a run-down dilapidated shed of the Holy Spirit. You're a *temple* of the Holy Spirit!

In light of this, *physical health is a spiritual matter.*

I think you need to take care of yourself because God is working in and through you and wants you to be well.

I think he wants you to be as well as possible to help him renovate the world.

Do you need to be Arnold Schwarzenegger? Nope. But you do need to pay attention to these three things:

1. Sleep. 2. Diet. 3. Exercise.

I know, I know. It's so obvious, right? But just like putting gas in your car, it's easy to forget about what we're supposed to pay attention to, even when it's important.

Sleep. Diet. Exercise.

Physical health is a spiritual matter.

THURSDAY - EXHAUSTED, BURDENED, HALF-DEAD BODIES

Yesterday I said that physical health is a spiritual matter.

Based on the feedback I got when I first published this devotional, it was a message a lot of us needed to hear. In today's fast-paced world, it's just so easy to put our physical well-being on the back-burner.

But if you are a follower of Jesus, you are a temple of the Holy Spirit. You're not a run-down dilapidated shed of the Holy Spirit. You're a *temple* of the Holy Spirit!

Because of that, I think you need to take care of yourself. God is working in and through you and wants you to help him renovate the world.

That message was yesterday. You were revved up! You were pumped! You thought about the big three (sleep, diet and exercise), made a mental note of which one you needed to attack, and set about your day!

Then today came along.

And with it... *excuses.*

But friends, know this: Excuses are a way of excusing yourself from taking action on the things that matter most.

The apostle Paul knew how easy it is to forget that our bodies are not our own. They belong the One who made them. That's why in 1 Corinthians 6:20 he said to "honor God with your bodies."

Don't let yesterday's motivation drown in today's excuses. You know what you need to do. And if you still need some get-up-and-go, soak in this dose of reality from best-selling author Geneen Roth: "Passion, strength, joy cannot take root in exhausted, burdened, half-dead bodies."[84]

So what do you need to do? Be a bit smarter about your diet? Go to bed a bit earlier? Go for a jog?

These aren't just physical issues, they're spiritual ones.

Excuses are a way of excusing yourself from taking action on the things that matter most.

So honour God with your body.

FRIDAY - WOOLLY SOCKS FOR A PROSTITUTE

One of the things I'm trying to improve in my own life is listening to God. I'm pretty good at talking to him. But listening? Not so much.

When I say 'listening' I'm not just talking about hearing an audible voice. I'm talking about those curious inner promptings that you don't quite understand at the moment, but which could very well be God directing you to act or think in a certain way for his glory.

A great example of this comes from a woman who worked at the Dream Center in Birmingham, Alabama. The Dream Center has a ministry to prostitutes.

One morning she was headed to work and had an inner "nudge" to get some woolly socks. Yup, woolly socks. She could have ignored it, but she didn't. So she went back in to her house and got them. And it's a good thing she did.

When she got to the Dream Center she discovered a prostitute passed out on the front steps. She called 911 and held the unconscious woman in her arms while she waited. As the woman regained consciousness she asked, "If I could get you anything, what would it be?"

The trembling prostitute answered, "A pair of woolly socks."

No word of a lie!

When she saw the socks she smiled and added, "They even match my outfit."[85]

Wow!

I firmly believe that if you consistently worship God; that if you consistently seek his will before your own; that if you consistently pray and read the Bible; that if you consistently look for ways to bring heaven to earth, that God will start communicating with you to help you do just that.

I like what it says in Psalm 37:4: "Delight yourself in the Lord, and he will give you the desires of your heart." Because the more you delight in him, the more your desires come into line with his own.

Pay attention. Listen. And respond.

If you need to shift your prayer life in a new direction, perhaps you should try doing a little less talking, and a little more listening.

SATURDAY - THE VINE OF YOUR SOUL

You often hear people talk about the "fruit of the Spirit."

It's a reference to what the apostle Paul says in Galatians 5:22-23 (ESV), that "the fruit of the Spirit is love, joy, peace, patience, kindness, goodness, faithfulness, gentleness, self-control."

The idea is that if you're a follower of Jesus and have the Holy Spirit living within you, these characteristics will start to happen in and through your life.

I think the biggest misunderstanding about the fruit of the Spirit is that you may have one or some of them, but not all of them. But that's not totally accurate.

It's "fruit" singular, not "fruits."

So if the Holy Spirit is working in and through your life, *all* of these characteristics will be growing in you. You may be more naturally inclined to some, and some may take longer to develop than others, but they will all be maturing in the vine of your soul.

I don't say this to make you feel bad. Lord knows, none of us are perfect, including me! I've had days when self-control and patience seem like birds who've flown into the window and are flailing around on the lawn, rendered temporarily useless. (Sorry for the visual.)

I say it because growing in your relationship with Jesus is a partnership. He's working at making you more like himself.

For your part, are you open to the change he's working within you? Or are you closed to some of these nine characteristics simply because you don't think they apply?

Look at this list: Love. Joy. Peace. Patience. Kindness. Goodness. Faithfulness. Gentleness. Self-control.

That's a description of the future you.

Today, watch for that one opportunity to grow and grab on. As a follower of Christ, God is maturing the vine of your soul.

SUNDAY...

MONDAY - DON'T BE AFRAID OF QUESTIONS

Amy Orr-Ewing is a director at Ravi Zacharias Ministries.

When she was applying to Oxford University she had to face a special interviewing committee. They saw that she was a Christian and this provoked a pointed line of questioning.

One of the interviewers asked, 'What are you going to do when you discover that your faith is based on a whole bunch of faulty assumptions?' Basically, the interviewer was saying, 'When you come to this fancy school, and the rigors of modern intellectual criticism come baring down on you and your naïve beliefs, are you going to fall apart?'

Orr-Ewing is super-smart and had heard these kinds of criticism before—criticisms, I should add, that are themselves naïve and misguided. Here's what she said:

"I believe that if something is true it will stand up to rigorous criticism."

The reason I tell you all this is because maybe you have questions about your faith. Maybe you've been challenged on something, or someone has told you that your beliefs are naïve or built on a faulty foundation.

But you don't need to be afraid of questions. In Psalm 119:160 we read, "All your words are true; all your righteous laws are eternal."

As Orr-Ewing stated to her Oxford interviewer, if something is true it will stand up to rigorous criticism.

Just as Christianity has... for thousands of years.

I've certainly found this to be true in my own faith. The more I've questioned, the more I've explored, and the more I've researched, my faith has become bigger, not smaller.

If you have questions, that's okay. Look faithfully for answers.

Your questions may be stepping stones to a faith that looks more like a castle and less like a house on sinking sand.

TUESDAY - WHAT MATURE PEOPLE DO

One of the unique things about being human is that we make tonnes of decisions every single day. Other creatures need to make decisions too, but I doubt they're aware of it as much as we are!

Some decisions are simple like: Do I wear jeans or shorts?

Others are hard, like: 'Do I sell my house?' or 'Should I end this relationship?'

And a lot are in-between: 'Do I tell my boss?' 'Should I let so-and-so know that I like them?' and 'Should I swipe my credit card one more time?'

The biblical writers are often talking about being "mature." Paul certainly does when he says he wants to "present everyone fully mature in Christ" (Colossians 1:28).

And I can't help but think there's a direct relationship between being mature and making wise decisions.

But life gets fast and confusing. So it's helpful to have a straightforward tool to help you navigate the conundrums that bombard your brain on a daily basis.

So that's what I'd like to share with you courtesy of John Ortberg. He says that when you're facing a decision and considering an option, ask yourself this: "Will this move me closer to God or further away?"

That's it.

The reason I like this is because it reminds us that we're supposed to make decisions that honour God. Maturity is like making the hockey team or getting an A in chemistry. It doesn't just happen. It's usually the result of deliberate hard work and honing your skills.

So as you approach today's tough decisions, ask yourself this: Will this move me closer to God or further away?

WEDNESDAY - KEEPING THE HAIRY GORILLA OUT

Several people pointed out to me recently how much bad news and trauma are coming at them every single day.

It seems that every time you turn on the radio, scroll social media, or watch the news, you hear about some catastrophe, murder, or story of society-gone-wrong.

The question people ask me is this: "Do you think there's more bad stuff happening these days, or do we just hear about it more than we used to because of instant reporting and the internet?"

Today's devotional isn't about answering that question. But I do want to highlight how the bad news and trauma in the world can be, in a weird way, like a car crash on the side of the highway. It's hard to look away.

And then we make it worse by watching shows and movies or consuming media and music that seem to revel in death and darkness.

Hopefully you don't think I'm hyper-sensitive. I'm not. I get my fair share of news, art, and culture as much as the next guy.

But I've come to learn that what we watch, read and listen to is a diet. Just how the food you put into your body impacts your well-being, the radio, books, social media, and news you consume impact your well-being in an even bigger way.

My point is this:

Watch your diet... your *invisible* diet.

If you don't want violent nightmares, don't watch shows that glorify killing.

If you don't want to keep beating yourself up, don't spend so much time on Instagram or Facebook comparing yourself to other people.

If you don't want a hairy gorilla in your house, don't open the door!

Proverbs 26:11 comes to mind: "As a dog returns to its vomit, so fools repeat their folly."

If you struggle with dark and heavy feelings, and also have a news, social media and radio diet of junk, don't keep going back for more.

Watch your diet.

A healthier you is waiting to say thanks, and to lead you to a more joy-filled life.

THURSDAY - READ TO UNDERSTAND (NOT JUST TO FINISH)

More. More. More.

That's a message you probably get on a daily basis. You need to have, get and be more! You should be doing more. More, more, more!

Granted, more can be a helpful solution—sometimes. More patience is good. And so is more kindness, sleep and cheesecake.

But what if the answer to greater wisdom sometimes had to do with...

Less.

If so, we'd probably all breathe a sigh of relief.

Today I'd like to suggest one super-practical spiritual habit that involves doing *less*.

You know that reading your Bible is a good thing. After all, it's the primary place where we learn about and encounter God's will.

But it's a big book. There's like a zillion pages. So we rush through trying to digest it all because more is better, right?

Maybe not.

When you rush through the Bible, you might get to the end, but you miss a lot. So instead, if you're rushing through and just not getting it, I think you should read less.

I'm not suggesting you don't read it every day; I think you should. But when you do read it, read a smaller chunk.

Read to understand (not just to finish).

Maybe even read the same paragraph three or four times. When Paul writes to the Colossians in 3:16 he says to "Let the message of Christ dwell among you richly..." He doesn't say to let the message of Christ whip in one ear and out the other or dance on the surface of your eyeballs for .02 milliseconds.

The word is *dwell*. Let the message of Christ *dwell* among you richly.

Sometimes more isn't better. It's just more.

When it comes to your Bible, and when you're rushing through and just not getting it...

Read less, better.

FRIDAY - IF YOUR DESIRES BE ENDLESS...

I've noticed something. Maybe you have too.

It seems that the more comforts people have, and the more money people have, and the more trinkets, toys and gadgets people have...

The more they want.

Maybe it has to do with the fact that when you focus on how much you have, you also focus on how much you don't have!

In the 1600's Thomas Fuller said that "If your desires be endless, your cares and fears will be too."[86] What I think he meant was that if you keep wanting more and more, you'll have more anxieties and fears in your life, perhaps because it's all an attempt to gain more and more control—something which, by the way, you can never achieve.

The bottom line is that the more content you are the more at peace you are. Maybe not one hundred percent of the time, but certainly a lot of the time!

So if you struggle to be content, and if you also struggle with the worry and fear that goes along with trying to give yourself a kind of security you can never actually achieve, you may want to try this.

Every time you wish for something you don't have, name one thing you're thankful you do. Simple, right?

So let's say you see your friend's new iPhone and get down about your yesterday's special from 2010. Or maybe you see someone else's picture-perfect graduation photos or super-meaningful job. What do you do?

You consciously name something you're thankful you *do* have. Maybe it happens when you're in the car, gym or trying to fall asleep. Wherever you are, name it.

Hebrews 13:5 (NLT) says, "Don't love money; be satisfied with what you have. For God has said, 'I will never fail you. I will never abandon you.'"

Wanting money and stuff is countered by the reminder that God will never fail or abandon you.

Every time you wish for something you don't have, name one thing you're thankful you do.

SATURDAY - WARRIORS NEVER GIVE UP

Over ten years ago I heard a sermon by my friend Brad Shoemaker. It has always stuck with me.

It was about David and Goliath. Most of us remember the highlights of the story.

Like Goliath mocking the Israelites. Like young David rising to the challenge. Like Goliath's fall.

But Brad pointed out a frequently forgotten detail. We find it just before the battle in 1 Samuel 17:40 (NLT): David "picked up five smooth stones from a stream and put them into his shepherd's bag. Then, armed only with his shepherd's staff and sling, he started across the valley to fight the Philistine."

Why *five* stones?

If David was so sure of himself, if he was so confident in God's victory, why didn't he take *one* stone for his sling instead of five?

I think David took five stones because of this: Even though he was confident God would help him win the battle, he knew it might take him more than one try.

Quite often in life, victory doesn't come fast or easy. Sometimes it seems you take two steps forward just to stumble back three. So whatever you're dealing with...

Never. Give. Up.

Getting knocked down a few times doesn't mean you've been defeated. Everyone gets knocked down. But it's the warriors who get back up. It's the warriors who re-load. It's the warriors who don't care about the dirt on their face because they can smell the approach of victory.

Friends, I'm not sure what you're dealing with in your life right now. But you're probably dealing with something. Whatever it is, remember that warriors never give up.

Failure doesn't mean defeat. Failure means you re-load for the glory of God.

SUNDAY...

MONDAY - MISSING OUT ON WHAT GOD WANTS TO DO

Reggie Joiner is passionate about helping young people develop their faith. Recently on a podcast I heard him tell a story about two girls in the fifth grade. They were in a store that sells beads to make necklaces.[87]

One girl started to take some and put them in her bag. As she did so she said to her friend, "Hey, you take some too—no one is watching."

The friend, who was surprised and didn't want anything to do with it, wasn't sure how to react. All she could remember was something she was taught at church a week or two earlier: "If you don't do the wise thing, you'll miss out on what God wants to do." So she just repeated it: "No. If I don't do the wise thing, I'll miss out on what God wants to do." This startled the friend because she hadn't heard that before. So she took the beads out of her bag.

Then they went up to the counter and just so happened to compliment the woman at the cashier on how pretty her beads were. (These were the very same style of beads they had almost shoplifted.) She was so touched by the compliment that she said, "Oh, I'm glad you like them. Here, let me give you some."

We often think that wisdom is about us knowing what's best. Yet none of us sees the whole picture. But when we act in a way that honours God—no matter what it is—we open ourselves up to a greater wisdom; we open ourselves up to the amazing things God wants to do in our lives.

In Ephesians 3:20 (NLT) Paul writes: "Now all glory to God, who is able, through his mighty power at work within us, to accomplish infinitely more than we might ask or think."

"Infinitely more than we might ask or think." Not "infinitely less" because you and I are so clever by ourselves. But infinitely more.

Wise people trust that God's way is best. Even when they can't see what's next.

What choices are you facing this week?

If you don't do the wise thing, you'll miss out on what God wants to do.

TUESDAY - A LIFE WITHOUT RISK

When I look back on my forty one years of life, I notice something. It's that risk can make you stretch and grow as a person. When we take a leap of faith or try something new, good things often happen.

Granted, sometimes making the safe choice makes sense—like saving up money for retirement or schooling, or getting the expensive bike helmets for the kids. But that's not really what I'm talking about here.

And I'm not talking about being foolish.

What I am talking about is being faithful. *Really* faithful. About putting big trust in God, living the abundant life Jesus offers you, and not always making the safe choice because it just makes you feel warm and cozy inside.

Recently I came across Ecclesiastes 11:4 which says: "Whoever watches the wind will not plant; whoever looks at the clouds will not reap." In other words, if you're always waiting for the perfect conditions, or if you're overly cautious, you'll miss out on the fullness of life.

Here's an anonymous poem someone sent me in an email. It says it well:

> *To laugh is to risk appearing the fool.*
> *To weep is to risk appearing sentimental.*
> *To reach out for another is to risk involvement.*
> *To expose feelings is to risk exposing our true self.*
> *To place your ideas, your dreams, before the crowd is to risk loss.*
> *To love is to risk not being loved in return.*
> *To live is to risk dying.*
> *To hope is to risk despair.*
> *To try at all is to risk failure.*
> *But risk we must, because the greatest hazard in life is to risk nothing.*
> *The man, the woman, who risk nothing does nothing, has nothing...*

Today is the first page in the next chapter of your life. Put big trust in God and live the abundant life Jesus offers you.

A life without risk is a live unlived.

WEDNESDAY - STARVE THE BEAST

Greed, laziness and vanity.

These are behaviours we often tolerate. Maybe we justify them so we don't have to change. Or maybe we just don't know *how* to change.

That's why it can be helpful to starve them!

Greed, laziness and vanity are like the proverbial monster under the bed from children's books. The more you feed and indulge them, the bigger and hungrier they get!

You can't solve greed, laziness or vanity by being more greedy, lazy or vain. You just make them bigger and scarier in your life.

So that's where the starving comes in.

For example, if you're prone to greed, you need to write a list of twenty-five things you're thankful for every day for a week. Seriously. If that's you, get a pen and paper. Or maybe you need to *not buy anything* outside of bare necessities for a month. In other words, starve the beast of greed.

If you're prone to laziness, you need to make a list of five ways to help or serve your neighbours in a practical way this week. And then do it. In other words, starve the beast of laziness.

And if you're prone to vanity, intentionally post a horrible picture of yourself on social media. In other words, starve the beast of vanity.

First John 1:8 (ESV) says, "If we say we have no sin, we deceive ourselves, and the truth is not in us."

What broken behaviour do you have within you that you pretend isn't there? Be honest. Then do three things:

1. Identify it.

2. Ask yourself: Do I *really* want to grow?

3. If the answer is yes, ask God to help you.

Don't feed the beast. Starve it.

THURSDAY - ONE HEARTBEAT AWAY

Revelation 20:12 gives us a look into the future: "Another book was opened, which is the book of life. The dead were judged according to what they had done as recorded in the books."

Friends, life isn't about getting comfortable; it's about getting ready. Because all of us are one heartbeat away from meeting our Maker.

FRIDAY - IF YOU'RE NOT GIVING UP SOMETHING

I think we can all agree on a few basic things. For example, that flooded basements and mosquitoes are annoying.

And I think we can also all agree that being a "giving person" is a good thing.

When we hear stories about helping others or self-sacrifice, something resonates. Physically or invisibly, we nod in agreement.

That said, I'm sure you probably think of yourself as a fairly giving person.

But are you?

I don't mean to be heavy-handed here. But it's an important question—at least if you claim to be a follower of Jesus.

Recently I was reading the story in the Bible about the widow's offering. A poor widow gives a financial offering at the temple in Jerusalem of only a few coins. Then some rich people give a tonne. She seems to have given a little and they seem to have given a lot.

But that's not how Jesus saw it.

Here's what he said: "Truly I tell you, this poor widow has put more into the treasury than all the others. They all gave out of their wealth; but she, out of her poverty, put in everything—all she had to live on." (Mark 12:43-44)

The reason I think her gift was so honoured was because she was truly giving up something. The rich people weren't actually giving because it didn't cost them anything.

I think we can apply this basic idea to our lives in general: *If you're not giving up something, you're not really giving.*

Maybe it's your time. Maybe it's your energy. Maybe it's your money. Maybe it's your comfort zone!

You see, when you give up something, you stretch yourself. You have to rely on God more, and therefore, he grows your faith in the process.

So today, as you think about the importance of helping and serving others, ponder the widow's offering, and remember this:

If you're not giving up something, you're not really giving.

SATURDAY - THIS MIGHT MAKE ME MR UNPOPULAR

Yesterday I talked about being a "giving person." Today I'm going to continue that theme. And I might become Mr. Unpopular in the process.

In fact, I wouldn't be surprised if some of you stopped reading this book after today!

But that's okay. It's healthy to push and challenge each other in a loving way from time to time.

It's a message for those who think they're too busy to serve and help others—and here it is: If you're too busy to serve, you're actually too lazy to set priorities.

(Crickets)

Now let me be clear. If you're in a crisis or struggling to keep your head above water in some other way, you need to focus on that. I get it.

But I think many of us aren't giving with our time, talent or energy simply because we're not willing to (a) identify godly priorities, and (b) rearrange our schedules to accommodate them.

Greg Stubbs is a small group leader for some youth at a church in Georgia. He has a big heart for young people. Not only is Greg a small group leader but he's in the military.

A few years ago he was deployed overseas. Thanks to modern technology Greg was still able to keep in touch with the young people in his group by email. A mom was so impressed with this that she told the pastor, Andy Stanley.

The next time Greg was home in Georgia, Andy asked him to join him at the front of the church as an example of setting priorities and serving others even when you have other important things going on.

Then he said that if anyone felt they were doing too much or were too busy to serve, that they should come to the front of the church and give their excuses to Greg.[88]

Bam!

My hope with today's devotional is to simply make you pause and ask yourself whether there's an area in your life where you're serving and blessing others. Maybe it's an official role through an organization. But it doesn't have to be. It could be informal, or with friends, at work, at school, or with your free time.

In Matthew 20:28 Jesus said that he "did not come to be served, but to serve..." I think the same is true for you and me. A part of the reason we are here on this earth isn't to *be* served, but *to* serve.

Are you somehow using your time, talent, treasure or energy to bless others? If not, you'll need to look at your schedule and make some changes.

SUNDAY...

MONDAY - LOW-DRAMA SPIRITUALITY

Miraculous healings! Huge crowds! Raising the dead!

It's so easy to think that spirituality only has to do with high drama— those moments, movements and miracles when people say, 'Wow!'

But more often than not, powerful spirituality has to do with *low* drama— the faithful person in prayer day in and day out; the tender, secure hands caring for children; the compassionate ear and shoulder to cry on; the lean-on-me friend; the pre-sunrise Bible reading; the attempts to bring integrity to the workplace.

Make no mistake about it: *Low drama spirituality has a highly dramatic impact*. Lives are helped. Prayers are asked and answered. And the souls of God's children are seasoned with goodness.

Psalm 112 speaks about someone who lives faithfully before God. As he trusts in God's goodness and provision it says that "His heart is steady" (Psalm 112:8). Wouldn't it be great to have a heart that is "steady," not only as you stand before God but as you interact with the people around you?

Low drama spirituality may not make the news. But that doesn't matter. We all have an audience of One.

Be steady. In a chaotic world, that's what many need most.

TUESDAY - IT'S NOT SUPPOSED TO INSULT YOUR INTELLIGENCE

Recently I was asked, "How do we know what to take from the Bible and what's not as important?"

It's a great question. Maybe you have it too. After all, the Bible can seem huge—and confusing.

Plus, it's easy to make the Bible "say" whatever you want it to say. I remember a friend jokingly telling me that the Bible condones suicide. "What on earth are you talking about?!" I said.

He explained: "Well, it tells us that Judas committed suicide, and it also tells us to 'Go and do likewise.' So there you have it!"

He was joking, of course. But he was also demonstrating what a lot of people do: Splice different parts of the Bible together out of context to make it say something it doesn't say. In his example, he was taking the account of Judas committing suicide in Matthew 27:5 and mushing it together with the saying to "go and do likewise" from the Good Samaritan in Luke 10:37, and coming up with something new (and inaccurate).

He made his point in a strange way. The Bible can be misused.

So how do you guard against it?

Sometimes on Sunday mornings I talk about this very thing. I like to highlight five principles from Heinrich Bullinger, a Swiss reformer from the 1500's, to guard against misusing the Bible.

They include better understanding the context of a passage, ensuring that your interpretation causes you to love God and your neighbours more (and not less), and ensuring that you are seeking God's will (and not just your own).

The good news is that the more you get into God's word, the more God's word gets into you. Or, put another way, the more you get into God's wisdom, the more God's wisdom gets into you.

The deeper you go into the Bible, the more it seeps into your soul. As that happens, its teachings become a more permanent part of who you are and how you live.

Yes, it takes some work. There's no magic pill that will make you perfectly understand everything in the Bible in one week. But things that are worthwhile take work.

As the very intelligent monk Thomas Merton wrote: "The Bible may be difficult and confusing, but it is meant to challenge our intelligence, not insult it."[89]

WEDNESDAY - MAYBE THIS WILL MAKE YOU LESS STRESSED

A new study suggests that going to church and worshiping God makes you less stressed.

The researchers at Vanderbilt University say that non-worshipers have higher levels of stress and more risks to their health. Marino Bruce is a research associate professor of medicine, health and society. He says, "We've found that being in a place where you can flex those spiritual muscles is actually beneficial for your health."[90]

But when I think through the possible reasons about why getting together with other people and worshiping God might be beneficial to our health, I'm not so sure it has to do with us flexing our spiritual muscles.

I think it's because worship reminds you that you're not in charge.

We humans get stressed. Big time. Imagine frizzy hair, cartoonish circles spinning in our eyes, and 3 a.m. worry-fests while staring bamboozled at the ceiling.

And a lot of that stress has to do with taking responsibility for things we're not responsible for. And for thinking we can control things we can't actually control. And for worrying about things that are beyond our understanding in the first place.

But when you sit in awe of God... When you pray to him... When you sing about his goodness... When you learn about his promises...

Your brain more clearly identifies and casts aside the lie that it's all up to you. There's only one Boss in life. And you're not it.

Psalm 95:6 (ESV) says: "Oh come, let us worship and bow down; let us kneel before the Lord, our Maker!"

So, worship. It reminds you that you're not in charge.

And it will probably make you feel less stressed—and more blessed.

THURSDAY - MAYBE THEY'RE NOT THE ONES WITH THE CLAWS

If you're a follower of Jesus, sooner or later you'll discover that forgiving someone is hard.

Forgiving easy things is a synch.

But the heavy lifting comes when you try to forgive someone who has truly wronged or hurt you. Maybe you still walk around with a chip off your shoulder. Maybe you have an invisible wound that causes your spirit to slump.

When I talk to people about forgiveness, a lot of them focus on how terribly the other person has acted. 'It's just so hard to forgive them,' they say. 'What they did was so wrong.'

That may be. But today I'd like to change your focus.

If you need help forgiving someone, think about how it could help *you*.

If you carry grudges and refuse to forgive others, doesn't that mean you continue to be controlled by the person who wronged you in the first place? By refusing to forgive someone, it can be like giving that person a continuing negative influence in your life.

Anger, resentment and bitterness are slices of soul-sucking real estate you don't need to own.

Forgiving doesn't mean forgetting. And it doesn't mean you condone what someone did. In the Bible, forgiveness flows out of an awareness that you and I are also broken and that God has forgiven us too. As it says in Ephesians 4:32, "Be kind and compassionate to one another, forgiving each other, just as in Christ God forgave you."

Forgiving someone is not some empty exercise. It minimizes the ongoing harm... to *you*.

If you've been wronged, and if anger, resentment and bitterness are gripping your heart, maybe they're not the ones with the claws.

Maybe you're the one who needs to let go.

FRIDAY - #LOOKATHOWGREATIAM

I knew a guy who would only pray in his closet with the door closed. It was because of what Jesus said in Matthew 6:6: "But when you pray, go into your room, close the door and pray to your Father, who is unseen. Then your Father, who sees what is done in secret, will reward you."

Jesus was not only teaching about prayer, but warning against hypocrites who like to put on a big show with fancy religious-sounding words.

And although I don't make a habit of going into an actual closet to pray, I do heed Jesus' advice to pray with simplicity and sincerity.

But today I'd like to apply this line of thinking to another part of your life and encourage you to do this:

Do something awesome for someone that can't be traced back to you.

The human ego loves to stuff itself. It's a hungry, self-serving beast. Think of Jabba the Hut, the large *Star Wars* gangster slug, and his insatiable desire for more. That's like our egos.

If we don't watch it, our giving can be about getting. We can do something nice for someone just because we love the praise. Or we can give to a charity simply because we benefit from the year-end tax receipt. Or we can boast about some gracious thing we've done on social media so our reputation gets a bit more padding.

#LookAtHowGreatIAm

So sometimes it can be good to do something for someone that can't be traced back to you. That way you know it's truly about giving, and not just about getting.

Praying in a closet takes you off the stage and ups the sincerity of your words as you kneel before the living God. In the same way, blind kindness and generosity are a stab in the gut to the gluttonous gangster called your ego.

Do something awesome that can't be traced back to you.

SATURDAY - ON YOUR FACE

I like to be practical. That's because we can wrongly think of faith as something theoretical which is somehow disconnected from our daily lives.

But it shouldn't be.

So I spend a lot of time thinking about things we can do on a daily basis that reinforce the daily reality of our beliefs.

One of those is *praying on your face.*

Yes, that's right. Praying on your face. Getting down on your knees, then lying on your stomach with your face to the ground [assuming you're physically well enough, of course!]—as if you're prostrating yourself before the Lord Almighty. Maybe not all the time, but sometimes.

Here's my rationale:

In *The Idea of the Holy*, Rudolf Otto describes how many people have lost a sense of the holiness, awesomeness and incredible power of God. He says that modern people "cannot even shudder properly."[91]

In other words, we have become so focused on the personal dimension of our relationship with God that we have lost a sense of his awesomeness and holiness. But listen to Psalm 68:34-35: "Proclaim the power of God, whose majesty is over Israel, whose power is in the skies. You are awesome, O God, in your sanctuary..."

Is there a personal and familiar aspect to our relationship with God? Absolutely. But that shouldn't eclipse our awareness of his holiness, awesomeness and power. If anything, it should intensify it, not diminish it.

So if you've lost a sense of the holiness, awesomeness and incredible power of God, do something that reminds you of that life-altering fact:

Pray on your face.

SUNDAY...

MONDAY - DESPITE THE ODDS

Who would you put in the following blank?

When I think of someone who is courageous, I think of
_____.

When I do it, my first instinct is to think about people who've done incredible things in the face of adversity.

Through the years I've known World War Two veterans, so I think of them. I also think about Moses who went up against the King of Egypt.

Courage is choosing to act despite the odds. And that's certainly true for them.

The reason I think of these examples is quite simply because I know about them. They're people I've talked to or read about in stories.

But most acts of courage go unseen. And they are still courageous.

The mom who breaks her back every month to ensure her kids are getting an education and that the mounting stack of bills are paid...

The man who sits alone in his apartment and refuses to give in to his angry thoughts...

The teenager who risks being shunned because she chooses to take a pass on spreading the hateful rumours about a friend...

The man filling out a new business loan application when all he can hear in his head are the words "You'll-never-amount-to-anything"...

The girl who reaches out to a friend from the past who she knows is being pulled down a path of addiction...

If you have blood and a pulse, you have the potential for courage. Why? Because you're not alone. If you are in Christ, you are powered by the Holy Spirit, and are a part of his army of light.

In the words of Psalm 27:14 (ESV): "Wait for the Lord; be strong, and let your heart take courage..."

Courage is choosing to act despite the odds.

TUESDAY - THE NUMBER ONE FACTOR FOR SPIRITUAL GROWTH?

I think the number one factor that contributes to your spiritual growth and to your maturity as a person is...

Difficult circumstances.

Granted, I don't have any data to back that up. But that's what I think after talking to hundreds of people, reading hundreds of books, and from my own personal experience.

First, difficult circumstances shatter the illusion that you can navigate life on your own without any help. And second, they bring you to your knees before God on a whole new level.

In Romans 5:3-4 (ESV) Paul writes, "suffering produces endurance, and endurance produces character, and character produces hope..." Since you've dealt with difficult circumstances (often multiple times) you learn to keep going, which deepens your character (through consistent spiritual practices and habits), which leads to hope (because those character-building habits remind you of the never-ending and big-picture goodness and provision of God).

Friends, I know that things can get tough. But don't give up. As hard as it might be, open yourself to the possibility that difficult experiences can be soul construction—or soul renovation—for a stronger, wiser and more faithful future you.

Life isn't just about what your circumstances are, but who you become despite your circumstances.

WEDNESDAY - A DAYTIME DISCONNECT?

Many people feel "disconnected" to God from 9 to 5.

Generally speaking, that's when you're at school, or at work, or going about the random tasks of life. (I realize that some of you work shift work but just go with me on this one.)

Maybe you think it's hard to feel close to God when you're studying algebra, working on a third quarter report, emptying a bedpan, or mowing the lawn.

But that time frame makes up a *huge* portion of our lives. And an important one too.

So let me share two thoughts with those who struggle with that time slot.

First, hard work honours God. You were given brains and a body. So no matter what you do, work hard. Be diligent.

Second, you can be an example to someone. More people than you know are hungry for someone with integrity, honesty and hope in their lives. Someone to trust, someone to share some goodness or light. So no matter what you do, maybe your 9 to 5 is an opportunity for you to be that person to somebody else.

In Colossians 3:17 (NLT) Paul writes, "And whatever you do or say, do it as a representative of the Lord Jesus, giving thanks through him to God the Father."

I think that's wisdom for us too. At school, at work, and beyond, try to be a representative of Jesus. None of us are perfect; I realize that. But when you try to represent the goodness, truth and love of God in who you are, the things you do will start to take on more meaning.

Just because you don't always feel connected to God that doesn't mean you can't be.

THURSDAY - WHY WE'RE SPONGES

If you put a sponge in murky water for three minutes, and then take it out and squeeze it, what is going to come out? Murky water.

And if you put another sponge in pure, clear water for three minutes, and then take it out and squeeze it, what is going to come out? Pure, clear water.

I say this because you and I are sponges.

We're powerfully impacted by what's around us. We absorb things from our environments, the people we interact with, and the values we're exposed to.

So it can be very easy to start to talk and act in a way that simply reflects our environments, the people we interact with, and the values we're exposed to.

That's why you need to be choosy about your choices.

In Colossians 2:8 Paul says, "See to it that no one takes you captive by philosophy and empty deceit, according to human tradition... and not according to Christ."

It's a warning to keep the eternal and steadfast Christ as your guide, and not the shifting values and opinions of a confused society.

So when you choose to be proactive about the kinds of things you think about, the people you interact with, and the values you have, you're doing your bit to ensure the water in your bowl is pure and clear.

Is it perfect? No. Can you control every aspect of your day? Of course not! (And don't even bother trying.) And you're right, our faith calls us into tough situations and to interact with all sorts of people as we seek to share God's light.

But one of the reasons we can start to feel defeated, and one of the reasons we can get perpetually sucked into ungodly thoughts and actions, is because we're naïve about how wildly impressionable we porous humans actually are.

Be choosy about your choices.

FRIDAY - A COMPANION OF FOOLS SUFFERS HARM

Lately I've been thinking about how wildly impressionable we humans are. It's not always a bad thing, but I think it really is the truth.

One study I read suggested that you're more likely to have warm and favourable thoughts toward someone you're talking to if you're holding a warm drink at the same time. Wow, talk about impressionable!

That's why your friendships matter.

In 1 Corinthians 15:33 Paul quotes an ancient poet and urges caution: "Bad company corrupts good character." Then in Proverbs 13:20 we read, "Walk with the wise and become wise, for a companion of fools suffers harm."

So my first question to you is this: Who are your friends?

And my second question is, do they chip away at your faith, or do they fortify your faith?

I'm not saying that you should only ever interact with people who just believe the exact same things that you do. What I'm saying is that peer pressure—in terms of our values and behaviour—continues to have an impact on us no matter what our age is.

If your friends are really supportive and full of God's hope, that's amazing. Consider this an affirmation.

But if not, maybe you need to widen the horizon of your friendships.

1. Who are your friends?

2. Do they chip away at your faith, or do they fortify your faith?

"Walk with the wise and become wise, for a companion of fools suffers harm."

SATURDAY - TIME TO JUGGLE UP THE PLAYLIST?

Over the past few days I've been talking about how wildly impressionable we humans are.

People say that children are sponges. But so are adults! (We're just better at hiding it.)

I read a study that said we're more likely to trust what someone is saying if they're wearing a white lab coat. Ever wonder why the people in the tooth-paste commercials are dressed like that? Is it because it's a great on-camera look? Probably not. I'm guessing it's because the advertisers have done their research and are trying to sway you! Yup, we're impressionable.

That's why the music you listen to matters.

Teaching people about how to live wisely according to God's will, Paul writes, "be filled with the Spirit, speaking to one another with psalms, hymns, and songs from the Spirit" (Ephesians 5:18-19).

Paul knows that music has a massive impact on the formation of your character and perspective.

So the question is this: What kind of music do you listen to? And then this: Does it chip away at your faith, or does it fortify your faith?

And I don't ask that question lightly. You might think I'm a puritan but I don't care—so let me be clear: Standards have gone waaay down. Music that celebrates and venerates violence, sexual promiscuity, apathy and which dishonours the Lord's name is in abundance.

The key is to keep your ears open, and not be blind (and deaf) to the fact that music has a massive impact on the formation of your character and perspective.

Your music matters. So what are you listening to? Does it chip away at your faith, or does it fortify your faith?

If you feel a bit convicted on this one, it's probably time to juggle up the playlist.

SUNDAY...

MONDAY - THE TRUTH ABOUT WHAT YOU CASUALLY SAY

What do you believe? Really? Not what you *say* you believe, but what you *actually* believe?

Sometimes you'll hear it said that how you spend your time and energy is the true measure of your true beliefs. Why? Because it's a practical demonstration of your actual priorities.

But today I'd like to suggest something else:

What you casually say is what you actually believe.

Here's an example. Let's say someone tells you they believe that Paul's words in Ephesians 4:29 aren't just for the Ephesians long ago—but for us as well: "Let no corrupting talk come out of your mouths, but only such as is good for building up, as fits the occasion, that it may give grace to those who hear."

But then what do they do? They malign others online. They guess their motives (often wrongly) and paint them as a villain.

Or maybe, in the intimacy of close friends, they trash talk someone in a way they would never do if they were physically standing in the presence of God.

What you say when your guard is down is often a clearer picture of your inner thoughts.

209

And guess what? Those are the moments people are watching. They're watching and putting the puzzle pieces together to figure out what you actually believe, and whether or not what you believe is worth living for.

Is Jesus God's Son? Did the resurrection happen? Is hope possible? Is love a command? Is the church God-ordained? Are our words for building up?

Let's examine our beliefs. Grow in godliness. And let our words reflect our hearts.

What you casually say is what you actually believe.

TUESDAY - INTEGRITY, NO MATTER WHAT

In 1985 a tornado ripped through Barrie, Ontario—the city where I live.

Just recently I was told about something that happened in the midst of that wicked storm. A Mennonite person saw a dollar on the sidewalk and returned it to City Hall. So if anyone had lost it they would be able to find and re-claim it.

Can you imagine doing that for a single dollar?!

Today, that dollar remains at City Hall. They framed it and hung it on the wall as an enduring testimony to personal integrity.

Integrity is about consistency.

Imagine yourself standing before God. Since you're before the Lord God Almighty, you're going to do your best to talk and act in a way that honours him. So integrity is trying to live with that same rigour even when you can't see God.

It's trying to consistently live for God's glory and not your own.

So what does that look like on the ground?

It's admitting when you're wrong even if it will cause personal embarrassment. It's standing up for God's truth even when it will make you unpopular. It's showing compassion toward someone—even if they rub you the wrong way—because they are made in the image of the God you serve.

What are you going to say and do today? Maybe Psalm 25:21 can be your prayer and guide: "May integrity and uprightness protect me, because my hope, LORD, is in you."

Integrity is about consistency. It's trying to live consistently for God and his glory... no matter what.

WEDNESDAY - NONE OF IT GOES TO WASTE

It's easy to get down in life. We wonder: "Am I making a difference?" or "How do I know if I'm living true to God's plan?"

A part of the reason we can get frustrated is because we can't always see the fruit of our labour. We live each day and don't know if the things we say or do make an impact in the long run.

Or do we?

Today I want to remind you about something that can lift your perspective back up to a horizon of hope.

Ephesians 1:10 tells us something about what God is up to in the world. It says that God's mysterious plan is "to bring unity to all things in heaven and on earth under Christ."

Woah. Go get a highlighter and flip open your Bible to Ephesians 1:10. It says that through the course of human history, God is bringing unity to all things. The word "unity" is a large idea that includes healing, wholeness, peace, reconciliation, harmony and abundant life.

So what does that mean for you?

It means that *no small act of faith goes to waste*. Everything you do that somehow contributes to that vision of unity—that honours God, that is in line with the teachings of Jesus, that is consistent with his vision for the world—somehow contributes to this wonderful unity that our Creator God is weaving together.

Every sincere prayer. Every act of forgiveness. Every word of truth that is spoken with respect. Every deed which makes our environment cleaner. Every project that makes our streets safer. Every action that cultivates healing in the human heart. Every deed of love toward a friend, family member, stranger or enemy. Every act of beauty or justice that muscles up against the ugliness of our bruised and bruising world.

You can't always see the end result. But God can. It's the unity of all things in heaven and on earth under Christ.

So are you making a difference? Yes you are. No small act of faith goes to waste.

THURSDAY - CREDIT WHERE CREDIT IS DUE

Imagine your best friend did something wonderful for you—like fix your broken garage door for free. They bought the parts, put in free labour, and even gave it a nice new paint job.

The next day, some people come over and admire your spectacular garage door.

What do you say? Do you say, "Thanks! I'm so lucky that it somehow got fixed"? or "I'm just glad it worked out"?

Of course not!

You'd give your best friend credit.

When it comes to God, I think we dishonour him when he does something wonderful for us and we don't give him credit.

Years ago, a friend of mine was thinking about going to seminary to be a pastor. He was short $3200 for his first year expenses. So he prayed: "God, if you want me to do this, please give me a clear sign."

The next day he got a letter from a cousin. A relative had passed away. And this relative wanted her money portioned out to the cousins. So here was his cut.

The letter included a cheque... for $3200!

What do you think he said? "That's so lucky that this problem somehow got fixed"? Or "I'm just glad it worked out"? Of course not! He gave God the credit.

In Psalm 61:1, David sings, "Hear my cry, O God; listen to my prayer..." You and I probably say that too. And when he responds in such a clear and generous way, why do we act like he doesn't exist?

This week, when God does something wonderful for you, give him credit.

Not only is it the right thing to do, but you'll remind yourself—and others —about how faithful God truly is.

FRIDAY - YOU WILL NEVER MAKE A GOOD IMPRESSION IF...

Most of us check the mirror in the morning, usually while combing our hair or brushing our teeth. Then we walk away from the mirror.

But not really.

A lot of us carry an invisible mirror around with us all day.

What I mean is that we're aware of ourselves. We're aware of the impression we're making. We want others to think well of us. Some of us to a greater degree than others. But I think it's pretty much true for most people.

Even the "rebel" who "doesn't care what anyone thinks" acts and speaks in a certain way to give an impression—that they don't care what others think (even though they actually do).

To varying degrees, most people are at least somewhat aware of the kind of impression they're making.

Recently I was reading something by C.S. Lewis. He said that "you will never make a good impression on other people until you stop thinking about what sort of impression you are making."[92]

This is what the apostle Paul was getting at when he wrote in 1 Corinthians 4:4 that "It is the Lord who judges me." He's wasn't condemning himself. He was saying that, in the end, what God thinks is more important than what people think.

Now don't go out and dress like a circus clown at your job interview and blame me or C.S. Lewis when you don't get the gig. It's good to be smart. But when it comes to being the best you God made you to be, your best impression on the world comes not from jumping through other people's hoops, but from knowing and trusting the deep rootedness of your worth and value in the One who made you.

What God thinks is more important than what others think.

Be at rest. Be you.

"You will never make a good impression on other people until you stop thinking about what sort of impression you are making."

SATURDAY - THE 7-DAY NO COMPLAINT CHALLENGE

Thou shalt not complain.

You're right. It's not one of the ten commandments. But the Bible certainly warns against complaining all the time.

I think about the ancient Hebrews complaining to Moses in the wilderness. Or Philippians 2:14-15 (NLT) where Paul says, "Do everything without complaining and arguing, so that no one can criticize you. Live clean, innocent lives as children of God, shining like bright lights in a world full of crooked and perverse people."

So today I'd like to suggest something very practical to help you complain less:

The 7-Day No Complaint Challenge.

I heard about the idea from Las Vegas pastor Jud Wilhite. Here's what you do. Take a bracelet (or watch), and every time you complain about something *irrelevant*, change it from one wrist to the other.

Granted, if you need to thoughtfully disagree with something or someone, there's nothing wrong with that. Feel free to thoughtfully disagree with a friend, co-worker or government policy decision until the cows come home.

But what this does is make you more aware of complaining about *irrelevant* things. Simply switching a bracelet or watch from one wrist to the other raises your awareness about how often you're complaining.

Wilhite explains his thinking like this: "Complaining is like scratching your arm when it's been in contact with poison ivy; it may bring some immediate relief, but it makes the situation worse in the end."[93]

Recently my eight-year-old daughter made me a bracelet. I'm going to use it for the next seven days.

So join me and take the 7-Day No Complaint Challenge.

It's not revolutionary. But I'm pretty sure it will make your words sound more like light, and less like death.

SUNDAY...

MONDAY - THAT'S WHAT NORMAL AWESOME PEOPLE DO

Before I became a pastor I had a number of different jobs—and therefore, a number of different bosses.

I saw different characteristics at work in each of them. Some were positive, and some were negative.

But one of the most problematic bosses was unpredictable. He was so inconsistent that he put everyone on edge. If he was having a bad day, it meant that everyone else was having a bad day too!

The reason I share this with you is because when you do good things consistently, it helps the people around you thrive.

I've always been inspired by Paul's advice to a young leader in 2 Timothy 4:2 (NLT). He encouraged him to tell people the good news about Jesus. "Be prepared," he wrote, "whether the time is favorable or not." In other words, do what you're supposed to do regardless of your circumstances.

To me, it's about consistency.

If you're feeling low about your parenting, maybe you need to get consistent with some tech-free family time. If you're feeling like your relationship is getting distant, maybe you need to get consistent and plan a regular date night. If you're feeling far from God, maybe you need to get consistent and actually schedule time every day to read your Bible.

You're no superhero. But you can get consistent.

Pastor Craig Groeschel often says this: "Successful people do consistently what others do occasionally."[94]

Do you want to be successful? I certainly do. And I also want the people around me to thrive.

One way to do that is to be consistent—regardless of your circumstances. That's what normal awesome people do.

"Successful people do consistently what others do occasionally."

TUESDAY - HOLD HIS HAND

Sometimes we can make our faith too theoretical.

And I kind of get that. After all, you can't see God the way you can see a street light. And many of us don't hear an audible voice from the Lord every time we pray.

As a result, God can seem distant. It happens. Not always, but sometimes. And then you start to wonder if God is really there. "God, are you there when I get criticized, again?" "Are you there when my day starts and I'm too busy to even think straight?" "Are you there when no one appreciates me?" "Are you there when I don't know if there's a point to my life?"

But he *is* there. He is *always* there. And here's a way to remember that fact: *Hold his hand.*

I know, sounds super-weird. But hear me out. In Psalm 73:23, Asaph writes: "Yet I am always with you; you hold me by my right hand." He says that God holds him by his right hand as a reminder that he is always with him.

So why not do the same thing to remind yourself that God is with you through the ups and downs? Imagine that God is holding your hand—and hold it back.

I mean it. When you're walking down the street, or making your way to your next class, or driving down the road, clasp your right hand. Remind yourself. Hold God's hand.

The things we physically do are acts of self-training. You're more likely to fall asleep when you lie down. You're more likely to feel better when you smile. And you're more likely to sense God's nearness when you hold his hand.

'Matthew, you're insane.' I know. But I think it could help you. Try it. Clasp your right hand. Remind yourself. And no matter what good, bad or ugly confronts you, you might just re-discover that the Lord Almighty is with you.

"Yet I am always with you; you hold me by my right hand."

WEDNESDAY - AREN'T ALL RELIGIONS BASICALLY THE SAME?

It's a good question. After all, we live in a diverse society, and a lot of religions speak about some kind of higher power and have a version of the golden rule.

I can't fully explore this issue in a short devotional. But it needs to be said that although there are some areas of overlap, Christianity is different.

And one of the main differences is Jesus.

Other religions also have a founder who is called a prophet and teacher (Buddhism has the Buddha and Islam has Mohammed). But Christianity says something more about Jesus.

He's God among us. Jesus says that he and God are one (John 10:30). Colossians 1:15 says that Jesus is "the image of the invisible God." And 2 Peter 1:1 calls Jesus "God and Saviour."

Why is this important? Because in Christianity, the question mark about God is turned into an exclamation point in Jesus.

Although there's a lot we don't know with our limited human brains, if you want to know the character of God, look to Jesus. If you want to know the teachings of God, look to Jesus. If you want to know God's dream for the world, look to Jesus.

Would I ever condemn someone from a different religion? Absolutely not. Would I respect and love them? Absolutely.

But I can also be confident that in Jesus something unique and world-changing has happened.

Jesus is the most influential and historically documented figure to ever walk planet earth. That impact continues to grow. There are 50,000 new Christians every single day. Jesus gives content to your questions about God. And he takes the mask off the mystery about God's vision for the world.

So follow Jesus. Closely.

In Christianity, the question mark about God is turned into an exclamation point in Jesus.

217

THURSDAY - GENEROSITY YOU DON'T DESERVE

Aren't all religions basically the same?

As I explained yesterday, it's a good question. After all, a lot of religions speak about some kind of higher power and have a version of the golden rule.

But there are significant differences. Yesterday I talked about the difference Jesus makes. And today I'd like to talk about something else:

Grace.

It means generosity you don't deserve. Say you shout at someone for no reason, but then they turn around and do something kind for you anyway. That's grace.

When it comes to how you are saved (or made eternally right with God, both in this life and the next), many religions say that it's all about how good you are. It's about your moral performance—living a kind life. "Look at how nice I've been, God is definitely going to let me into heaven."

But Christianity is different.

We're all sinful people. (Sorry to break it to you, but it's the truth.) We don't love God, other people, or ourselves as we should. And because of that, none of us can ever be morally good enough to perfectly please a perfect God.

So that's where grace comes in. When you confess your sin to God, and put your faith in Jesus as the Lord of your life, he *gives* you forgiveness. He *gives* you salvation. He *gives* you eternity. He *gives* you heaven.

That's why the crucifixion and resurrection of Jesus are so important. When you put your trust in him, he does for you what you can't do for yourself. He takes (and pays for) your sin, and in return *gives* you...

Everything.

Ephesians 2:8-9 lays it out: "For it is by grace you have been saved, through faith—and this is not from yourselves, it is the gift of God..." As it is sometimes said, "God's riches at Christ's expense."

How amazing is that? It doesn't matter where you live, how much money you have, what colour your skin is, or whether you're male or female. It also doesn't matter whether you've been in jail, littered, struggle with addiction, or have a pile of unmentionable secrets.

God's grace in Jesus is equally accessible to all.

If you want or need to know more, talk to your pastor or let me know. Either way, be confident—not in what you've done, but in what Jesus has done for you.

With Jesus you have everything. Without him, you don't.

FRIDAY - NEVER TAKES A HOLIDAY

Holidays are awesome. A few of my family's habits while on vacation are making S'mores (not to brag but I'm kind of an expert), smacking mosquitoes, reading, and getting caught up with friends.

So today's devotional is something for you to think about, whether you have some holidays come up, or even just a weekend.

Here it is: Faith never takes a holiday.

Yes, we take a break from work or school. And yes, we take a break from our normal routines. But we don't take a break from God.

Maybe it seems obvious, but it's way too easy to let our brains turn to mush when we downshift for a holiday, long or short. It's as if we think the beach, BBQ party or backyard are watered-down-faith zones.

But they're not.

I know you're trying to have some you time, but other people still need a friend... even when you're on holidays. Prayer and Bible reading still root you in God... even when you're on holidays. And the world still needs Jesus' grace and truth... even when you're on holidays.

In a powerful passage about what a life of Christian love is like, the apostle Paul writes, "Never be lacking in zeal, but keep your spiritual fervor, serving the Lord" (Romans 12:11).

What if the beach was where someone heard a word of hope? What if the shopping mall was where new life happened? What if your extra time was someone's just-in-time?

You never take a break from God. And God never takes a break from you. Phew!

So keep on the lookout. You never know where you'll be needed next. Faith never takes a holiday. And neither does the grip of a gracious God.

SATURDAY - HOW'D NOT COMPLAINING GO?

Seven days ago I proposed the 7-Day No-Complaint challenge.

The idea was simple. Wear a watch or bracelet, and every time you complain about something irrelevant, switch it to the other wrist. Quite simply, it makes you more aware of how much you're complaining—and hopefully helps you dial down the useless verbal diatribes.

But what about me? How'd it go?

I think it went pretty well. I used a bracelet my daughter made me. And it definitely ping-ponged back and forth several times. On a few occasions it made me pause and ask, 'Is this a legitimate complaint, or am I just being a jerk?'

But here's what I also found: Complaining people seem to create more complaining people. Maybe that's why Paul quotes the Greek poet Menander in 1 Corinthians 15:33: "Bad company corrupts good character."

Being around people who complain a lot is like being shot with a poisonous dart loaded with ingratitude.

So what do you do?

First, simply be aware of it. That's half the battle.

And second, in your dealings with others, be wise about who's infecting who. Instead of being infected with negativity, infect with positivity.

With love, with faith, with truth, and with gratitude.

Our 7-Day No-Complaint challenge is technically over. But maybe it's just beginning...

SUNDAY...

MONDAY - SPECIAL AGENT... YOU?

I heard a story about someone who took an exam to join the civil service. One of the questions was this: "Do you think you are a special agent of God?"[95]

As you can imagine, it was designed to weed out potential "crazies" from the civil service. I get where the hiring committee was coming from.

But if you're a follower of Jesus, you actually are a special agent of God.

Writing in the first century, the apostle Peter said, "But you are a chosen race, a royal priesthood, a holy nation..." (1 Peter 2:9, ESV). That sounds like "special agent" status to me!

I think God communicates with us all the time. You may not hear an audible voice, but as you mature as a Christian, you will come to increasingly trust the inner promptings that (a) are consistent with biblical teachings, and (b) benefit others. Let me give you an example.

I often get a strong urge to pray for someone. It can hit me when I'm driving my car, sitting at my desk, or lying in bed. I think to myself, 'I wonder why that person just popped into my head?' Over time, I've come to trust that this is God calling me to pray for someone.

So I do it. And I think you should too.

One time this urge was so strong that I dropped to my knees in the middle of the kitchen right then and there and pleaded to God for a particular person. I later learned that they were going through an intense spiritual battle that very same day!

When God summons you to prayer, answer him. Wherever you are. He can use your obedience in that very moment for healing, for hope, and for the good of one of his children.

If you're a follower of Jesus, you are a special agent of God.

TUESDAY - "GOD WITH SKIN ON"

There was a stretch in 2017 when the news bombarded us with stories of massive destruction: fires in British Columbia, Canada, tropical storm Harvey in the southern United States, flooding in Bangladesh, India and

221

Nepal, and Hurricane Irma slamming the Caribbean and heading toward Florida.

There were—and are—many reasons to be concerned. But in these types of situations, what can you do?

Several years ago a Tornado hit Lafayette, Tennessee. In response, people from a nearby church in Nashville got together to pick up trees, haul away debris, and offer general assistance.

A newspaper asked one of the helpers why they came. This is what he said: "We want to be God with skin on."

Brilliant! He wasn't claiming to be God. He was talking about sharing the presence of God with those who hurt.

I'm not sure where you live. Many of you are in North America. I'm guessing you're pretty spread out. But some of you are close to problems in your own communities. If so, check with local agencies about how to help. But what do the rest of us do?

First, we can pray.

Second, we can heed the advice of authorities about where they need specific kinds of assistance.

And third, we can send money.

If others were watching your town go through a disaster, isn't that what you would want them to do?

Proverbs 3:27 offers this advice: "Do not withhold good from those to whom it is due, when it is in your power to act." You can't do everything, but you can do something.

If you're close to a disaster—or far away—use your knees, ears, arms and wallets. Like the God-with-skin-on helper from Tennessee, you can share the presence of God with those who hurt.

WEDNESDAY - "WHEN I WAS IN PAIN"

A seventy-eight-year-old grandmother was living alone when she had a stroke and fell in her bathroom.

She was paralyzed. And alone. For three days. On a cold, hard bathroom floor.

A neighbour eventually checked in on her and called an ambulance. For the next six months she was under the constant care of doctors until she died.

Her grandson really struggled with this. Where was the silver lining? How could any good come out of this?

Toward the end of his grandmother's life, he asked her what she had thought about while lying on the bathroom floor. Here's what she said:

"I've never been closer to God my whole life than when I was in pain."[96]

When it comes to our own lives, we often bump into painful experiences —or crash into them!—and ask, "Why would God let this happen?"

That's a big question, and I don't want to dismiss it. But today I think we can learn something from this seventy-eight-year-old grandmother.

If we're open to the possibility, difficult experiences can draw us closer to God—not push us farther away.

Those moments are when we're brutally aware of our dependence on him. Those moments are when the illusion of our own control and self-sufficiency is shattered into a thousand irreparable bits. Those moments are when our prayers are raw, and our trust is stretched.

Writing to Christians in ancient Rome, Paul had an incredible outlook. He told them that "suffering produces endurance, and endurance produces character, and character produces hope..." (Romans 5:3-4, ESV).

Don't let difficult experiences crucify your faith. If you're open, God can use them to resurrect a faith that has more endurance, character and hope.

THURSDAY - THEN YOUR SCHEDULE MAKES YOU

How is your routine?

If you're thoughtful about it, your daily routine can help you live out your priorities in a real and tangible way. In fact, at first you make your schedule, but then your schedule makes you! What I mean is that if you don't craft it in the right way, it will have a reverse debilitating impact on your daily life.

So...

Do you want to get in shape? Schedule it in and tie up your shoes or get to the gym. Consistently. Do you want to get back to worship? Set your alarm on Sunday and head to church. Consistently. Do you want to improve your marriage? Set some mutual goals and schedule time to make them happen. Consistently. Do you want to get outside your comfort zone? Take an evening, research volunteer opportunities, and get out there. Consistently.

People who stagnate think things through over and over again. But they fail on the follow up. People who grow, however, still think things through. But they do something about it.

Psalm 90:12 (ESV) says: "So teach us to number our days that we may get a heart of wisdom." It's a request for God to make us aware of how limited our time on earth is, so that we can gain wisdom for how to go about our lives in a godly way *today*.

Putting into practice a routine that honours the limited time you have, and which helps you achieve godly priorities, is one of the most practical ways for you to grow as a disciple of Jesus.

At first you make your schedule, but then your schedule makes you.

FRIDAY - 151,600 PEOPLE EVERY DAY

We live in the age of distraction. Researchers even talk about "DAF – Directed Attention Fatigue." Our brains have to work incredibly hard to wade through the information that is hurtling toward us at breakneck speeds.

The result is that we're mentally tired. When that happens, it's not only hard to live out our priorities, but to even know what they are! It's hard to stay focused when you're bamboozled.

Here's why all of this is important: Every one of us is *one heartbeat away from meeting our Maker*. It could happen at any time. Psalm 103:14-15 (NRSV) says, "As for mortals, their days are like grass; they flourish like a flower of the field; for the wind passes over it, and it is gone, and its place knows it no more." God is eternal. But you and I are not.

Not to alarm you, but about 151,600 people die every single day on planet earth.

So doesn't it make sense to ensure you're ready?

The number one thing you need to do is get right with God. You do this by acknowledging your sin and brokenness to him, asking him to forgive you, putting your trust in Jesus as the Lord of your life, and accepting what he has done for you on the cross. After that, start to learn more about his teachings as you join in on the work he's doing to renovate the world and bring heaven to earth.

Tomorrow I'll talk about other important relationships. But your relationship with God is the biggie!

It's easy to be bewildered and confused by the pace of our modern society. It tires us out pretty quickly. So you need to step back, take stock, and remind yourself what's truly important.

I'm not saying your death is imminent. I just don't have that information. But if it is, are you ready?

All of us are only *one heartbeat away* from that incredible, awesome encounter.

SATURDAY - PRIORITIZING KEY RELATIONSHIPS

Yesterday I said that life was unpredictable and short, and that all of us are one heartbeat away from meeting our Maker. Not to be morbid, but it's true!

Because of that, getting right with God is our number one job. But today, I'd like to talk about something else along the same vein:

Prioritizing others.

We all know that relationships are important. But since life can be so hustle-bustle, it's helpful to take a step back and remind ourselves about what's what.

First, your family is important. When speaking to the young Timothy, the apostle Paul said that "Anyone who does not provide for their relatives, and especially for their own household, has denied the faith and is worse than an unbeliever" (1 Timothy 5:8).

Then in Galatians 6:10 he stressed the importance of "doing good to all people, especially to those who belong to the family of believers." There is a consistent thread through the Bible that when God's people are obedient to him, the family of believers provide for each other.

But it doesn't end there. Caring for others is an ever-expanding ripple in the Christian faith.

We see this in the story of the Good Samaritan where Christ teaches us that we're to show mercy to our neighbours—who are essentially anyone in need.

In light of all this, we're to prioritize our families, our church, and organize our lives so that we're available to show mercy to others, even if they're strangers, and even if they look or believe differently than we do.

Is this a tall order? Yes. Are many people too busy to live it out? Yes. But is it also wisdom for living well? Yes it is.

Tom Landry was a famous NFL football coach. Someone once asked him how he could be so calm under pressure. He said, "Well, I have my priorities in order. First, God. Second, my wife. Third, my kids. Fourth, football. So if I lose on Sunday I've got a lot left over. There's a lot of people who, if they lose on Sunday, don't have anything left over."[97]

Don't let life zoom by without prioritizing key relationships. It's not always easy. But you'll sleep better at night. Dr. Henry Cloud says this: "At our very core we are relational beings... The soul cannot prosper without being connected to others."[98]

SUNDAY...

MONDAY - CRYING OUT FOR A DIVINE EXPLANATION

Does God even exist?

I personally think that's the one question that changes everything.

Are we here on purpose, or by chance? Is there something after death, or not? Is there right and wrong, or is it all relative? Do truth, beauty and love have meaning? And do they make a difference?

I think all of these questions underlie a bigger one: Does God even exist?

In 2017 at the church I pastor, I explored three of the big arguments for the existence of God.

One is the argument from the stars. It basically goes like this (and keep in mind that I'm radically condensing here): In 1929 Edwin Hubble started exploring the stars. He found that the universe was massive—and expanding. He traced this expansion back to one moment—a big explosion; a "big bang"—when all space, matter, time and energy came into existence.

When it comes to logic and the scientific method, a central idea is this: Something can't come from nothing. Babies don't just appear. They come from somewhere. If there's a knock on your door, something had to cause it. So what do you find when you apply that logic to the universe?

The evidence points to an intelligent mind, a Creator, outside of the physical matter of the universe.

Frances Collins is an award-winning scientist who mapped the human genome. He says, "The Big Bang cries out for a divine explanation. It forces the conclusion that nature had a defined beginning. I cannot see how nature could have created itself. Only a supernatural force that is outside of space and time could have done that."[99]

All of a sudden, Genesis 1:1 doesn't sound so strange: "In the beginning God created the heavens and the earth."

Whoever you are, follow the evidence. Philosopher Alvin Plantinga says there are over twenty solid arguments for the existence of God. What I like about this one, is that tells us that our universe is here on purpose.

And so are you.

Asking honest, thoughtful questions often results in discovering honest, thoughtful answers.

[To find a summary of my teaching series called "Does God Even Exist?" go to www.MatthewRuttan.com/Resources]

TUESDAY - IN SPITE OF YOU

Some streams of thought are simply polluted. They contaminate your brain.

For example, always talking negatively about yourself is like this. (This usually happens inside your head.) Instead of living confidently as a child of God, you continually berate yourself and chip away at your self-assurance with a non-stop, self-defeating monologue.

When it comes to Christianity, another polluted stream of thought is that God would never save you (because you always mess up) and would never use you (because you're so imperfect).

If you think like that, you need to ask yourself where that thinking comes from. Then you need to identify it and throw it out the window.

In his book *The Problem of God*, British Columbia Pastor Mark Clark says this: "God doesn't save you and use you *because* of you but in *spite* of you."[100]

I like that. God saves you and uses you for wonderful things in this world not because you're so awesome—but because he is!

After talking about using our talents to serve others, the apostle Peter says this: "To him be the glory and the power for ever and ever." (1 Peter 4:11). That's significant. Why? Because it's not about bringing ourselves glory, but God!

Today, don't be down because you have a history of messing up and because you know you're imperfect. Be up because God can do more in and through you than you could ever do by yourself.

All you have to do... is say Yes.

WEDNESDAY - DRY PATCHES AND WHAT TO DO ABOUT THEM

If you believe in the God of the Bible, you know it's important to cultivate your relationship with him.

But it's not always easy. Dry patches come and try to expand their real estate in your soul. And you're not quite sure how to beat them back.

If you can relate to this, here's some advice. Did you ever injure your leg and need a crutch? Put quite simply, the crutch gives you stability you can't give yourself while you regain your strength.

That's like the Psalms in the Bible.

So here's something I do to give me spiritual stability when a dry patch hits. Find a powerful psalm, maybe Psalm 51, 23 or 121. Then read through one or two verses at a time, then pray based on what comes to mind.

Here's an example from Psalm 121: "I lift up my eyes to the mountains—where does my help come from? My help comes from the LORD, the Maker of heaven and earth."

Stop there. Since it starts with an acknowledgment that all help comes from God, praise and thank him for the help he gives you in your own life. Then go back to the text:

"He will not let your foot slip—he who watches over you will not slumber..." This verse is about God protecting and watching over you. So thank God very specifically for how he is protecting and watching over you. Then go back to the text.

Do you see how it works?

Dry patches are normal. They don't mean you're inadequate. They mean you're human. So one simple-yet-powerful tip is to use the psalms as a crutch. Read, pray, repeat.

The psalms give you stability you couldn't give yourself, just like a crutch, while you regain your strength.

THURSDAY - TENSION

Tension. Nine times out of ten it's no fun. In fact, when talking about family, friends, team, church or work, I don't think I've ever heard someone say, "Hey everybody, I love tension!"

And yet, it happens—a lot!

So today I'd like to suggest that tension can actually be an opportunity.

In their book *Lead Small*, Reggie Joiner and Tom Shefchunas write that "Tension is actually the platform that gives you an opportunity to demonstrate that this is a safe place."[101]

When they say "safe place" they're talking about an environment where relationships of mutual respect and trust can be built.

If you start to act irrational, blurt out crazy talk, or blow up every time things get a little tense, people will learn that you can't handle tension, and that it's not a safe place to be honest, share a different opinion, or disagree.

In Romans 12:18 (ESV) Paul writes this: "If possible, so far as it depends on you, live peaceably with all." When he talks about living "peaceably" he doesn't mean we should never disagree and sweep problems under the rug. I think he means we should trust God so much, and be so confident in who we are in Christ's love, that we are not easily frightened by different opinions, strong feelings, or uncertain territory.

When a bit of healthy tension comes up, you don't need to explode or run for the hills. It may be an opportunity to expand the steadfastness of your soul. The result might just be relationships that have more mutual respect and trust.

FRIDAY - DOES JESUS NEED TO BE MORE CHRISTLIKE?

I sometimes see posts from a satirical website called *The Babylon Bee*. They put out funny stories about faith, Christianity, the church and our culture. They're not real stories. They just make them up, usually basing them on current issues for a laugh.[102]

For example, one story was about how a guy was really praying to hear from God—while his Bible remained unopened right in front of him!

More recently I saw one about a woman who read the actual Gospel stories of Jesus and was very offended by them (and him). She went on record to say that Jesus "should be more Christlike."

That's correct. After reading what Jesus actually said and did, and realizing that a lot of what he said and did contradicted what she herself thought was right, she accused Jesus of not being enough like... himself!

The story was written to be funny, but it was a commentary on what a lot of us do. We think we know more than anybody else what it means to be Christlike... and sometimes even more than Jesus himself!

So what's my point?

When it comes to being more Christlike, humility and maturity grow each other.

I'm not saying that you shouldn't be confident about certain things. And I'm not saying that all interpretations of Jesus and the Bible are true. But I am saying that we're all works in progress. The more humility, the more maturity; and the more maturity, the more humility.

In Philippians 2:7 we read that even Jesus humbled himself taking on "the very nature of a servant."

Are you right sometimes? Yes. Are you wrong sometimes? Yes. Do all of us have work to do to be more Christlike? Yes.

The ones who have every single detail figured out, and who seem to know what Jesus should say and do even when it wasn't what Jesus said and did, are often the ones who have locked him outside.

SATURDAY - THE LANGUAGE OF GOD?

Are we just here by chance, or by design? Are we the result of randomness, or is there an orchestrated intelligence to life on earth?

A lot of people feel that chance and randomness are the order of the day. But are they sure? The question we need to ask is this: Where does the evidence point?

One of the powerful arguments for God's existence is that life, our universe, and our world shows evidence of being wonderfully designed. The argument is that creation is so perfectly sophisticated, complex and beautiful that it points to a divine Designer—to God.

Theoretical physicist Paul Davies says that "the appearance of design is overwhelming." Frances Collins, the award-winning scientist who mapped the human genome refers to the intelligent, sophisticated information woven into even the smallest aspects of the universe as "the language of God."

'Maybe,' some respond. 'But it can still be chance.'

Really? Can you really say that after looking at the actual mathematics?

Davies says that the chance of our universe coming into existence like it is, is like a marksman aiming at a coin and hitting it. But the coin isn't in the next room. It's on the other side of the observable universe, twenty billion lightyears away!

Where does the evidence point? It points to a divine Designer—to the God who created the universe, and who created you and me on purpose.

Over the door of his famous physics laboratory, scientists James Clerk-Maxwell put Psalm 111:2: "Great are the works of the Lord; they are pondered by all who delight in them."

When you ponder how amazing life is... When you ponder how amazing the universe is... You don't find *fewer* reasons to believe in God, you find *more*.

Take notice of the unparalleled beauty, sophistication and intelligence woven into life around you. It is "the language of God." And one of the messages I think it communicates to us is this: 'Do not be afraid. I am right here with you.'[103]

SUNDAY...

MONDAY - YOUR SECOND WIND

I workout three or four times a week. And let me be honest with you. It's not my favourite thing to do.

I like how it makes me feel, and there are definitely some beautiful trails to bike and paths to run. But before I start, I usually have to convince myself it's a good idea.

Recently I was on the elliptical machine. I was fervently watching the little digital clock on the screen, and it seemed like my workout was taking *forever*.

But then I realized something. I was focused more on *what* I was doing instead *why* I was doing it.

I remembered that exercising helps me think more clearly; it helps me be a better husband and dad; and it makes me more effective as a pastor and leader. Those thoughts gave me a second wind. So I closed my eyes and went for gold!

When it comes to your life, what are you doing on a day-to-day basis that is getting you down? What is that difficult or monotonous thing that keeps you staring at your feet?

I'm not suggesting that your problems are easily squashed. But I am suggesting that we often need reminders about *why* we're doing what we're doing to make the daily battles a little less overwhelming.

In Colossians 1:11 (ESV) Paul prays this: "May you be strengthened with all power, according to his glorious might, for all endurance and patience with joy..."

That's my prayer for you too. When you focus on living, working and breathing for God's glory and Christ's kingdom, I think you get an injection of strength, endurance and joy.

In your day-to-day life, the *what* is important, but so is the *why*. It's your second wind. And it's always at your back.

TUESDAY - STOPPING PROBLEMS FROM PUTTING DOWN ROOTS

Have you ever noticed how the Bible is packed with statements about God wanting us to worship, glorify and serve him?

And have you ever thought to yourself, 'Doesn't that seem kind of selfish? Why is the all-loving God so consumed with his own glory?'

Well, it's actually for our benefit. Let me explain.

In the summer of 2017 I conducted a marriage for two people in their twenties. One of the things I talked about during the ceremony was that when you put God at the centre of your marriage, it's harder for problems to get to the centre. Will you have some? Sure you will. But since your focus is on God, the problems can't take over.

That same idea applies to us as individuals. When you put God at the centre of your life, it's harder for problems to get to the centre.

The more we worship, glorify and serve God, the more we open ourselves to the joy God gives. That's part of what I take from Psalm 16:11 (ESV): "You make known to me the path of life; in your presence there is fullness of joy; at your right hand are pleasures forevermore."

I don't think God wants you to worship, glorify and serve him because *his* joy depends on it—but because *yours* does.

When God has the prime real estate on your priority list, problems have no space to permanently put down roots.

WEDNESDAY - LIKE YOU'RE ACTUALLY TALKING TO THE KING OF KINGS

The famous Billy Graham says that prayer is the "sweetest work of the soul."[104]

If that's true, why do so many people struggle with it?

One of the continual refrains I hear is that prayer is hard work and that it's easy to get distracted.

So today I'd like to offer super-practical advice to those who are stuck when it comes to talking to the Almighty.

First, have better posture.

And second, speak out loud.

Now I know that God doesn't only listen to those with good posture and to those who talk out loud. (It's important for us to be clear on that point.) But I think that staleness in our prayer life sometimes happens because we forget what we're actually doing.

So this advice is to help you re-focus on who you're talking to.

In 1 Timothy 6:15 (ESV) God is called "the blessed and only Sovereign, the King of kings and Lord of lords." That's serious stuff! If the Queen came to your house, would you mumble away to her in a distracted way while half falling off the couch?

I doubt it!

So if you're stuck in your prayer life, start your conversation with the King of kings by snapping to attention, and speaking to him like you would a King—a powerful King who loves you and wants the best for you.

There's an old joke that when Jewish people pray, they stand. And when Roman Catholics pray, they kneel. And that when Presbyterians pray, they slump! Lol (That could work for Uniteds, Baptists, Anglicans, Methodists, and several independent churches as well, but you get the gist.)

This isn't about how much attention God gives you—but about how much attention you give God.

Pray like you're actually talking to the King of kings.

THURSDAY - SECRECY STRANGLES

All of us struggle with something.

But many of us keep it secret.

Some of you struggle with over-spending.

Some of you struggle with pornography.

Some of you struggle with body image.

Some of you struggle with over (or under)-eating.

Some of you struggle with addiction.

Some of you struggle with gambling.

Some of you struggle with fidelity.

Some of you struggle with excessive worry.

Some of you struggle with harmful thoughts.

Some of you struggle with _____.

I'm not here to judge or depress you.

I'm here to let you know that *secrecy strangles.*

When you struggle with something and keep it a secret—when you don't tell another living soul—you feed the beast. It gets bigger, not smaller. When it comes to your struggles, secrecy strangles your freedom.

And it can strangle your joy too.

In 1 Chronicles 29:17 (NLT), David prays to God and says, "I know, my God, that you examine our hearts..." David knows that God sees what is inside our hearts.

So even though you might think you're alone with your struggles, you're not. God knows what's going on. And I believe he wants you to be healthy and free.

One of the ways I think you can start to break the stranglehold is to tell it to someone you trust.

They don't need to be a professional, have a leather couch, or know the perfect answer. But they need to be someone you trust, and someone who cares about you.

So reach out.

Sometimes your next best step toward greater health and freedom is easier than you think.

FRIDAY - BACK OF THE LINE!

I remember being in a huge line up for the Tim Horton's coffee shop. My friend and I were about the twentieth and twenty-first people in line.

But then, out of nowhere, some guy saw a two-foot gap between person two and three near the front... and cut in! He budded!

So my friend yelled out, "Hey buddy, the rest of us mind!" The budder pretended not to hear. So again, he called out, "Hey you, the rest of us were here first. Back of the line!"

Most people—regardless of country or culture—have a basic sense of morality, of right and wrong, deep within them. For example, most people know that it's wrong to cut in line, and that it's right to wait your turn.

Have you ever wondered where that comes from? It comes from God—the Maker of morality.

In Romans 2:15 (NLT), Paul explains that even those who don't believe in God "demonstrate that God's law is written in their hearts." In other words, God has planted a deep, basic sense of right and wrong inside humanity.

It doesn't come from society in general, or from evolution, or from majority thinking. So it has to come from an outside source—from God.

I'm telling you this for two reasons.

First, God wants us to live in a way that honours him.

Second, since this deep basic morality is in *all* people it means you have something in common with those who don't share all your beliefs. It can be treasured common ground as you build relationships and start to intro-duce others to the powerful ways Jesus amplifies and clarifies how life can be lived in an abundant, world-changing way.

God's basic compass of right and wrong is planted deep within your heart; it pulses through your veins. Use it to help heal the world.

SATURDAY - AT THE END OF YOUR ROPE

Have you ever felt like you were at the end of your rope? Like you had no energy, patience or resources left?

Those are often the times that we call out to God the most. Because we have no energy, patience or resources left, the illusion of our own self-sufficiency is shattered. We realize we can't do it on our own; that whatever we're currently doing isn't working; and that we need outside help.

In those times, God seems particularly fond of revealing himself as the rope at the end of your rope. He offers some help, direction or answered prayer, and things often start to get better.

If that's been the case for you, here's the key: When things improve, keep calling out to God with that same robust fervour that you had when the world seemed like it was coming to an end.

Just because everything is hunky-dory, it doesn't mean you need God less.

So stay on your knees, push deeper into the Bible, and keep your eyes wide open to the ways God is directing you on an hourly basis.

And do you want to know what happens when you do that? You discover that God is powerfully present and directing your life—not only when you're walking through the valley of the shadow of death, but when you're living in the lush pastures on the other side.

When Proverbs 3:5 (ESV) says, "Trust in the Lord with all your heart, and do not lean on your own understanding," it doesn't mean twenty-five percent of the time. It means one hundred percent of the time.

God is the rope at the end of your rope. It's human to trust him when you're desperate. It's discipleship to trust him when you're not.

SUNDAY...

MONDAY - ANNOYING PEOPLE

People can be really... annoying!

Who knows, maybe you think *I'm* annoying. Maybe people think *you're* annoying! Either way, you and I live our days with other people—many of whom rub us the wrong way.

You know who I'm talking about!

It could be someone at work, school or church. It could be someone on your team, or in your family or friendship circle.

The thing with people who annoy us is that they turn us off of whatever they're saying, regardless of what they're actually saying. They could have a great idea, but since it's coming *from them*, we immediately discount it.

Some people can summon a strong mood within us, and when that happens, we stop listening, and we also stop being our best. Ravi Zacharias says, "A mood can be a dangerous state of mind, because it can crush reason under the weight of feeling."[105]

Proverbs 17:24 says, "A discerning person keeps wisdom in view..." Here's something I take from that passage: Intelligent, faithful people try to focus in on what's right and try not to get distracted—not only from their own fluctuating moods, but from the frustrating people around them.

Don't let someone's bad manner distract you from their good ideas.

In a variety of situations, and with a variety of (sometimes annoying and frustrating) personality types, a discerning person does their best to keep wisdom in view.

TUESDAY - THE FAITH OF INDIANA JONES

In the movie *Indiana Jones and the Last Crusade*, Harrison Ford plays Indiana, the adventure-prone professor of archaeology.

At one point he comes to the edge of a massive cliff and needs to cross the huge gorge in front of him. But there's no bridge! It's definitely too far to jump across. So he checks his map again. It confirms that a bridge is there —but he can't see it! It makes you wonder, has it been destroyed? Is the map wrong?

The scene is tense because time is running out and Indiana needs to get to the other side to save his friend.

He stands there sweating, wondering what to do. At this point he realizes he needs to take "a leap of faith."

So he closes his eyes and takes a dramatic first step out into what looks like an abyss... and his foot comes down on something hard!! As he opens his eyes and starts to walk, the angle of the camera shifts, and we see that there was a bridge there all along. We just couldn't see it because it was an optical illusion.

But only after he took that first leap of faith could he see the path ahead.

Hebrews 11:1 (NRSV) gives us a definition of faith. "Faith is the assurance of things hoped for, the conviction of things not seen."

"...the conviction of things not seen." Like a way ahead; like what life will be like on the other side of that tough decision; like tomorrow...

If you're waiting for a perfectly clear sign from God, maybe you're not living by faith. Maybe you're not trusting God's promises to be with you, to guide you, to provide for you, and to love you.

Just as Indiana Jones discovered, sometimes you need to take that first leap of faith before the path reveals itself.

WEDNESDAY - THANKFUL IN A HELLISH EXPERIENCE

During World War Two, Corrie ten Boom and her family sheltered many Jews who were fleeing the Nazis.

In 1944 the Nazi police seized Corrie, her sister Betsie, and their father. They ended up in a concentration camp, all the while holding firm to the promises of God.

One day they moved into Barracks 28. The sewers were backed up. The mattresses were soaked with urine. And when they went to bed, they got bitten because the beds were swarming with fleas.

In a near panic, she and her sister wondered what to do. But then Betsie realized that God had given them the answer that very morning while reading 1 Thessalonians 5:18: "...give thanks in *all circumstances*..." (emphasis added)

So they made a list. They were thankful that they hadn't been separated, that their Bibles weren't seized, and that they were crammed in with so many women so that they could minister to and encourage so many.

Then Betsie suggested they even be thankful for the fleas! After all, it said to give thanks in *all* circumstances—not just nice ones. Corrie wasn't sure. But she did it anyway.

As time went on they realized they had a lot of freedom in Barracks 28. So they started a worship service. Then another. People were hearing the eternal message and hope of Jesus—people who hadn't heard it before. Women were encouraged and helped in the midst of this hellish experience.

Then one day they realized why they had such incredible freedoms. It was because of the fleas! The guards didn't want to walk into those rancid conditions so they kept their distance.

Upon learning this, Corrie remembered their prayer of thanksgiving in *all* circumstances—even in flea infestation.

What about you? Are you able to give thanks in all circumstances? I encourage you to push yourself.

When you make the effort, I think God reminds you that no matter what you're dealing with, he's always loving you, he's always providing for you, and he's also guiding you.

It's human to be thankful when things are good. It's discipleship to be thankful when times are tough.

THURSDAY - THREE TIPS TO GO DEEPER

Yesterday I shared the powerful story of Corrie ten Boom and her ability to be thankful even in hellish experiences.

Following the lead of 1 Thessalonians 5:18 where Paul says to "give thank in all circumstances," she was even able to thank God for the fleas in a World War Two concentration camp. It might seem strange, but they enabled her to help and minister to so many people.

In light of Corrie's inspiring example, I'd like to give you a few ideas to help you go deeper with your own gratitude.

The reason it makes a difference is because when you intentionally cultivate gratitude, you become better able to handle adversity.

First, make a list. When you're having a terrible week, sit down and make a list of what you're thankful for. Life itself... a home... Netflix... enough money for food... whatever.

Second, you can go for a walk (or drive) and simply recite what you're thankful for. Your car... fresh air... the gift of music to soothe your soul...

Third, when it comes to your prayer life, you can spend several days just offering prayers of thanksgiving. 'Thank you, God, for what Jesus did for us... for faith... for my friend who is always willing to listen...'

When you're feeling very UN-grateful, I know this stuff is hard. It's probably the last thing you want to do. But when you intentionally cultivate gratitude, your faith grows. Why? Because you're consciously reminding yourself of three of God's promises.

That no matter what you're going through he's always loving you.

That no matter what you're going through he's always providing for you.

That no matter what you're going through he's always guiding you.

And that helps you handle whatever (temporary) adversity you're dealing with. So when you're having a tough week, intentionally go deeper with your gratitude. It'll make you stronger and remind you that God is still at work.

It's hard to be faithful if you're not thankful.

FRIDAY - IF YOU GLORIFY THE PAST

I'm no stranger to nostalgia. I like looking back and remembering the good ole days.

But is there a point when looking back too much is harmful?

I believe that *if you glorify the past you handcuff the present*. In other words, if you put too much stock in what has happened in the past, you undermine the potential and power of what can happen next.

It's just too easy to strap on some rose-coloured glasses and make an idol out of those golden yester-years (even if they weren't so golden).

I think this was one of the things Paul was getting at when he wrote, "I press on toward the goal for the prize of the heavenly call of God in Christ Jesus." (Philippians 3:14, NLT) With God, there is always good and meaningful work to do. Your horizon always has hope.

It's good to visit the past from time to time. But don't stay there. If you think your best days are behind you, they will be.

So press on toward the goal.

If you glorify the past you handcuff the present.

SATURDAY - CHEAP DIVERSITY VS RICH DIVERSITY

"Diversity" is a big deal these days. It's the idea that we should be accepting of people from different cultures, backgrounds and beliefs. For me, it brings to mind Psalm 133:1 where it says, "How good and pleasant it is when brothers live together in unity!"

But there are two kinds of diversity. There's cheap diversity. And there's rich diversity.

Cheap diversity is when people acknowledge there are different backgrounds and beliefs in a society, but no one actually talks about the meaningful differences within these different backgrounds and belief systems.

In an effort to get along and "be nice," cheap diversity just focuses on what people have in common—and intentionally downplays anything that makes people different. At its worst, it even pretends no real differences exist. It's like asking everyone to put on a mask.

Rich diversity, on the other hand, goes deeper. It also acknowledges that there are different backgrounds and beliefs in a society, but it is open to exploring the differences in a meaningful way.

I remember working with a guy in Toronto at a financial company. He was Jewish, I was Christian. He'd ask me about my faith, and I'd ask him about his. We'd also tell jokes, talk hockey, and enjoy a beer together on Fridays after work.

And do you know what? We got along great! It would have been naïve to pretend we were the same. Were there similarities? Of course. But it would have been cheap and disrespectful to pretend our faiths and lives had no meaningful differences.

In a world desperate for peace, cheap diversity isn't the answer. I think we can get closer to the reality of diverse peoples living together in unity when we're honest about our differences, willing to talk about them, and mature enough love and respect one another in the process.

SUNDAY...

MONDAY - GETTING UNSTUCK

Do you ever feel like you're stuck? Like what you're doing on a day-to-day basis isn't getting you closer to your goals?

If so, you're not alone. But don't fear. There's hope!

Consider Moses. After he led the Hebrews out of slavery in Egypt he found himself stuck. He was serving as a leader and judge to the people and was spending every waking hour settling disputes.

So his father-in-law Jethro gave him some advice. "What you are doing is not good," he said. (Sometimes it takes family to tell you like it is!) Jethro went on to tell him to appoint more judges and spread out the workload. That way they would only have to bring the difficult cases to Moses. "That will make your load lighter," he said. (Exodus 18:17, 22)

Moses modified his methods to better accomplish his mission.

Now here's how this applies to you: Sometimes you need to modify your methods to better accomplish your mission.

Maybe you want to nurture close family relationships, but what you're doing isn't bearing fruit. If so, you probably need to modify your methods. Maybe you want more financial balance, but what you're doing isn't working. If so, you probably need to modify your methods. Maybe you want to make a better impact at work, but what you're doing isn't working. If so, you probably need to modify your methods.

What is it for you? What's your goal? If you're not getting traction, maybe you need a different pair of shoes. Even Moses had to adapt.

Sometimes you need to modify your methods to better accomplish your mission.

TUESDAY - LIFE'S GOLDEN SWEET SPOT

In high school I loved to sit around and play guitar and sing with my friends.

Sometimes the best part was coming up with harmonies. When we hit the right notes it was like sliding into a golden sweet spot.

But since we were pretty new at it, our guitar chords would occasionally be out of whack, and our harmonies would be... well, how do I say it? Not good!

In music they call it dissonance.

The art of life is harmony. And I'm not talking about music. What I mean is that you hit a golden sweet spot when your beliefs and actions are in tune with each other.

In Mark 12:33 Jesus says the first commandment is to love God "with all your heart..." He means your whole being. So if you want to love God with your whole being, but are living in a way that contradicts that desire, you're living with dissonance because your beliefs aren't matching your actions. It goes against the kind of deep soul-satisfying harmony you can experience in life.

This idea is even picked up by the American Heart Association: "Examine your values and live by them. The more your actions reflect your beliefs, the better you will feel..."[106]

I echo that!

What are you doing today that is inconsistent with your beliefs?

When your actions reflect your beliefs, you slide into that golden sweet spot called harmony. You may not get it right every time. But when you keep practicing, and when you keep leaning on the Lord for help, the music your life makes can move mountains.

WEDNESDAY - ABSTRACT FAITH DIES

I live close to an amusement park called *Canada's Wonderland*. It has roller coasters, rides, and sugary-foods galore.

I first learned about it in T.V. commercials when I was small. I could even tell you where it was, what the sign looked like, and the names of some of the big rides.

But it wasn't until I went there in person that I really got a first-hand look at how awesome it was. Initially, *Canada's Wonderland* lived in my mind as an incredible-yet-abstract idea. I had to go there myself for it be personal.

This same transition needs to happen for your faith to come alive. Faith that is abstract dies. But faith that is personal thrives. Here's the difference.

Your faith is abstract when you generally "believe" in God, but don't live differently as a result. You haven't stepped out on faith and onto the path of Jesus. In James 2:19 (NLT) it says, "You say you have faith, for you believe that there is one God. Good for you! Even the demons believe this..." You may even think the Bible is important and go to church sometimes—but there's still a distance, a disconnect. Don't feel too special about that kind of "belief." Even the demons believe!

Faith that is personal, on the other hand, means that you've committed yourself to God, and that you live your life differently as a result.

It means that you go out of your way to worship and pray on purpose. It means that you go out of your way to stand up for someone who is treated unjustly. It means that you spend your money wisely. It means that Jesus is more than a nice guy: He's an actual Saviour whose teachings impact your decisions and direction.

When you start to live like that, it's like walking into a whole new world for the very first time. Do you just "believe in God"? Or are you following Jesus? There's a difference.

Abstract faith dies. Personal faith thrives.

THURSDAY - LIVING IN THE TIME OF GOD'S PATIENCE

Every day a faithful, big-hearted woman I know wakes up, looks out her window, and says, "One more day, Lord, one more day."

She's referring to the fact that Jesus hasn't returned yet. As a result, we have—at least—one more day.

There's a lot of speculation about when Jesus will victoriously return to judge the world and make everything new again. In addition to wondering when it is going to happen, people wonder...

Why is it taking so long? What's the delay? Why isn't it happening sooner?

These questions get louder as the world around us stumbles more and more like a drunk coming out of a pub at midnight.

But 2 Peter 3:9 gives us the answer: "The Lord is not slow in keeping his promise, as some understand slowness. Instead he is patient with you, not wanting anyone to perish, but everyone to come to repentance."

God works on his own timetable. He's not in a hurry like you and I are. He is patient with us, not wanting anyone to perish, and instead wanting people to turn from their sin and brokenness and embrace his promise, eternity and goodness in Christ.

Maybe his patience is for someone you care about. Maybe his patience is *for you*.

The Mennonites have a saying: "We are living in the time of God's patience." In light of those words, Jesus' delay isn't because God *doesn't* care, but because he *does*.

And since God cares about the spiritual well-being of the people and world around us, so should we.

FRIDAY - JERKED UP BY THE COLLAR

What do you expect when you worship God?

Some of us expect to give something—whether it be our time, talent, money, voice, or prayers. But many of us expect to get something too—whether it be teaching, or friendship, or inspiration, or even comfort.

Today I want to focus on the idea of comfort. Don't get me wrong: I don't have anything against a bit of comfort. But I do have something against a lot of it.

Will Willimon tells the story about a young man on the Duke University Campus who had never been to chapel and didn't have any intention of going. He said that things in his life were going pretty well and he didn't want to get "jerked around" by God in and through a worship service.

That student knew, on a deep level, that God can use worship to speak to people, direct their lives, and sometimes make them change their course— what he called being "jerked around."

In light of that, Willimon wondered if he should put a warning sign above the entrance way to the chapel: "Please don't risk coming in here if you don't want to be jerked up by the collar and moved to somewhere where you haven't been before."[107]

It makes me think of Romans 12:2 (ESV): "Do not be conformed to this world, but be transformed by the renewal of your mind..." Because that renewal often happens through worship.

You can't be allergic to personal renewal and a disciple of Jesus at the same time.

To those who don't have a church to worship in, I think you should find one. Things happen there that don't happen anywhere else. And to those who already have a church to worship in, I think you should be open to how God may want to speak to you, direct you, and sometimes renew and alter the course of your life.

Special things happen during worship. So this Sunday, expect to hear from God. Expect a renewing of your mind that just might impact everything else.

SATURDAY - FERTILIZING JOY

Joy.

It's listed as one of the "fruit of the Spirit" in Galatians 5:22-23. That means it's something God grows in you when you become a Christian: love, *joy*, peace, patience, kindness, goodness, faithfulness, gentleness and self-control.

For some, joy grows quickly. For others, not so much. But is there anything you can do to fertilize the upward expansion of joy in your attitude and outlook?

Yes there is.

You can intentionally spend time with people who consistently see the goodness of God at work, even through the various ups and downs of life. These people have hope—consistently.

Now let me be clear. I'm not one of those people who thinks you should "only spend time with people who make you happy." That stuff drives me crazy. It feeds into a theory of relationships that is wildly shallow.

What I'm talking about here is intentionally spending time with people who consistently see the goodness of God at work, even through the various ups and downs of life. These are people who focus on and trust that God is a steadfast provider, Saviour, healer and teacher... even when they can't see all the pieces to life's puzzle.

But why should you spend time with these people?

Because they remind you that God is good, even when you can't see it. Because they teach you how to scan the horizon for hope, even when it doesn't come naturally to you. Because they show you that difficulties are temporary and don't have to define who you are.

So if you want to fertilize the upward expansion of joy in your attitude and outlook, intentionally spend time with people who consistently see the goodness of God at work, even through the various ups and downs of life.

When you do, not only will you experience more joy, but you just might start to be that joy-filled inspiration to somebody else.

SUNDAY...

MONDAY - FAITH ISN'T ABOUT CONVENIENCE

Years ago my brother told me a story that has always stuck with me.

In an effort to be financially disciplined he used an "envelope system" for his money. When he did his monthly budget, he put different amounts of money into different envelopes. One for groceries, one for gas, one for entertainment—that sort of thing.

It was all about spending money wisely and sticking to the plan.

One day he drove across Nashville to buy a CD. When he got there he realized he hadn't taken money from his "entertainment envelope" ahead of time. So instead of using a credit card, he drove all the way back home, got the money, and drove all the way back to the store to buy the CD. Talk about discipline!

He stuck to the plan even when it was inconvenient.

There's a word of wisdom in there for us too. We may or may not be employing the "envelope system," but I think we experience spiritual growth when we stick to a plan even when it's inconvenient.

What's your plan? Is it drawing closer to God? Or prioritizing certain relationships? Or living in a certain kind of way? Or contributing to your community? Or growing as a disciple of Christ?

Whatever it is, life has zillions of inconveniences. They whisper in your ear that the easy way out and the path of least resistance is always the best option. But are you going to let those nattering minions perpetually dive bomb your eyes and throw you off track?

Or are you going to stick to your guns? Proverbs 25:28 (NLT) says, "A person without self-control is like a city with broken-down walls."

Today is a new day. And sometimes the battle plan needs to be insanely simple: Stick to your guns.

Faith isn't about convenience. It's about Christ.

TUESDAY - A REST... FROM SCREENS

Writer Lettie Cowman tells about a traveler who visited Africa and used a group of guides and carriers to carry their supplies as they hiked and explored.

On the first day she was impressed because they went a huge distance. But the next day the carriers refused to move. The leader said that on the first day they had traveled too far too fast. As a result they were now waiting for their souls to catch up to their bodies.

How many of us are living lives where we feel the same way—that our souls need to catch up to our bodies![108]

As you can tell by now, I feel passionately about how important rest is. But it's not just me. In the August 2018 issue of *National Geographic Magazine*, Robert Stickgold of Harvard Medical School said that "We are now living in a worldwide test of the negative consequences of sleep deprivation."[109] Yup, it's a problem.

In Mark 6:31 Jesus saw all the activity flustering around the disciples and said: "Come with me by yourselves to a quiet place and get some rest." He knew they needed to rejuvenate if they were to be effective in what they had to do.

So I've been offering some advice about rest in our modern lives. Today my suggestion is to *create boundaries for screen time*.

Sometimes we fail to realize how much media can stimulate our brains. In many situations it can keep our mind on high-alert even though we're trying to relax.

So during the time you've set aside to rest, why not turn your phone off for a certain period of time. Maybe don't check email before 8am or after 6pm. Perhaps don't check social media when you're with your family on an outing. Or maybe sub-out a TV show for a board game or pick-up match of baseball.

Many of the forms of technology around us are so new and so powerful that we still don't know all of their effects—either positive or negative.

So as we learn how to rest, set boundaries for screen time.

People who know when to disconnect are often the ones who know when to connect to what matters most when it really matters.

WEDNESDAY - GETTING YOUR HEAD IN THE GAME

When I was small my Little League team would say a cheer right before we ran onto the field. It was a way to rally ourselves and focus on what we were about to do.

Maybe it seems strange, but it can be good practice to have a ritual before you read your Bible too. It's a way to rally and focus yourself on what you're about to do.

Too often, we read our Bibles as if nothing is going to happen as a result. We think and act like they're dusty words on a page that are far removed from our daily lives.

So you need something to shift your thinking—to help you remember you're not just reading the Bible, but receiving a word from God.

What kind of ritual am I talking about?

I simply recite Isaiah 40:8 every time I open my Bible: "...the word of our God stands forever." It gets my head in the game and focuses me on what I'm about to do. In a simple-yet-powerful way, it reminds me that I'm not just reading the Bible, but about to receive a word from God himself. Isaiah 40:8 draws our minds heavenward into a wide open space, teaching us that even though our lives are temporary, God's word and wisdom stand forever!

Here are some others you might find useful: "Your word is a lamp to my feet and a light for my path" (Psalm 119:105). "For the word of God is living and active. Sharper than any two-edged sword..." (Hebrews 4:12).

Why not give it a try? It's simple. But it gets your head in the game.

Reading the Bible is not about checking off a religious box. It's about receiving a word from God.

As Isaiah 40:8 says, "the word of our God stands forever"! Approach your Bible reading—and your life—confident that this is true.

THURSDAY - IT ALL GOES BACK IN THE BOX

Jesus told his followers to avoid storing up "treasures on earth." These are things that don't last—things like homes, money, and material things.

Are they evil in and of themselves? Of course not. As a means to an end, they can be useful. But as ends in themselves, they can be distracting and devastating.

Instead, in Matthew 6:20, Jesus says we should store up "treasures in heaven." He's referring to things that don't rust or fade. Treasures in heaven are things that honour God but are invisible—things like faith, redemption, godly priorities, and the fruit of the Spirit that is growing within you: love, joy, peace, patience, kindness, goodness, faithfulness, gentleness and self-control (Galatians 5:22-23).

This is a reminder we all need, especially because we live in such a material world. One of the messages our society preaches is that we're supposed to live in the moment, and get what we want when we want it so we can enlarge our personal happiness in the short term.

But according to Jesus, that's missing the point.

One man was teaching another how to play the board game *Monopoly*. The new guy had never played it. But he picked it up quick and accumulated boardwalks, homes, properties and money out the wazoo.

At the end of the game he was so incredibly happy. He started shoving all of the *Monopoly* money into his pockets while speculating about the new stuff he was going to buy.

That's when the first man explained the misunderstanding. The *Monopoly* money only had value while they were playing. When the game was over it was worthless and went back in the box.[110]

How many of us approach life like this? If we're not careful, we can spend our time, money and energy on things that have no lasting value. One day it will all go back in the box.

Look at your life. Don't store up treasures on earth. Instead, store up treasures in heaven.

FRIDAY - PRICELESS!

In our society, the words "rich" and "poor" have dual meanings. On one hand, someone is "rich" when they have a lot of money, and someone is "poor" when they don't.

But we also think people are "rich" when they have wisdom and strong friendships. In the same way, someone is "poor" when they neglect what's truly important in life.

I think the *MasterCard* "Priceless" commercials are so successful because they pick up on this dual meaning of the word "rich."

I remember one of them where a frizzy-haired girl is eating cereal. The narrator talks about how her parents can use *MasterCard* to buy books (for $30) and shoes (for $26) and a globe (for $18) to help her learn and be successful in life.

Then she lifts up her cereal bowl to take a drink and dumps it all over herself. Then the narrator says, 'Remembering to take it one day at a time: Priceless. There are some things money can't buy. For everything else there's *MasterCard*."[III]

The underlying message is that, although money can help you buy some things, the most important things in life are priceless.

In a similar way, when it comes to your faith, "rich" and "poor" are re-defined. Jesus says we should store up "treasures in heaven." And in 1 Timothy 6:18, Paul writes about being "rich in good deeds."

That's the kind of wealth to shoot for.

Because of the richness of Christ, you have an inexhaustible warehouse of wealth inside of you. A treasure chest without a bottom. And you can spend your days giving it away.

Giving away your talent to build up the kingdom. Giving away words of kindness and truth and wisdom. Giving away patience whenever it is needed. Giving away prayers for the hurting. Giving away time for that person who needs a friend.

That's someone who is rich. Rich in good deeds.

I can only imagine God looking upon people like that—upon people like you—and describing what your contribution to the world is like...

Priceless.

SATURDAY - THE ALMIGHTY KILL-JOY?

A lot of people think of God as an Almighty Kill-Joy. As if he never wants you to have any fun. As if he wants you to continually flagellate yourself and stick a pin in the balloon of your excitement and happiness.

This is a radical misunderstanding of God. Does God think you should do whatever you want whenever it feels good? Of course not. But despite what you may have thought, God's commands are so that you can get *more* out of life—not less.

In Jeremiah 7:23 we read what God said to the Hebrews as they left Egypt: "Obey me, and I will be your God and you will be my people. Walk in all the ways I command you, that it may go well with you."

That it may go *well* with you. The same holds for us today.

New York pastor and speaker Tim Keller says, "You harm yourself when you prioritize anything more than God."[112]

So...

When we put our jobs before God, we are twisting the order of things and inviting more difficulty into our lives.

When we put our hobbies before God, we are twisting the order of things and inviting more difficulty into our lives.

When we even put our families before God, we are twisting the order of things and inviting more difficulty into our lives.

The more closely you follow his commands, the more you'll discover that God isn't the Almighty Joy-Killer, but the Almighty Joy-Giver. He wants you to get *more* out of life—not less.

The Lord isn't deflating your joy—he's inflating it.

SUNDAY...

MONDAY - TIS ONLY A FLESH WOUND!

Most people have some annoying habits. Sometimes they're no big deal.

But sometimes those habits are actually hurtful. Maybe you're perpetually insensitive. Or maybe you're quick to criticize or trample on someone's well-meaning ideas.

And here's why it can be hard to identify the hurtful habits you may have.

It's because people aren't usually quick to tell you what they are. Why? Because they don't want to hurt your feelings. And they probably don't like conflict.

It makes me think of the Black Knight in an old *Monty Python* movie. King Arthur cuts off both of his arms in a battle, but the Knight continues to jump around enthusiastically as if nothing is wrong, proclaiming, "Tis only a flesh wound!"

He was lying to himself, downplaying the magnitude of the problem!

Sometimes we do the same thing. We lie to ourselves, downplaying the magnitude of the problem. We think we have it all together, and turn a blind eye to any hurtful habits we may have in the process.

So what should you do?

Proverbs 17:17 (NLT) says, "A friend is always loyal, and a brother is born to help in time of need."

So find a friend you trust who can speak to you candidly. Give them some warning about what you want to talk about, get together, and ask, "Where do you think I have room to grow as a person?" After they share, don't defend yourself. Just thank them. And pray on it.

"A friend is always loyal, and a brother is born to help in time of need."

TUESDAY - EVEN IF EVERYONE IS DOING IT

When I was learning how to drive a car, the instructor didn't just teach me what was in the driver's manual. He taught me other tips too.

One of those tips was to go "with the speed of traffic."

'When you're driving on the highway,' he explained, 'and everyone is going a bit faster than they should be, it can—within reason—be safer to just "go with the flow" instead of driving the actual speed limit.'

I think that's the approach many of us take when it comes to morality as well, to deciding the difference between right and wrong. Instead of consulting what God thinks, we can just cruise along "with the speed of traffic"—simply because that's what everyone else is doing.

But a leader in ancient Christianity named Augustine offered a clear corrective that still resonates today: "Wrong is wrong even if everyone is doing it. Right is right even if no one is doing it."

I like that. Right and wrong flow from the all-knowing and all-wise heart of God, not the latest opinion polls.

I don't want to come across as a stick-in-the-mud. In fact, I struggle with this too. The momentum of our society can be so strong that blending in is simply the path of least resistance. But as God's people, we need to seek his will first. As it says in Isaiah 5:20, "Woe to those who call evil good and good evil, who put darkness for light and light for darkness..."

Are you in the process of making a big decision? Are you wondering if your life is headed in the right direction? Does anyone ever ask you to give some guidance or advice?

If so, seek God's eternal teaching, not our society's temporary trends. "Wrong is wrong even if everyone is doing it. Right is right even if no one is doing it."

WEDNESDAY - HOW TO BE WEALTHY (WITHOUT ANY MONEY)

According to Mother Teresa, the spiritual poverty in the western world is *worse* than the physical poverty in Calcutta.

She said, "You in the West have millions of people who suffer such terrible loneliness and emptiness... These people are not hungry in the physical sense, but they are in another way. They know they need something more than money, yet they don't know what it is. What they are missing really is a living relationship with God."[113]

Mother Teresa tapped into the fact that there is a spiritual void in many people's lives—a void they try to fill with money, possessions and stuff.

But in the Bible, Paul teaches that people who are rich in this life shouldn't put their hope in money. It's a hope that is both false and fleeting. Instead, they should put their hope in God. His command is for people to "be rich in good deeds, and to be generous and willing to share" (1 Timothy 6:18).

How's that for counter-cultural? You get rich by *giving*—not getting. But I don't think we'll ever be able to actually live that way if we don't have that "living relationship with God."

When a relationship is dead, there is no communication. When a relationship is dead, there is no joy. When a relationship is dead, there is no trust.

But when a relationship is living, there is communication; there is joy; and there is trust. And since you have so much, you also have much to give away.

Do you want to side-step the spiritual poverty of our time? Then put your hope in God, and "be rich in good deeds" and "generous and willing to share."

You get rich by giving not getting.

THURSDAY - LEAVING A LEGACY OF WEALTH

We're probing the idea of how to be wealthy (without any money).

In 1 Timothy 6:18 Paul writes, "Command them to do good, to be rich in good deeds, and to be generous and willing to share."

With that in mind, today I want to ask you this question: Do you spend so much of your time and money on yourself that you can't bless or help anyone else when the opportunity arises? Here's why that question is important.

If you're going to be "rich in good deeds" and "generous and willing to share" you need the mental and physical resources to step in and step up when required.

Unfortunately, so many of us are focused on ourselves that when an opportunity arises to help someone else it feels more like a burden than an opportunity. And so many of us are financially stretched (and undisciplined) that when an opportunity arises to bless someone materially, we just can't do it, or don't want to.

It's hard work to come back into balance. I need to work at it all the time. And I realize it takes discipline to free up money for the benefit of others.

But the end result doesn't just help others—it helps *you*.

Do you want to know what happens to people who go out of their way to give practical help and hope to the people and relationships around them? They become rich. Are they happy every single moment of their lives? No they're not. But that's not the point. The point is to glorify God and get in on the ways Jesus is renovating the world.

Think through today's key question: Do you spend so much of your time and money on yourself that you can't bless or help anyone else when the opportunity arises?

As you ponder it, remember that the greater joy in life isn't being perpetually happy with lots of stuff. It's glorifying God, and getting in on the wonder-filled ways Jesus is renovating the world.

That's leaving a legacy of wealth.

FRIDAY - WHEN "MORE! MORE! MORE!" ISN'T THE ANSWER

In yesterday's devotional I talked about how to be wealthy (without any money).

Let's push further on that same theme. Why? Because thinking this stuff through helps us live more abundant lives.

In 1 Timothy 6:6 Paul says that "godliness with contentment is great gain." In other words, true wealth is the result of living a godly life alongside an attitude of contentment.

What I'd like to focus on is that word "content."

Our society isn't really good at teaching contentment. In fact, it often seems to preach a philosophy that we continually need "More! More! More!" Twenty-four hours a day!

In the *U.S. News & World Report*, Linda Kulman wrote how Americans shell out more for garbage bags than ninety of the world's two hundred and ten countries spend for everything.

And in a book called *Money*, Bob and Rusty Russell say that in 1900, the average person wanted seventy-two different things and considered eighteen of them essential. Today the average person wants five hundred things and considers one hundred of them essential![114]

Unfortunately, it seems that the more we have, the more we want. And the more we have, the more we think we have to have.

So my question is this: Are you content with what you have?

I'm not saying we shouldn't sometimes treat ourselves or want some nice things. But what I am saying is that if we are *never* satisfied, and if we are *always* looking for the next best thing, maybe we simply don't trust that God will provide for us.

Maybe we're more in love with material things that won't last than we are with spiritual things that will.

In verse 10 Paul writes: "Some people, eager for money, have wandered from the faith and pierced themselves with many griefs." Don't let that be you. Work on being content. Trust that God provides. And the result will be "great gain" in your life.

SATURDAY - ACTIVELY LOOKING FOR OPPORTUNITIES

We've been exploring how we can be wealthy (regardless of how much money we have).

Our main verse has been 1 Timothy 6:18. Paul says: "Command them to do good, to be rich in good deeds, and to be generous and willing to share."

So far I've asked you some critical gut-check questions. They're supposed to help you evaluate whether you're truly in a good position to be "rich in good deeds" and "generous and willing to share."

Here's today's question:

Are you actively looking for opportunities to do good deeds?

The key words are "actively looking."

For too many of us, we start the week in a hurry. We feel behind before we even get out the door. Plus, we can get stressed about what so-and-so said or X, Y, or Z.

That kind of a mindset turns our thoughts inward toward ourselves instead of outward toward other people.

So when an opportunity comes up to do a good deed for someone, instead of seeing it as an opportunity, we can see it as a burden. It's just one more thing to do.

So here's what I encourage you to do:

Start your week with a different frame of mind. Pray for God to open your eyes to the good deeds that can be done. See them not as a burden, but an opportunity.

Immature people tend to think that challenges are problems to be avoided. Mature people tend to think that challenges are opportunities to be seized.

Here's a prayer to get you started:

Dear God,
Free me from the tyranny of a rushed life.
Remind me that you're in control, no matter how much I spin and scurry.
Open my eyes to the opportunities to do good and be generous,
So that I can fly into today and tomorrow with your wings of purpose.
I pray these things in name of Jesus, the ultimate Giver.
Amen.

SUNDAY...

MONDAY - NO MATTER THE CHAOS AROUND YOU

We live in turbulent times.

In North America, over forty million people are diagnosed with Generalized Anxiety Disorder. There seems to be sabre-rattling between big nations. There are natural disasters. Terror attacks continue. Plus, the past one hundred years have been plagued with global conflict.

All of this amplifies the need for peace. But how do we get there?

And how do followers of Jesus help make it happen?

Last week I was drawn to 2 Chronicles 7:12-14 (ESV). When King Solomon had finished building the beautiful temple in Jerusalem, God spoke these words to him:

"I have heard your prayer... if my people who are called by my name humble themselves, and pray and seek my face and turn from their wicked ways, then I will hear from heaven and will forgive their sin and heal their land."

Since God was talking about the temple, his people are to be a people of worship. They are to humble themselves, pray, seek his face, and turn from their wicked ways. And then, God will hear, forgive, and heal their land.

I realize that was 3000 years ago, and that the Jerusalem temple has been built, destroyed, rebuilt, destroyed and rebuilt again. But there is something enduring about those words.

No matter what is happening in the society around us, we can be a people of worship, of humility, of prayer, of seeking God's face, and of turning from our evil ways and back toward the path of love.

That is a legitimate way to advance world peace. No matter what age we live in.

You can't always have a say in what happens *around* you; but you can have a say in what happens *through* you.

Let's be a part of the healing our world so desperately needs. No matter the chaos around you, Christ can shine through you.

TUESDAY - WHEN TRAUMA AND DANGER COME

In 2008 it rained for days and days in northern England.

A family in Chester-le-Street went out for a walk. The three-year-old daughter, Laura, wanted to jump in the puddles. So that's just what she did. She ran toward a puddle at the side of the street and jumped!

Then she disappeared.

Laura's parents ran over and quickly realized what had happened. There had been so much rain that the gutters were full and had popped off the grate cover. When Laura had jumped, she went right down the hole.

Thinking quickly, the father, Mark Baxter, figured that the gutter emptied into the river one hundred yards away. He ran as fast as he could, jumped into the river, and pulled out his little girl before it was too late.

In an interview afterward, Mark said that worst-case-scenarios had come into his head. But he refused to think the worst.

For her part, three-year-old Laura said that when she found herself in the rushing water, she immediately did the "star float." She had been taking swimming lessons and was taught to do that if she ever experienced unexpected danger.[115]

Here's why I say all this.

Life is full of trauma and danger. And at some point, all of us will have to deal with our fair share. What I love about the Baxter's story is that in a crisis they were able to be at their best. They didn't let worst-case-scenarios or panic determine their actions. They rose to the occasion.

In Romans 15:13 (ESV), Paul says this: "May the God of hope fill you with all joy and peace in believing, so that by the power of the Holy Spirit you may abound in hope."

People who "abound in hope" are those who have been so filled up by God, that in the midst of trauma and danger, they summon the hopeful best within themselves—not the despairing worst.

If you need motivation to keep growing in your journey with Jesus, this is it. Trauma and danger come. And when they do, you want the best to come out of you, not the worst.

Not only for yourself, but for the people around you.

WEDNESDAY - TEMPTATION IN THE AGE OF THE QUICK FIX

Because you're human, you get tempted.

Like many other people you get tempted to do or pursue something that seems good at the time, but will immediately or eventually lead to harm in your own life or in the lives of the people around you.

Some temptations are obvious. Like the temptation to steal something, or flirt with someone you shouldn't, or cheat, or over-spend, or gossip.

But here's something I think we all need to do when trying to make good decisions (and not sloppy ones that will come back to haunt us).

Wait.

We live in the age of the quick fix. And I think Satan preys on our weakness to want instant everything. I imagine him whispering into our ears, 'Don't think about it, just do it! Now! What are you waiting for? Are you chicken?'

But bad short-term decisions often lead to hurtful long-term consequences.

Here is how James 1:14-15 (NLT) says it: "Temptation comes from our own desires, which entice us and drag us away. These desires give birth to sinful actions. And when sin is allowed to grow, it gives birth to death."

Yikes! I want my actions to give birth to life, not death! So if you're facing temptation, and especially if you have a habit of rushing into things...

Wait.

Seek God's will, and be thoughtful. Bad short-term decisions often lead to hurtful long-term consequences.

THURSDAY - SATAN

A lot of people don't think about Satan very much. Sure, they read about him in the Bible sometimes, and hear an allusion to him in a movie now and then.

But he probably doesn't really figure into their daily thoughts.

But that's the thing. He often *does* figure into our daily thoughts. It's just that we're not aware of how he works.

Jesus calls Satan the "father of lies" (John 8:44). And the lies he plants often go unchecked. Why? Because we think the lies in our own heads are coming from us—and not from the Evil One.

But what if they were?

Don't get me wrong. I'm not saying you're possessed. And I'm not saying Satan is the author of every bad thought you have. But you need to be confident about who you are as a follower of Jesus. This helps you stand strong and identify the Deceiver's lies before they take root.

If you belong to Christ you are... a child of God, a member of his very own body, loved, a citizen of heaven, salt of the earth, God's co-worker, God's temple, valuable, chosen to do good works, redeemed and forgiven, seated with Christ in the heavenly realms, able to access God directly through the Holy Spirit, and able to do all things through Christ who gives you strength!

If that's who you truly are, why in the world would you ever allow the smallest thought of self-deprecating and self-defeating discouragement to enter your head?

God encourages. Satan discourages. Remember that.

Maybe this Satan stuff is new to you. Maybe you've never taken it seriously. Maybe you think I'm crazy. But if Jesus takes Satan seriously, so should we. It's important for us to live life with both eyes open. Satan's greatest achievement in modern times is convincing thoughtful people he's not really there.

So stand tall. Be unafraid. Root yourself in the truth of who God made you to be.

Living in the light of that truth crushes the head of the one who would love to suck the confidence from your soul.

God encourages. Satan discourages. Who are you going to listen to?

FRIDAY - DRUNK ON NOVELTY?

One of the invisible values of our society is novelty.

That means we often prioritize and cherish ideas that are *new*.

Now don't get me wrong. I'm a big fan of new ideas. The problem is when new ideas aren't necessarily good ideas. When we're star-struck with the "latest and greatest," we get drunk on novelty, forfeit our better judgment, and adopt a naïve philosophy of change for the sake of change.

My friend Grant Vissers has a podcast. In one of the episodes he interviews Frank Bealer, author and CEO of Phase Family Centres. Here's what he said: "Sometimes change feels like progress, but it's not always true."[116]

What I like about Bealer's insight is that it challenges the idea that novelty, change and progress are undeniably linked.

Sometimes they are. But sometimes they aren't.

It's up to you and me to use our brains to make decisions and lead our lives in a way that honours good, godly ideas—and not just novel ones.

Proverbs 19:2 (NLT) says, "Enthusiasm without knowledge is no good; haste makes mistakes."

When a new idea comes along—and you find yourself wanting to go "all in"—ask yourself whether you're drunk on novelty and hastily wading into what might be a mistake, or whether you've thought it through and are basing your decisions and actions on a truly good and godly idea.

"Sometimes change feels like progress, but it's not always true."

SATURDAY - JUDGING AN IDEA ON ITS ABUSE

There are a lot of good ideas out there. But a lot of these good ideas are told to us by flawed people or by flawed organizations.

Let me tell you what I mean and then what it means for you.

Some people discount your ideas simply because you've been inconsistent with how you live out your values (or don't live out your values).

Some people discount ideas within Christianity because some Christians aren't as loving as they should be.

Some people discount ideas from the government because that same government (or political party) didn't follow through on their commitment.

That can be really frustrating. I'm with you on that one.

But according to an ancient leader in the church called Augustine, "We are never to judge a philosophy by its abuse."

In other words, just because some people aren't able to live up to a certain idea or standard, that doesn't mean that idea or standard is wrong.

For example, Jesus tells us to love our enemies and to pray for those who persecute us (Matthew 5:44), and to love our neighbours as ourselves (Mark 12:31). I'll forever be working on that. But just because I sometimes miss the mark, that doesn't mean Jesus is wrong.

So what does this mean for you?

It means that you and I need to work at figuring out the truth of things, instead of just discounting an idea because it's been abused, or because it's being promoted by someone we don't like, or by someone who is flawed.

Instead, let's judge it by whether it is consistent with the character of God, and whether it will help us be a blessing to the people around us.

As Augustine said, "We are never to judge a philosophy by its abuse."

SUNDAY...

MONDAY - MEET ADVERSITY, YOUR TEACHER AND TRAINER

A bunch of people were put in a room and each given the same short story to read. It was about a young man who went through several difficult hardships.

Then they were given a pencil and were invited to cross out anything in the story they thought would result in the young man having "a better life."

So they went through and crossed off things you'd expect—like accidents, relationship difficulties, and health problems.

Then they learned that the young man had later reported that it was *because* of his many hardships that he was able to have a better life. They taught him courage and perseverance and faith. He was an overcomer. And you can't be an overcomer if you don't have anything to overcome.

Then the people were asked if there was anything they'd change about what they had crossed out.

I'm not suggesting that we want difficult things to happen. But what if we looked at them in a different way?

What if your willingness to lean on God and overcome a difficulty resulted in... a more faithful you, a more steadfast you, a wiser you, a more helpful you—ready and willing to assist someone overcome a difficulty and have hope for a new day?

Use adversity as a teacher and trainer instead of a death sentence.

You gotta admire the perspective of James in the Bible: "Consider it pure joy, my brothers and sisters, whenever you face trials of many kinds, because you know that the testing of your faith produces perseverance" (James 1:2-3).

What difficulty have you faced? Use adversity as a teacher and trainer instead of a death sentence.

TUESDAY - STRIKE ME BLIND IN ONE EYE!

Today I share a story I've adapted from William White.[117]

It's about two business men. Their stores were across the road from one another and they had an incredible rivalry.

When one made a big sale, he'd walk over to the other man's store to boast about it. And the other did the same. This went on month by month and year by year.

So one day God sent an angel to one of the business men. "The Lord God has chosen to give you a great gift," the angel said. "Whatever you desire, you will receive. Ask for riches, long life, or healthy children, and the wish is yours. There is one stipulation," the angel cautioned. "Whatever you receive, your competitor will get twice as much. If you ask for one thousand gold coins, he will receive two thousand. If you become famous, he will become twice as famous."

The angel smiled. "This is God's way of teaching you a lesson."

The business man thought about it for a minute, and then said, "You will give me anything I request?" The angel nodded. Then the man's face darkened as he gave his answer:

"I ask that you strike me blind in one eye."

All of us can get angry. There are times when our anger is justified. But there are times when it isn't.

If left unchecked, it will start to darken how you see the world. Not only will it have a negative impact on the people around you, but it will have a negative impact on you as well.

James 1:20 (NLT) says, "Human anger does not produce the righteousness God desires." Anger tends to feed itself—and not with faith, hope and love.

So if you have a deep unsettled anger, or even if you have a penchant for letting your frustrations fester, take steps to deal with it.

Bring it to God. Talk to a friend. Read the gospels and be reminded of who you were created to be.

Smoldering anger is a flame-throwing boomerang. It doesn't just hurt others—it hurts you.

WEDNESDAY - SIFTING FOR WISDOM IN THE AGE OF "EXPERTS"

Do you sometimes feel like we live in a time that is saturated with "experts"?

There are food experts and weather experts and psychology experts and sports experts and economy experts. They share their wisdom on talk shows, books and blog posts.

I think a lot of that is great. We can really benefit from the research and insight of smart people.

But it can also be intimidating, especially when we want to know something about God or God's will for our lives. We can wrongly assume that we can only get that insight from a spiritual or religious "expert"— someone who has had years of formal training.

Now is it true that teachers, authors and pastors have good wisdom to share? Of course they do. (Full disclosure: I'm a pastor!)

They're a valuable part of the mix. But they're not the only ingredient.

One of the best ways to know more about God or God's will for your life is to simply talk to a friend who is also trying to follow Jesus. As I read the Bible, and as I watch relationships unfold around me, what I notice time and time again is that God uses normal people to help other normal people in extraordinary ways.

This doesn't mean your friend's voice is the same as God's voice; but humble godly friends can help you clarify some of your thinking about God.

Proverbs 12:15 (NLT) says, "Fools think their own way is right, but the wise listen to others." There is something *wise* about admitting you don't have all the answers. There is something *wise* about the search. There is something *wise* about proactively listening to someone else on the path.

If you want to know more about God or God's will for your life, be proactive. One of the things you can do is simply talk to a friend who is also trying to follow Jesus. Tell your story. Listen to theirs. Ask questions. Maybe share a laugh. And perhaps a cry. And pray.

God can use normal people to help other normal people in extraordinary ways.

THURSDAY - GOD'S GOT THIS

"Faith" is a word that is easy to throw around. "Journey of faith," "Faith in God," "Have a little faith."

But what does it mean?

Hebrews 11:1 (ESV) says this: "Now faith is the assurance of things hoped for, the conviction of things not seen." Can't argue with that. It's in the Bible!

But in flushing out the wider biblical vision which circles around the person of Jesus, Ravi Zacharias provides further clarity. He says that "faith is a confidence in the person of Jesus Christ and in His power, so that even when His power does not serve my end, my confidence in Him remains because of who He is."[118]

To me, that's the "assurance of things hoped for" and the "conviction of things not seen." I am confident in who Jesus is and in his power regardless of what's happening in my life. His wisdom and goodness isn't limited to my own ability to see and measure it.

If we believe in God only to get from God, it's not really belief—it's a fast food spirituality that is about our wants instead of his will.

Hard things happen in life. Through them all *trust God*. Confusing things happen in life. Through them all *trust God*. Surprising things happen in life. Through them all *trust God*.

One day all difficulties will come to an end—but you won't, and neither will God. So root your faith not in your temporary conditions, but in an eternal relationship.

There's a saying out there I sometimes hear: "You've got this!" I get the sentiment. And I appreciate it.

But the heart of faith—the "assurance of things hoped for" and "the conviction of things not seen"—isn't so much that "You've got this," but that God does.

Through the storms of life, that's the greatest hope of all.

FRIDAY - BACK TO BASICS

Recently my six-year-old son and I grabbed our baseball gloves and went out to the front lawn to play catch. He's been getting better and better. So we've gotten into the habit of backing up further and further away from each other so that it's more of a challenge.

But we hadn't played catch in a while. So when we resumed our usual far-away positions, he kept missing—and he kept getting frustrated.

So to fix the problem, we moved closer—almost too close. This way, he could catch everything. As a result, his confidence went up. Soon we were back at our previous far-away positions making great catches and having a tonne of laughs.

Most people I know want to make progress in their faith. So they pile up different religious practices. I'm not knocking that. But if you're not ready for it you can end up getting frustrated. You keep dropping the proverbial ball and your mental energy goes into feeling bad about yourself instead of dialing in to the Lord.

Sometimes you need to simplify your practices to move forward.

If this is you, get back to basics. It's like my son and I standing six feet apart playing catch. Slowly say the Lord's Prayer each morning. Read a few paragraphs of the New Testament or a Psalm before bed. Go to church on Sunday.

There's a beautiful line in Psalm 119:2 that says, "Blessed are they who keep his statutes and seek him with all their heart." It says to seek him with all your heart. But it doesn't reference pace or speed.

If your spiritual house is on the brink of breakdown, ensure your foundation stones are set firmly in place, and get back to basics.

Sometimes you need to simplify your practices to move forward.

SATURDAY - BUT YOU SHOULDN'T GET MORE CRANKY

In a prophecy about the Messiah's birth, Isaiah said that Jesus would not only be called "Prince of Peace," but "Wonderful Counselor" (Isaiah 9:6).

But rarely do we think of Jesus as a counselor. Maybe that's because we (a) don't pay him to listen to us, and (b) can't picture him with a leather couch.

Even still, it's a helpful way to think about one of his roles in your life: Counselor. Even though the back-and-forth is different than it would be with someone you'd find through Google, speaking honestly with Christ as if you were in a counseling relationship, and listening to his wisdom and direction through what he says in the Gospels, is a powerful ongoing conversation that directs your thinking and decision-making.

As you go deeper with him through his wonderful counseling, the more you discover the peace of which he is the Prince.

My friend Matt Brough wrote a book called *Let God Be God*. In it he says, "If you are spending time with Jesus, you will get angry at injustice from time to time, but you shouldn't get more cranky."[119]

I love that. If your journey of faith keeps leaving you more and more cranky, it's probably because you're either not being fully honest with your Counselor about what you're going through, or you're unwilling to listen to his words of wisdom.

In therapy relationships, the counselor is way more effective when the patient is brutally honest. So as you think of Christ as your Counselor, be more honest than you're currently being. Let him work. And receive back his words with authority as you ponder them in the Gospel stories.

Think of Jesus as the Wonderful Counselor he is. And you'll increasingly discover the peace of which he is the Prince.

SUNDAY...

MONDAY - SURVIVING A FIRING SQUAD

Before he was a writer, Fyodor Dostoevsky was arrested by the czar of Russia and sentenced to death by firing squad.

Leading up to the day of his execution, Dostoevsky became acutely aware of the gift of life. He savoured every moment, every meal, every memory. He knew he had only so long to enjoy life on earth.

On the appointed day he was blindfolded and taken before the firing squad. In a moment of terror, the guns went off.

But he didn't die!

After his blindfold was removed, he learned that the bullets were blanks. It had been a cruel psychological trick, a kind of torture.

From that day forward, Dostoevsky was a new man. He was even more thankful for normal things like the warm sun, and more gracious toward others. His senses had been heightened, and he carried that passion and attention to detail into his writing.

He also carried a deep gratitude and appreciation for being fully alive—for his second lease on life.[120]

It sounds like 2 Corinthians 5:17 (NLT): That "anyone who belongs to Christ has become a new person. The old life is gone; a new life has begun!"

If you belong to Christ, things are now different—you've got new eyes, new ears, and a new voice to speak hope to the people around you.

If you belong to Christ, you are unceasingly thankful because even though you deserve the worst, God gives you his best.

If you belong to Christ, you've got a new lease on life, and are summoned to live it out in a way that brings heaven closer to earth.

"Anyone who belongs to Christ has become a new person. The old life is gone; a new life has begun!"

Be awake. Be thankful. Be a blessing.

You've already come out the other side of death. So live today like you're fully alive.

TUESDAY - WHEN YOU KNOW WHAT'S IMPORTANT...

There was a young boy who really wanted a new BMX Bike for Christmas. But his parents knew it was expensive and weren't keen on it.

One night his mom even caught him praying about it. She criticized him because there were so many other things he should be praying about instead.

The next morning the mom went downstairs and admired their beautiful nativity scene. But she saw that something was wrong with it. The wise men and shepherds were there. So were Joseph and Jesus.

But Mary was missing.

She went closer and noticed a note where Mary would normally be. The note said, "Dear Jesus, if you ever want to see your mother again, you had better get me that BMX bike."[121]

It's a funny little story that highlights how we can so often make our faith exclusively about getting what *we* want instead of what *Jesus* wants.

In Matthew 20:28 Jesus said that he "did not come to be served, but to serve..." So if we are the kind of people who want to follow Jesus (instead of ignore him) we are probably going to want to live our lives less like consumers and more like Christ.

Here's another way to think about it. When you *know* what's important, you *do* what's important. Since we *know* what's important to Jesus we *do* what's important to Jesus. That's why we serve.

Instead of making our faith exclusively about getting what *we* want, let's do some honest soul-searching and ask whether we're living our lives in a way that advances what *Jesus* wants.

When you *know* what's important, you *do* what's important.

WEDNESDAY - THE VIEW FROM THE TOP

Every day we're faced with choices about what route we're going to take. These come in the form of decisions. A lot of them are simple. You don't even have to think about them.

But there are also *difficult* choices. These are choices like whether to do the right thing or the easy thing; whether to stand up for someone who is being treated unfairly or look the other way; or whether to sacrifice some of your energy and love for some greater purpose.

It's easy to make the choice that makes life easier for you in the short term. But life isn't about being easy. In fact, if you want to be wiser, have stronger relationships, and be closer to God, it's often going to take work.

Proverbs 13:4 (NLT) says, "Lazy people want much but get little, but those who work hard will prosper."

I really enjoy watching some of those old T.V. episodes of *The Waltons*—not because they represent a better or more faithful era, but because so many of the episodes are about developing personal integrity.

One of the characters was Grandpa Walton. He didn't just live on the Blue Ridge Mountains of Virginia, they lived in him. And one of his expressions went like this:

"When you come to a mountain, there's two things you can do. You can either go around it or climb over it. The first way is easiest, but you miss the view from the top."

When it comes to the decisions you have to make, some of them seem like mountains—big and intimidating. The question you need to ask yourself is this: What route are you going to take?

"When you come to a mountain there's two things you can do. You can either go around it or climb over it. The first way is easiest, but you miss the view from the top."

THURSDAY - A SURPRISING KIND OF FATIGUE

Fatigue comes in many different forms.

Not getting enough sleep can leave you tired.

Being stressed can leave you tired.

I think that not eating well or exercising can also leave you tired.

But there's another kind of tired that I want to tell you about. And you definitely don't need it dragging down your soul.

In 2 Corinthians 1:12 (NLT), Paul writes this: "We can say with confidence and a clear conscience that we have lived with a God-given holiness and sincerity in all our dealings."

Wouldn't it be great if you and I could look back on each day and say the same thing? That with confidence and a clear conscience we lived with a God-given holiness and sincerity in all our dealings?

One of the outcomes of living like that would be less fatigue. Why?

Because it's tiring to live your life in a way that contradicts what you know is right. It's like trying to swim upstream.

Kyle Idleman says it like this: "It's exhausting trying to live in a way that violates your heart."[122]

Are you fatigued? Maybe you just need more sleep. Maybe you're stressed. Maybe you're eating too much junk food and are stagnant most of the time.

But maybe you just need to look at your day-to-day life, and make some changes so that the way you live more closely reflects your beliefs—so that you end more of your days with a clear conscience, and a confidence that you've done your best to be godly and sincere in your dealings.

As Idleman reminds us, "It's exhausting trying to live in a way that violates your heart."

FRIDAY - STOP IT

In John 8:44 Jesus calls the Devil "a liar and the father of lies." As a deceiver, he loves to convince God's children that they are less than who they truly are. So stop beating yourself up. The Devil doesn't need another ally.

SATURDAY - THE COURAGE TO FACE RIDICULE FOR GOD

Over time we have kind of lost sight of the fact that when Joseph married Mary he stepped into a world of ridicule. After all, she would have given birth to Jesus *less* than nine months after their marriage.

That might not be too uncommon today, but back then it was a serious issue.

If Mary's pregnancy had been the result of unfaithfulness it could have been punishable by death; it would have brought shame on their families; and it could have risked Joseph's business and reputation. Who would've believed that God himself was the baby's father?!!

But Joseph had courage in the face of ridicule. He followed God's command and "took Mary home as his wife" (Matthew 1:24). He cared more about what God thought than what other people thought.

And so can you.

In our society, with each passing year, your faith is going to make you stand out. And you'll sometimes face ridicule for your beliefs. Because of that it's tempting to downplay the importance of—and never talk about —your faith.

But don't give in.

Joseph had the courage to face ridicule for God, and so can you.

If you just go with the flow and do what everyone else is doing your life and faith will probably be shallow. But they can be more meaningful if you simply, humble and confidently stand firm in your faith.

Worship God with joy. Be boldly generous in all things. And don't hesitate to tell the truth about what life really means to you.

Joseph had the courage to face ridicule for God—and you can too.

SUNDAY...

MONDAY - THE BEGGAR AND THE KING

Elisabeth Elliot tells us a story about a beggar and a King.

A beggar was sitting at the side of the street with his hat outstretched asking for money.

Then he noticed that the King himself was coming, complete with his whole entourage. This was his lucky day! How could the King refuse to give him something?

So he stretched out his hat. But the King, instead of *giving* something, *asked* for something! The beggar was surprised and shocked. But wanting to be a loyal subject, he looked into his hat and fished out three small grains of rice and gave them to the King who smiled and went on his way.

At the end of the day, the beggar looked into his hat to see what was there after his full day of begging. To his amazement, there, in the place where the three grains of rice had been, were three small grains of pure gold!

At that moment he realized what had happened. When he gave the King the three grains of rice, the King had mysteriously replaced them with a greater gift.

Considering this, and considering his own initial reluctance to give, the beggar thought, 'O, how I wish I had given him all!'

In this story, you and I are the beggar, and Jesus is the King.

How often do we hesitate to give him our time, our talents, our service, our money, our energy and our courage? Maybe we think it's because it will cause us to lose something. We think we'll lose something of temporary value, when we'll really gaining something of eternal value. But as it says in Acts 20:35: "It is more blessed to give than to receive."

He gives us so much more than we give him.

'O, how I wish I had given him all!'[123]

Don't hesitate to be generous to God and others. God gives us so much more than we give him.

TUESDAY - THE GREAT DISARMER

This week you will meet someone who upsets you. They might upset you a little. Or they might upset you a lot.

Maybe they're in your own family and say something to rub you the wrong way. Or maybe they're a friend, classmate or co-worker whose actions scratch the invisible chalkboard of your brain. So how do you keep your head? How do you respond as your *best* you, instead of the *reactive* you who is probably going to regret what you said or did?

Proverbs 14:29 (NLT) says, "People with understanding control their anger; a hot temper shows great foolishness." It means that when you react to people and situations with a hot temper it's evidence of your own foolishness. But people of understanding control their anger.

That's the key. Understanding. It's The Great Disarmer.

When someone upsets you—once, twice, or time and time again!—try to learn more about them and their situation. What is at the root of their words? What has happened in their past that has contributed to their outlook?

Chances are, they're wrestling with something you just can't see. That doesn't excuse bad behaviour, but it does slow you down from judging, wagging your tongue, or being hurtful when you don't have all the facts.

They've had tough experiences that contribute to who they are. Just like you.

Henry Wadsworth Longfellow says, "If we could read the secret history of our enemies, we should find in each man's life sorrow and suffering enough to disarm all hostility."

Those who pursue understanding are the ones who pursue peace—not only with others, but within themselves.

WEDNESDAY - IN THE SHADOW OF A STINGY GOD?

Theologian Kosuke Koyama once said in a speech that "every Christian must decide whether we serve a stingy God or a generous God."

I wasn't in the audience when he said that. But my guess is that he was talking about how our understanding of God impacts how we treat other people. If we think we serve a stingy God, we'll be stingy toward others. And if we think we serve a generous God, we'll be generous toward others.

At this point you're probably guessing what I'm going to say next—that God is generous and so we should be generous toward others.

I could. But I won't.

Instead, I'm going to say that you need to be generous toward *yourself*.

In Psalm 23:3 David says that God "restores his soul." What if God wanted to restore your soul as well—but you kept cutting him off at the pass?

Are there days when you're run ragged? Sure. Are there days when you're tired to the bone? Of course.

But make those days the exception not the rule.

What if you took the full hour for lunch? What if you decide to not beat yourself up when you get your next bad grade? What if you took a twenty-four-hour break from social media and the game of constant comparison? What if you treated yourself to an evening out? What if you got together with a friend to just laugh?

As Koyama said, "every Christian must decide whether we serve a stingy God or a generous God."

Yes. God is generous.

So why not inhale some of the restoration God can work in your soul and be generous... to yourself.

THURSDAY - THE BATTLE PLAN

Psalm 95:1 (ESV) says, "Oh come, let us sing to the Lord; let us make a joyful noise to the rock of our salvation!"

It's no secret that I like statements of truth which are clear, practical, and to-the-point. I came across one of these recently by author and speaker Lysa TerKeurst. Here it is:

"My battle plan. Worry less. Worship more."[124]

Isn't that great?

I like it because it reminds us that life isn't a walk in the park—it's a battle. And if you want to worry less in the midst of that battle, you are well advised to worship more.

One of the reasons that's important is because worship draws our eyes away from ourselves and our obsessively worrying ways, and back to God, our un-moving, un-intimidated and never-failing Lord—the "rock of our salvation!"

Do you feel like life is getting away from you or getting you down? If so, adopt a battle plan:

Worry less. Worship more.

FRIDAY - HURTING TRUMPS BUSYNESS

Writer, speaker and scientist Alister McGrath says that "To love God entails loving what God loves."[125]

So who does God love?

God loves the emotionally needy. God loves the braggart. God loves the one we overlook. God loves the forgotten. God loves those who are struggling.

1 John 3:18 says, "let us not love with words or speech but with actions and in truth."

That's why you love the emotionally needy. That's why you love the brag-gart. That's why you love the one you usually overlook. That's why you love the forgotten. That's why you love those who are struggling.

When we think of people who are "needy" we often think of people in extreme situations. And that certainly applies to them. But there are people around you every day in very normal situations—people like you—who need a word or touch of grace.

I know you're busy. And that some days get away from you. And that some days you get it wrong.

But if someone is hurting, *hurting trumps busyness.*

That's part of what it means to be a disciple.

SATURDAY - "I JUST DON'T SEE GOD WORKING IN MY LIFE"

Over the years I've spoken with some people who have told me something like this:

"I just don't see God working in my life."

Because of that, they stop looking, and they stop expecting him to be working in their lives. So let me offer some advice:

When you *do* the work of God, you *see* the work of God.

I'm not saying that God won't show up wherever or whenever he pleases. But what I've found is that when you go out of your way to serve and help other people, you start to see God's presence and work in your life in more powerful ways.

The apostle Paul gives some advice in Philippians 2:4 (ESV): "Let each of you look not to his own interests, but also to the interests of others." He then goes on to encourage his readers to be like Jesus in humble self-sacrifice.

When that happens—through helping others in practical ways, volunteering, going out of your way to feed, love or encourage someone—not only do you see God's work more clearly, but your days feel more full of purpose.

And that's huge: Purpose. Especially in a time when a lot of people aren't sure if they have any.

Serving or helping others gives you a stronger sense of purpose. So do the work of God. When you do, you'll start to *see* his work on a more regular basis.

SUNDAY...

MONDAY - WHEN YOUR FAITH BECOMES A PUNCHING BAG

"You know that Jesus wasn't a real person, right? You know he was just based on ancient myths, right?"

That's what a friend said to me in university.

And do you want to know how I replied? It was a *really* profound response that made them stop in their tracks, change their mind, and immediately embrace the truth. I said: "Um... well... ah... what did you say?"

See what I mean? What an amazing rebuttal! (Not!)

Every once in a while I come across arguments against the historical existence of Jesus.

Some say that there are stories in the Bible that are contradictory. Some—like my friend—say that Jesus is just based on some ancient myth, paralleling other ancient hero figures like Horus or Mithras. So my question for you is this: How would you respond to those challenges?

After that experience with my friend, I put myself through the torture of reading some books by the supposed "experts" who said these things. I discovered what many others have found. That the more I explored the origins and content of the Bible, the more reliable it seemed. Plus, the Jesus-is-a-myth argument doesn't hold up to historical scrutiny. One author said he came up with the theory after reading the Egyptian Book of the Dead. But when actual Egyptologists questioned the details he was forced to say he couldn't remember where he had read them! And he was the one who many other people had based *their* opinions on!

Today, no serious historian doubts that Jesus was a real historical figure. H.G. Wells was an atheist historian who said, "Jesus Christ is easily the most dominant figure in all history."

The Christian faith can sometimes seem like a punching bag. So as details about your faith get challenged, how will you humbly defend your beliefs?

I think that one of the concluding words of encouragement from the letter to the Hebrews is a great piece of perspective for you and me too: "The Lord is my helper; I will not be afraid. What can mere mortals do to me?" (Hebrews 13:6)

If you don't intentionally build yourself up in faith, someone else will be more than happy to try and tear you down.

TUESDAY - WHEN WE REFUSE TO SILENCE OURSELVES

A lot of us want to hear from God. We want a word of direction or some understanding or the living waters of encouragement. But how many of us are willing to create some quiet space in our lives to listen?

When Jesus is teaching in Matthew 11:15 he says, "He who has ears to hear, let him hear." That line unsettles me a bit. If some people have "ears to hear" it must mean that other people have ears but don't hear!

When it comes to hearing from God, I don't want that to be me. What about you?

Do you need serious direction? Do you need understanding? Do you need the living waters of encouragement?

Create some time in your schedule, read your Bible, pray... and listen.

I sometimes wonder if God's apparent silence in our lives is because we refuse to silence ourselves.

But when we do, not only do we create mental space to more clearly hear his voice, but we create a readiness in our souls to listen.

What if you don't hear from God, not because his life is filled with too much rush and noise, but because yours is.

WEDNESDAY - ONE HABIT TO LIVE MORE SIMPLY

I love simplicity.

And I love things that go along with the idea of simplicity—things like sincerity and practicality.

Maybe I really like simplicity because I know that (a) life can get complicated, and (b) I find it very hard to achieve!

Writing to the Corinthians Paul says that "we behaved in the world with simplicity and godly sincerity..." (2 Corinthians 1:12, ESV). There seems to be a straightforwardness about that way of life—a lack of pretension, an un-budging faithfulness, and peace of mind. Sounds good to me!

But like many noble pursuits, it's easier said than done. So *how* do we live more simply?

One suggestion from professor and writer Richard J. Foster is to *develop a habit of giving things away*.

Owning too many things complicates our lives. Things need attention and fixing. Plus, having a lot of things tends to convince us that we actually *need* every single one of those things—and that we *need* even more!

But we usually don't.

Foster says that most of us could probably give away fifty percent of what we owned and still wouldn't be inconvenienced in any significant way.[126]

I'm guessing that for many of us developing a habit of giving things away won't make us more impoverished. It will make us more free.

Do you want more simplicity? Do you want to live "in the world with simplicity and godly sincerity"? I'm not saying you need to be a monk in the desert. But if you need practical help to simplify your life, develop a habit of giving things away.

THURSDAY - WHEN I PRAY "COINCIDENCES" HAPPEN

William Temple was an English bishop known for many things including his teaching and writing. A few years ago I came across something he said that has really stuck with me.

"When I pray, coincidences happen. When I don't, they don't."

Today's devotional is not overly complicated. My point is (a) that the supposed "coincidences" you experience after you pray aren't necessarily coincidences; and (b) that those "coincidences" should encourage you to keep coming back to our answering-God in prayer as you see him actively working in your life.

In Psalm 145:18 David says, "The LORD is near to all who call on him, to all who call on him in truth."

So seek God's will in prayer, honestly and wholeheartedly. The supposed "coincidences" you experience after you pray aren't necessarily coincidences! They should encourage you to keep coming back to our answering-God in prayer as you see him actively working in your life.

He answers. He encourages. He is near.

"When I pray, coincidences happen. When I don't, they don't."

FRIDAY - ENJOYING THINGS WITHOUT OWNING THEM

As far as I can tell, Jesus didn't own very much. The Gospels don't tell us anything about a storage unit for his overflow belongings.

As I write this I'm aware that in comparison to him I have a lot of stuff. I have a house and a car in the driveway. I have a room full of books, a few guitars, more clothes than I can wear in a week, and a few sentimental things from my childhood that I just don't want to throw away.

And on my snazzy little laptop I read these words of Jesus from Luke 12:15 (NLT): "Beware! Guard against every kind of greed. Life is not measured by how much you own."

I don't think I'm a greedy person. But maybe I am.

Why do I have all this stuff? Why do I often want more stuff? Is it just because I'm bombarded with commercials every day reminding me about what I don't have? Or is there some deep desire within me that thinks owning stuff will make me comfortable, or in control, or successful, or good?

Two days ago I talked about simplicity. Today, I'd like to do the same with another word of advice from Richard J. Foster.

He says that we can cultivate simplicity in our lives *by enjoying things without owning them.*[127]

Ownership can be an obsession in our culture. It's an illusion that gives us false security and draws us away from depending on God to provide for us.

Do you want to cultivate more simplicity and peace of mind in your life?

Enjoy a ride in your friend's car without wishing you owned it yourself. Borrow a book. Take a walk through the park.

Jesus said: "Beware! Guard against every kind of greed. Life is not measured by how much you own."

Tomorrow I'm still going to own my stuff. But I want to use it in a way that glorifies God, helps me serve Jesus, and which doesn't distract me from what's most important.

As you go about your day, try to enjoy things without always having to own them.

SATURDAY - WHAT IF IT WAS SOMETHING ANNOYING WITHIN OURSELVES?

Something a lot of people enjoy is getting together with friends and family. But let's be honest. There's also a lot of people who *don't* enjoy that!

Why? Because certain people can drive us crazy. Some have attitudes, habits and opinions that drive us up the wall!

In the Bible, Christians give evidence of the Holy Spirit within themselves with the qualities of "love, joy, peace, patience, kindness, goodness, faithfulness, gentleness and self-control" (Galatians 5:22-23, ESV). From what I see, it doesn't seem to exclude gatherings with friends and family!

So in an effort to help us out a bit, let me share an insight I once read. I think it was from the Christian psychiatrist M. Scott Peck, but I can't be sure.

One of the reasons certain people really annoy us is because, deep down— on a subconscious level—they remind us about something annoying *within ourselves.*

Impatient people, the argument goes, frustrate us because they remind us of our own impatience. Unloving people frustrate us because they remind us of our own lack of love. Brash people frustrate us because they remind us of our own lack of self-control.

Kind of changes how you look at people, doesn't it?

So as you get together with people, and as you get worked up under the collar about so-and-so, remember that all of us are imperfect. There's only one perfect Person—and none of us are him.

All humans are a work in progress. Including you.

SUNDAY...

MONDAY - THE KINTSUGI KING

We don't tell people everything. Well, at least most of us don't.

One of the places this is most obvious is on social media. We log on to Facebook and scroll through the pictures of what people *want* us to see. And then we post pictures of what *we* want people to see. It happens in our conversations too. People ask us how we're doing and we reply by saying the things we *want* them to know. It seems that many of us are scared to death of our brokenness.

I read about something called Kintsugi. It's a ceramic restoration process from Japan where broken ceramic pieces are reassembled. The bits are sealed back together—but not in a way that hides the cracks. It's done so that the cracks stand out. Intentionally.

And the cracks are filled with *gold*. You'd think that this re-furbished Kintsugi pottery would be less valuable. But no. People love it. It usually sells for more than it originally cost!

Usually, we hide our cracks. Just outside polite conversation and cropped out of Instagram posts. But God sees the original. And I think he takes your cracks and fills them with gold. Here's what I mean.

In *The End of Me*, Kyle Idleman writes "Flaws are openings."[128] He means that the flaws in your life are the places where God can enter in and do some of his best work. I don't expect you to turn around and make a poster board of your brokenness on Twitter or in today's conversations.

But why not think of your flaws as openings?—openings being filled with God's gold.

I love what God says to the prophet Jeremiah: "I am the Lord, the God of all mankind. Is anything too hard for me?" (Jeremiah 32:27) He is powerful. And able. And willing. Whatever your hurt, and whatever you hide, God can heal and make you whole.

Don't discount yourself. But more importantly, don't discount God. He is the Kintsugi King. And he does great work.

TUESDAY - WITHOUT FOOD WE CAN LIVE FOR WEEKS... BUT HOPE?

Unfortunately, we live in a time of increasing despair.

In April 2016 a front page *New York Times* article titled "U.S. Suicide Rate Surges to 30-Year High," highlighted the sobering fact that overall suicides rose twenty-four percent between 1999 to 2014. The increase in the last eight years was double that of the first seven (which means it's getting worse, faster). The suicide rate tripled for girls ages ten to fourteen, and rose in almost every other racial and gender category.

Various people tried to explain it. Some said it must be due to economic factors or low job prospects. But not a single person mentioned faith or God. Only one, Harvard professor Robert Putnam, mentioned the word "hopelessness."

It's easy to get sucked into the prevailing hopeless outlook of the culture around us. It's as if there's a turbo-charged magnetic pull with the strength of ten roller coasters invisibly careening through every home.

So we need to constantly remind ourselves that we are, when we are at our best, people of hope. As it says in 1 Peter 1:3, "he has given us new birth into a living hope..." But this doesn't mean shallow optimism or look-the-other-way denial.

To be hopeful is to have confidence that God's plan will be revealed in the end —that one day, all things will be made beautiful again, and that you and I can be a part of God's sneak-peek foretaste of that beauty in the here and now.

It's easy to be overrun with cynicism. After all, that's the turbo-charged magnetic pull with the strength of ten roller coasters invisibly careening through your home. But don't give in. As G.K. Chesterton said, "A dead thing can go with the stream, but only a living thing can go against it."

When he was a boy, Hugo Gryn was a prisoner at the Auschwitz concentration camp. Even in the middle of a dire situation, his father went to great lengths to observe the special Sabbaths and Jewish festivals. On a particular evening his father took a piece of string and put it in a bit of butter so they could have a Sabbath candle.

Hugo exclaimed: "Father, that is all the butter we have!" But his Father calmly replied: "Without food we can live for weeks. But we cannot live for a minute without hope."[129]

WEDNESDAY - THE ONES WHO WILL BE REALLY HAPPY

Serving and blessing people is a faithful thing to do. After all, Jesus himself was a servant. But it can be difficult and involves sacrifice and re-arranging your priorities.

So maybe you're still not convinced. So let me appeal to the smiley-face part of you that runs on...

Happiness.

Albert Schweitzer was a doctor who started a hospital in Africa. Not only did he kick-start and work in the hospital, but he put on music concerts to fund it as well.

Writing to Christians in the ancient world, the apostle Peter said that "Each of you should use whatever gift you have received to serve others..." (1 Peter 4:10) Schweitzer certainly embodied that principle one hundred percent!

One year he was invited to address the graduating class from Eton College. He said, "I don't know what your destiny will be. Some of you may be actors, politicians, teachers, doctors, surgeons, but I do know this: the only ones among you who will be really happy are those who have sought and found how to serve."[130]

Later, the students asked him about his sacrifices. He dismissed their inquiries and said, "It's not a matter of sacrifice, it's a matter of happiness, actually: happiness consists in service, in giving yourself here and now to that which is worthy and above your own self-interests."

To Schweitzer, service wasn't primarily about sacrifice—although it definitely was that too. For him, it was a matter of personal happiness.

Those who are happiest are those "who have sought and found how to serve."

So do it for Christ. Do it for others. Do it for the kingdom come.

But also do it for you.

THURSDAY - THE MESSIAH IS LIVING AMONGST YOU

In Matthew 22:44 (ESV) we read, "Therefore you also must be ready, for the Son of Man is coming at an hour you do not expect."

In light of those words, let me share a story about a monastery in the forest. The monks prayed, fasted, and did acts of kindness.

But the Abbot who ran the monastery was worried. They were getting smaller in number and the building was starting to fall apart.

So he went to see his wise old friend to see if he had any advice about how the monastery could be saved.

"I just don't know," he said. But as the Abbot went to leave, the wise old man stopped him: "Oh, just one more thing. I forgot to tell you that the Messiah is living amongst you."

"What?!" The Abbot was surprised. They were awaiting the return of the Messiah, of Jesus, and they assumed they would recognize him. But could this be true that he was already living amongst them?

The Abbot returned to the monastery and told the monks. They wondered who it could be. Could it be brother Peter? His faith was strong, but he sometimes lost his temper. It couldn't be him. Or could it? Or maybe it was brother Anthony. He was very patient and kind, but his breath was bad. Surely it couldn't be him! Or could it?

Because they didn't know who it was, the monks started treating each other with profound respect. Their words were full of humble and God-honouring truth. And their actions were full of love and self-sacrifice.

After all, any one of them could be the Messiah. And they all wanted to treat the Messiah well.

As always, tourists and visitors came to see the monastery. As they did, they noticed how things had changed—how they treated each other with great respect, with such truth and love.

It was so compelling that three of the young visitors wanted to stay. The next year that number doubled. Soon, the monastery was vibrant and thriving again.

The wise old man had told the Abbot that the Messiah was living amongst them. Perhaps the Abbot misunderstood his friend's meaning...

But it was nevertheless true.[131]

FRIDAY - CHILD-LIKE WITHOUT BECOMING CHILD-ISH

I'm on a subway. You probably are too. I don't mean a literal subway, but a real one nevertheless. The pace of life accelerates and the world around us becomes blurry.

Too fast to take it all in. Too fast to stop. Too fast to smell the roses. Zoom! (I think we just ran over fifty of them.)

Psalm 90:1 says, "I will tell of all your wonderful deeds." But to do that we need to disembark. And pause. And wonder.

Wonder.

Wonder isn't in a rush. Wonder doesn't pretend to have all the well-groomed answers. Wonder doesn't oppress. Wonder expands the lungs. Wonder opens her eyes.

Wonder gets off the subway and wades in to the smells, sounds and sights of a world longing to be lived.

Recently a precious and wise friend of mine said this: "The task is to become child-like without becoming child-ish." (He told me not to give him credit for the quote because he's sure he heard it somewhere else!) But it's genius. Think about it:

The task is to become child-*like* without becoming child-*ish*.

Ever wonder why Jesus, referring to the children around him, said that his kingdom "belongs to such as these"? (Mark 10:14) A child lives in the now. Is able to accept a gift. And delights in... wonder.

Yesterday my son and his friend chased a ladybug around the backyard for five or ten minutes. Literally. They marveled, they laughed, they were blown away... by a ladybug.

The task is to become child-like without becoming child-ish.

Today, pause. Get off the subway. Wonder. For the kingdom belongs to such as these.

SATURDAY - YOUR JOHN 3:16 MOMENT

I wrote today's devotional after a man in my congregation passed away. As I walked away from his room—and away from a body that was no longer home to a beating heart—I felt the need to ask you this question.

Are you ready for your own death?

Unfortunately, a lot of people don't think about it until it's too late.

In previous eras, people thought about death a lot more than they do now. Life was harder, disease was rampant, people died younger.

But today, it's a topic people avoid. For many people, life has become comfortable, and longer. And since our increasingly secular society isn't sure what to say about death (or the possibility of an afterlife)—some people avoid saying anything at all.

So what do you need to do to be ready?

First, get right with God. It's eternally important to place your faith in Jesus as God's Son, to ask for God's forgiveness for your sins, and to trust what Jesus has done for you on the cross. It's a life-changing and joy-giving thing to do of unending significance. So if you're still unsure about it, you need to figure it out pronto.

Second, get right with others. Do you have something important to say to someone you care about? A word of love or forgiveness? Don't wait.

Third, reassess your priorities to ensure they're aligned with your faith in Jesus. And live by them.

John 3:16 says, "For God so loved the world that he gave his one and only Son, that whoever believes in him shall not perish but have eternal life."

How you respond to that statement is your John 3:16 moment. And it's the moment that matters most.

The parishioner I just told you about had a strong faith in Christ and trusted deeply in the sovereignty of God. The night before he died, he was tired but calm when he said this: "I am ready for my eternal rest."

What confidence! What faith! What hope!

Your John 3:16 moment is the moment that matters most.

Are you ready?

SUNDAY...

MONDAY - NEVER UNDERESTIMATE YOUR IMPACT

My dad, Eric, died in November 2014. He was 64.

As I look back, I think about the kind of dad he was. He was a great dad. But to be honest, he probably wouldn't have won a dad-of-the-year award. He was more low-key than that. Plus, he wasn't perfect. Just as you and I aren't perfect.

But that doesn't mean he wasn't a great dad. And it doesn't mean he didn't have a huge impact on my life.

For years he went to work, cut wood to heat our house, took my brothers Deric and Jason and me to hockey and drama and musical performances, volunteered as a baseball and hockey coach, loved my mom day-in and day-out, and cared for his parents.

But that's not all...

He taught me that standing out isn't important—but that working hard is (no matter what you do). He taught me that making family a priority means making sacrifices. He taught me that you can take life seriously and be silly at the same time. He taught me how to paddle a canoe, and that sometimes you just need to tune out the criticisms of other people. He taught me that experiences are more important than stuff.

In light of that, and as I type these lines, I can remember our family sitting around a dancing campfire at Kel-Mac campground as he played harmonica into the dark, still sky.

Proverbs 22:6 (ESV) says, "Train up a child in the way he should go; even when he is old he will not depart from it." And there's the thing. Never underestimate your impact on the life of someone who's watching you. You may not end up in a history book. But that's okay.

Someone is in your life right now. Someone is feeling the impact of your words and actions. Someone is watching and learning how you navigate life, make decisions, and walk into an uncertain tomorrow.

For years my dad loved that old Randy Travis song, "Forever and Ever, Amen." He would walk around the house whistling it. So maybe that's a good note to end on:

Never underestimate your impact on the life of someone who's watching you. That impact will endure... forever and ever, amen.

REFERENCES AND NOTES

1. This is my good friend Jeff Einboden who I mention later on in this same forward.
2. C.S. Lewis, "On Obstinacy in Belief," *C.S. Lewis: Essay Collection* (London: Harper-Collins, 2000), 213-14.
3. I had originally thought this statement was by English bishop and New Testament scholar N.T. Wright. But I can't find where he said it, so perhaps I made it up. I'm not sure!
4. As told by Donald W. McCullough, *The Trivialization of God: The Dangerous Illusion of a Manageable Deity* (Colorado Springs: NavPress, 1995), 127.
5. You can find Matt's podcast here: https://www.spiritualityforordinarypeople.com/
6. I have heard this quote several times and always attributed to Frankl. I believe it is from his book *The Unheard Cry for Meaning: Psychotherapy and Humanism*.
7. Nora Young, *The Virtual Self: How Our Digital Lives Are Altering the World Around Us* (Toronto: McClelland & Stewart, 2012), 89.
8. Serena B. Miller with Paul Stutzman, *More Than Happy: The Wisdom of Amish Parenting: Simple Parenting Principles for the Modern World* (New York: Howard Books, 2015), 105.
9. As quoted in: John Ortberg, *All The Places to Go—How will you*

know? God has placed before you an open door. What will you do? (Carol Stream: Tyndale House, 2015), 40.

10. This quote is from TerKeurst's book *The Best Yes: Making Wise Decisions in the Midst of Endless Demands*. But I have to admit, I haven't read the whole thing. I saw TerKeurst put this on social media. And then she confirmed with me that it was from *The Best Yes* through an Instagram conversation. The book was published in 2014 by Thomas Nelson.

11. See particularly chapters 13 to 15 in: Robert D. Putnam, *Bowling Alone: The Collapse and Revival of American Community* (New York: Simon and Schuster, 2000).

12. As discussed in: John Ortberg, *Soul Keeping: Caring for the Most Important Part of You* (Grand Rapids: Zondervan, 2014), 46.

13. As told in: Max Lucado, *Outlive Your Life: We Were Made To Make A Difference* (Nashville: Thomas Nelson, 2010), 48-49.

14. As told in: Richard J. Mouw, *Uncommon Decency: Christian Civility in an Uncivil World* (Downers Grove: IVP Books, 2010), 78.

15. M. Scott Peck, *The Road Less Travelled: A New Psychology of Love, Traditional Values and Spiritual Growth* (New York: Simon & Schuster, 1978), 88.

16. Dietrich Bonhoeffer, *The Cost of Discipleship* (New York: Touchstone, 1995), 283.

17. The exact address for that specific blog is: www.matthewruttan.com/2018/04/10/is-there-evidence-for-the-resurrection

18. As told in: Kyle Idleman, *Grace from the Cross* (Grand Rapids: BakerBooks, 2018), 62-64.

19. Oswald Chambers, *My Utmost for His Highest*, updated edition (Grand Rapids: Discovery House, 1992), entry for January 6 (no page number).

20. You can read about Frankl's experience in: Viktor E. Frankl: *Man's Search for Meaning* (Boston: Beacon Press, 1959).

21. As quoted in: Stephen Seamands, *Give Them Christ: Peaching His Incarnation, Crucifixion, Resurrection, Ascension and Return* (Downer's Grove: IVP Books, 2012), 99.

22. Max Lucado, Anxious for Nothing: Finding Calm in a Chaotic World (Nashville: Thomas Nelson, 2017), 24.

23. *In Christ Alone* was written by Keith Getty and Stuart Townend. The words to *How Great Thou Art* were written by Carl Gustav

Boberg, with English translation by Stuart K. Hine. The words to
Shine Jesus Shine were written by Graham Kendrick. And the
words to *Good Good Father* were written by Pat Barrett and
Tony Brown.

24. As told in: Tony Campolo, *Let Me Tell You A Story: Life Lessons from
Unexpected Places and Unlikely People* (Nashville: Thomas Nelson,
2000), 21.

25. This scene was from the last episode in Season Two, "Christmas
at Downton Abbey." It was directed by Brian Percival and written
by Julian Fellowes. The original air date was December 25, 2011.
The show was co-produced by Carnival Films and Masterpiece.

26. This was posted by pastor and best-selling author Tim Keller on
Twitter on June 20, 2013. In the comments to the Tweet he
suggests it is a paraphrase of something he read in one of C.S.
Lewis' books. You can see the original Tweet and thread here:
https://twitter.com/timkellernyc/status/347750511484747776

27. As told in: Tony Campolo, *Let Me Tell You A Story: Life Lessons from
Unexpected Places and Unlikely People* (Nashville: Thomas Nelson,
2000), 183.

28. Mark Batterson, *The Power of If (Excerpts from If)*, (Grand Rapids:
BakerBooks, 2015), 27.

29. Francis Chan & Lisa Chan, *You And Me Forever: Marriage In Light of
Eternity* (San Francisco: Claire Love Publishing, 2014), 126.

30. *Bruce Almighty* was released in 2003 and was produced by
Spyglass Entertainment, Universal Pictures, Shady Acres
Entertainment, and Pit Bull Productions. It was directed by Tom
Shadyac and written by Steve Koren, Mark O'Keefe and Steve
Oedekerk.

31. "Unanswered Prayers" was released on the *No Fences* album in 1990
by Garth Brooks on Capital Nashville. It was written by Garth
Brooks, Pat Alger and Larry Bastian.

32. As quoted in: Timothy Keller, *The Freedom of Self-Forgetfulness: The
Path to True Christian Joy* (Leyland: 10Publishing, 2012), 22.

33. Carl F. George with Warren Bird, *How to Break Church Growth
Barriers: Capturing Overlooked Opportunities for Church Growth*
(Grand Rapids: Baker Book House, 1993), 41.

34. I recall reading a version of this story in a Max Lucado book. But
I can't remember which one! The version I tell here is my own
take on the same idea.

35. Billy Graham, *Nearing Home: Life, Faith and Finishing Well* (Nashville: Thomas Nelson, 2011), 84-85.

36. As told in: Craig Groeschel: *The Christian Atheist: Believing in God but Living as If He Didn't Exist* (Grand Rapids: Zondervan, 2010), 69-70.

37. I came across this fact in: Carl F. George with Warren Bird, *How to Break Church Growth Barriers: Capturing Overlooked Opportunities for Church Growth* (Grand Rapids: Baker Book House, 1993), 58-59.

38. As told in: Tony Campolo, *Let Me Tell You A Story: Life Lessons from Unexpected Places and Unlikely People* (Nashville: Thomas Nelson, 2000), 216-220.

39. Groeschel talks about this concept in his book: Craig Groeschel, *The Christian Atheist: Believing in God but Living as If He Didn't Exist* (Grand Rapids: Zondervan, 2010).

40. C.S. Lewis, "On Obstinacy in Belief," *C.S. Lewis: Essay Collection* (London: Harper-Collins, 2000), 213-14.

41. As told in: Harold Kushner, *Who Needs God* (New York: Summit Books, 1989), 154.

42. Toni Birdson & Tami Heim, *@StickyJesus: How to Live Out Your Faith Online* (Nashville: Abingdon Press, 2010), 131.

43. Toni Birdson & Tami Heim, *@StickyJesus: How to Live Out Your Faith Online* (Nashville: Abingdon Press, 2010), 131.

44. The episode was posted on June 6, 2017. You can listen in here: https://www.spiritualityforordinarypeople.com/jen/

45. This idea is expressed in: Timothy Keller, *Encounters with Jesus: Unexpected Answers to Life's Biggest Questions* (New York: Dutton, 2013), 143ff.

46. C.S. Lewis, *Mere Christianity* (Macmillan, 1960).

47. Ravi Zacharias: *Jesus Among Other Gods: The Absolute Claims of the Christian Faith* (Nashville: Thomas Nelson, 2000), 129.

48. I've seen or heard this statement from Groeschel in a few different contexts including Twitter. I believe I also heard him say it in his Leadership podcast. You can check it out here: https://www.life.church/leadershippodcast/

49. As quoted in: Scott Cooper, *I Don't Want To Go To Church: Practical Ways To Deal With Kids and Religion (Whether You're Religious Or Not)*, (New York: Paulist Press, 2007), 106.

50. Margaret Feinberg, *Fight Back With Joy: Celebrate More, Regret Less,*

Stare Down Your Greatest Fears (Brentwood: Worthy Publishing, 2015), 35.

51. Timothy Keller, *Making Sense of God: An Invitation to the Skeptical* (New York: Viking, 2016), 233.

52. Jean Vanier, *Becoming Human* (Toronto: House of Anansi Press, 1998), 163.

53. Ace Collins, *GrATTITUDE: Practicing Contagious Optimism for Positive Change* (Grand Rapids: Zondervan, 2010), 133.

54. As told in: Richard J. Mouw, *Uncommon Decency: Christian Civility in an Uncivil World* (Downers Grove: IVP Books, 2010), 52.

55. Ann Voskamp, *One Thousand Gifts: A Dare to Live Fully Right Where You Are* (Grand Rapids: Zondervan, 2010).

56. The words to *Amazing Grace* were written by John Newton.

57. As told in: Philip Yancey, *Vanishing Grace: What Ever Happened to the Good News?* (Grand Rapids: Zondervan, 2014).

58. Atul Gawande, *Being Mortal: Medicine and What Matters in the End* (Doubleday Canada, 2014), 122, 123.

59. "Cray Button" was written by Solomon Olds, Jacob Olds, Joshua Olds, Nathan Currin, Derek Mount, and Riley Friresen. You can check out their website at http://ff5music.com/

60. As quoted in: John Ortberg, *All The Places to Go—How will you know? God has placed before you an open door. What will you do?* (Carol Stream: Tyndale House, 2015), 116.

61. As told in: Mark Batterson, *The Grave Robber: How Jesus Can Make Your Impossible Possible* (Grand Rapids: BakerBooks, 2014), 69.

62. I read about Valerie's inspiring story on www.FaithIt.com

63. Jud Wilhite, *The God of Yes: How Faith Makes All Things New* (New York: Faith Words, 2014), 144.

64. These two approaches to life are played out by Tim Keller in his book *Prodigal God: Recovering the Heart of the Christian Faith* (New York: Riverhead Books, 2008), 37ff.

65. Someone emailed me this story from Addison and McGlone so I'm not sure about the original source.

66. Rick Warren, *What On Earth Am I Here For?* (Grand Rapids: Zondervan, 2014), 24.

67. This is from Tolstoy's book *A Confession*.

68. Kennon L. Callahan, *Living in Grace* (North Charleston: CreateSpace Independent Publishing Platform, 2013), 35.

69. Luke Timothy Johnson, *Living Jesus* (San Francisco: HarperSanFrancisco, 1999), 4.
70. The song "Speak Life" was written by Toby Mckeehan.
71. After I originally published this devotional online, I received an email from a pastor in Ethiopia, Zeb Mengistu, confirming that it was true.
72. Viktor E. Frankl: *Man's Search for Meaning* (Boston: Beacon Press, 1959), 58-59.
73. Tomas G. Long, *Preaching From Memory to Hope* (Louisville: Westminster John Knox Press, 2009), 29.
74. Max Lucado, *Before Amen: The Power of a Simple Prayer* (Nashville: Thomas Nelson, 2014), 52.
75. Mark Batterson, *The Grave Robber: How Jesus Can Make Your Impossible Possible* (Grand Rapids: BakerBooks, 2014), 221.
76. As quoted in: Kevin Myers and John C. Maxwell, *Home Run: Learn God's Game Plan for Life and Leadership* (New York: Faith Words, 2014), 60.
77. I've seen this quote attributed to Kimmel on social media.
78. As told in: John Ortberg, *All The Places to Go—How will you know? God has placed before you an open door. What will you do?* (Carol Stream: Tyndale House, 2015), 70.
79. As told in: Craig Groeschel, *Altar Ego: Becoming Who God Says You Are* (Grand Rapids: Zondervan, 2013), 93.
80. Words: Luke 23:42. Music: REMEMBER ME, Jacques Berthier (1923-1994), Taizé Community (France). Words: public domain.
81. Kevin Myers and John C. Maxwell, *Home Run: Learn God's Game Plan for Life and Leadership* (New York: Faith Words, 2014), 150.
82. David Kinnaman & Gabe Lyons, *Good Faith: Being a Christian When Society Thinks You're Irrelevant and Extreme* (Grand Rapids: BakerBooks, 2016), 111.
83. I heard Mark Clark talk about this in a talk he delivered to the Canadian Church Leaders Conference at Connexus Church in Barrie, Ontario in June 2017. You can find out more about Pastor Clark here: http://www.pastormarkclark.com/about/
84. Geneen Roth, *Women, Food and God: An Unexpected Path to Almost Everything* (New York: Scribner, 2010), 177.
85. Mark Batterson, *The Grave Robber: How Jesus Can Make Your Impossible Possible* (Grand Rapids: BakerBooks, 2014), 39-40.
86. As quoted in: Andy Stanley, *How To Be Rich: It's Not What You Have.*

It's What You Do With What You Have (Grand Rapids: Zondervan, 2013), 59.

87. I heard Reggie Joiner tell this story on a Think Orange Podcast. You can listen to the podcasts here: http://orangeblogs.org/thinkorangepodcast/

88. As told in: Andy Stanley, *Making Vision Stick* (Grand Rapids: Zondervan, 2007), 41-43.

89. Thomas Merton, *Opening the Bible* (Collegeville: The Liturgical Press, 1970), 14.

90. The article, written by Jim Patterson and published on the Vanderbilt University website, was posted on May 31, 2017. You can read it here: https://news.vanderbilt.edu/2017/05/31/worship-is-good-for-your-health-vanderbilt-study/

91. I've got to be honest. I used to own this book and made a note of this quote. But now I can't find it!

92. C.S. Lewis, *Mere Christianity* (New York: HarperCollins, 2001), 226-27.

93. I read about this in: Jud Wilhite, *The God of Yes: How Faith Makes All Things New* (New York: Faith Words, 2014), 72-73.

94. As posted on Twitter on May 12, 2016: https://twitter.com/craiggroeschel/status/730753084167589888

95. As told in: M. Scott Peck, *Further Along The Road Less Travelled: The Unending Journey Toward Spiritual Growth* (New York: Simon and Schuster, 1993), 82.

96. As told in: Craig Groeschel, *The Christian Atheist: Believing in God But Living As If He Doesn't Exist* (Grand Rapids: Zondervan, 2010), 100-101.

97. I can't recall when I specifically heard this, but it was a quote from a radio program on Life 100.3FM in Barrie, Ontario.

98. As quoted in: Andy Stanley and Bill Willits, *Creating Community: 5 Keys to Building a Small Group Culture* (Colorado Springs: Multnomah Books, 2004), 36.

99. Frances S. Collins, *The Language of God: A Scientists Presents Evidence for Belief* (New York: Free Press, 2006), 67.

100. Mark Clark, *The Problem of God: Answering a Skeptic's Challenges to Christianity* (Grand Rapids: Zondervan, 2017), 82.

101. Reggie Joiner and Tom Shefchunas, *Lead Small: Five Big Ideas Every Small Group Leader Needs to Know* (Cumming: Orange, 2012), 50.

102. You can check them out at: https://babylonbee.com/

103. Further reading about the dialogue between science and faith can be found in John Lennox's article "Challenges from Science" in: Ravi Zacharias, author and general editor, *Beyond Opinion: Living The Faith We Defend* (Nashville: Thomas Nelson, 2007); and "Science Increasingly Makes the Case for God" by Eric Metaxas at http://ericmetaxas.com/media/articles/science-increasingly-makes-case-god/, published on March 25, 2014, but which first appeared in the *Wall Street Journal* on December 25, 2014; and the chapter "The Problem of God" in: Mark Clark, *The Problem of God: Answering a Skeptic's Challenges to Christianity* (Grand Rapids: Zondervan, 2017); and the chapter "Science Has Disproved Christianity" in: Tim Keller, *The Reason for God: Belief in an Age of Skepticism* (New York: Riverhead Books, 2008).

104. Billy Graham, *Nearing Home: Life, Faith and Finishing Well* (Nashville: Thomas Nelson, 2011), 40.

105. Ravi Zacharias: *Jesus Among Other Gods: The Absolute Claims of the Christian Faith* (Nashville: Thomas Nelson, 2000), vii.

106. "How to Manage Your Stress," *USA Today*, March 7, 2001, http://usatoday30.usatoday.com/news/health/2001-03-07-stress-tips.htm.

107. As told in: Arthur Van Seters, *Preaching and Ethics* (St. Louis: Chalice Press, 2004), 52.

108. As told in: John Ortberg, *Soul Keeping: Caring for the Most Important Part of You* (Grand Rapids: Zondervan, 2014), 130.

109. Michael Finkel, "Want to Fall Asleep? Read This Story" in *National Geographic Magazine*, August 2018. The quote appears on the cover.

110. I forget the location of this exact reference, but I think I heard Max Lucado use this *Monopoly* analogy. It was probably him because he's in the habit of saying awesome stuff.

111. I looked up this commercial online. You can see it here: https://www.youtube.com/watch?v=fsz3BjKbOMk

112. Timothy Keller, *Making Sense of God: An Invitation to the Skeptical* (New York: Viking, 2016), 91.

113. Mother Teresa of Calcutta, *Life in the Spirit: Reflections, Meditations, Prayers*, ed. Kathryn Spink (San Francisco: HarperCollins, 1983), 31.

114. Rob Russell with Rusty Russell, *Money: A User's Manual* (Sisters: Multnomah, 1997), 82.

115. N.T. Wright, *After You Believe: Why Christian Character Matters* (New York: Harper One, 2010), 22-24.

116. Vissers' interview with Bealer was posted on July 27, 2017. You can listen in to the interview, and find other helpful content on the Young Church Leaders Podcast here: http://youngchurchleaders.org/2017/07/27/yclp-007-frank-bealer-myth-balance/

117. This story is found in: William R. White, *Stories for Telling: A Treasury for Christian Storytellers* (Minneapolis: Augsburg, 1986), 122.

118. Ravi Zacharias: *Jesus Among Other Gods: The Absolute Claims of the Christian Faith* (Nashville: Thomas Nelson, 2000), 58.

119. Matthew D. Brough, *Let God Be God: Give Control to the Only One Who Can Set You Free* (Blythe Thicket Books, 2016), 78.

120. As told in: Tony Campolo, *Let Me Tell You A Story: Life Lessons from Unexpected Places and Unlikely People* (Nashville: Thomas Nelson, 2000), 73.

121. As told in: Tony Campolo, *Let Me Tell You A Story: Life Lessons from Unexpected Places and Unlikely People* (Nashville: Thomas Nelson, 2000), 60.

122. Kyle Idleman, *AHA: Awakening, Honesty, Action* (Colorado Springs: David C. Cook, 2014), 148.

123. Unfortunately I have lost the original source and location for Elliot's story.

124. As posted on Twitter on December 9, 2017. Find the Tweet here: https://twitter.com/LysaTerKeurst/status/939637301663141894

125. I've seen this quote attributed to McGrath on Twitter.

126. See Richard J. Foster, *Celebration of Discipline: The Path to Spiritual Growth* (San Francisco: Harper and Row, 1978), 79.

127. See Richard J. Foster, *Celebration of Discipline: The Path to Spiritual Growth* (San Francisco: Harper and Row, 1978), 80.

128. Idleman talks about this idea and Kintsugi in: *The End of Me: Where Real Life in the Upside-Down Ways of Jesus Begins* (Colorado Springs: David C. Cook, 2015), 37-38.

129. As told in: Thomas G. Long, *Preaching From Memory to Hope* (Louisville: Westminster John Knox Press, 2009), 132.

130. This story is told by John N. Gladstone in a sermon called "The Only Time You Have Is Now." It is published in: Michael P.

Knowles, ed., *The Folly of Preaching: Models and Methods* (Grand Rapids: William B. Erdmans, 2007), 178.

131. A version of this legend appears in the prologue to: M. Scott Peck, *The Different Drum: Community Making and Peace* (New York: Simon and Schuster, 1987), 13-15.

ABOUT MATTHEW RUTTAN

Matthew Ruttan writes the "Up!" daily devotional, pastors Westminster Presbyterian Church in Barrie, Canada, won 'best blog' by the Canadian Church Press in 2015, detests mosquitoes, and hopes to own a rowboat one day. He loves Jesus, writing songs, Ketchup Chips, and believes that if you have a life-changing faith, your faith should be changing your life. He and his remarkable wife Laura are navigating the sacred trust of raising three wonder-filled children.

Learn more at www.TheUpDevo.com or www.MatthewRuttan.com

facebook.com/MatthewRuttanUp

twitter.com/theupdevo

instagram.com/theupdevo

Made in the USA
Columbia, SC
28 November 2018